# MARX'S THEORY OF THE GENESIS OF MONEY

## How, Why and Through What Is a Commodity Money?

SAMEZŌ KURUMA
*translated with an introduction by E. Michael Schauerte*

**Outskirts Press, Inc.**
**Denver, Colorado**

Marx's Theory of the Genesis of Money
All Rights Reserved.
Copyright © 2009 E. Michael Schauerte
V5.0 R1.1

Outskirts Press, Inc.
http://www.outskirtspress.com

ISBN:   978-1-4327-2731-4 paperback
ISBN:   978-1-4327-3052-9 hardback

Outskirts Press and the "OP" logo are trademarks belonging to Outskirts Press, Inc.

PRINTED IN THE UNITED STATES OF AMERICA

# ACKNOWLEDGEMENTS

In translating this book I have benefited from the advice and encouragement of Dr. Ken Kuruma (the author's son) and Dr. Teinosuke Otani. Both patiently responded to my stream of questions and invited me into their homes for many enjoyable afternoon conversations. I am very grateful for their help and friendship over the past three years. (I should note, of course, that neither bears any responsibility for whatever errors might remain in my translation or for the content of my introduction.) I also want to thank my wife Yuko for her patient understanding towards my time spent studying the "genesis of money" – instead of generating more of it myself – and for taking care of Emma and Mia on those afternoons when I was out visiting Kuruma *sensei* or Otani *sensei*.

# CONTENTS

|  | Introduction | 1 |
|---|---|---|
|  | A Note on the Text | 29 |
| Part One | Theory of the Value-Form & Theory of the Exchange Process | 31 |
|  | Preface | 33 |
| I. | Theory of the Value-Form & Theory of the Exchange Process | 35 |
| II. | Why is the Want of the Commodity Owner Abstracted from in the Theory of the Value-Form? (A Response to the View of Kōzō Uno) | 69 |
| 1. | Uno's First Argument | 73 |
| 2. | Uno's Second Argument | 95 |
| 3. | Uno's Third Argument | 113 |
| Part Two | Marx's Theory of the Genesis of Money (A Discussion with Teinosuke Otani) | 127 |
| 1. | The Questions "How, Why and Through What" (The Genesis of Money) | 129 |
| 2. | Riddle of the Money-Form and the Riddle of Money | 137 |
| 3. | Difference between the First and Second Edition of *Capital* | 151 |
| 4. | The Significance of the "Why Question" (The Particularity of Commodity Production and the Essence of Value) | 161 |
| 5. | In What Sense is the Simple Value-Form "Accidental"? | 169 |
| 6. | The "Detour" of Value-Expression | 173 |

7.      The Meaning of the "Formal Content of the   187
Relative Expression of Value" (Hegel's The-
ory of Judgment and Marx's Theory of the
Value-Form)

8.      How the Development of the Value-Form   197
Unfolds (Neither a Historical Development
Nor the "Self-development of a Concept")

9.      The Meaning of Abstracting from the Indi-   203
vidual Want of the Commodity Owner (Nobuteru Takeda's Criticism of Kuruma)

10.     What is the "Dialectic" in the Case of the   213
Value-Form?

       References   217

# INTRODUCTION

"Beginnings are always difficult in all sciences," Karl Marx warns the reader in his preface to *Capital*, noting that the first chapter of his book will therefore present the "greatest difficulty." What is the nature of this difficulty? And how can we overcome it?

The Japanese Marxian economist Samezō Kuruma (1893–1982)[1] argued that once we become aware of the exact nature of the difficulty we will have already largely overcome it. Kuruma emphasized, in particular, the need for the reader of *Capital* to understand how and why Marx frames each theoretical question in the beginning chapters in a particular way. This involves understanding the manner in which Marx sets aside those elements not directly relevant to a given theoretical question, in order to pose the question in a "pure" and hence answerable form. For Kuruma, once we have understood a theoretical question and grasped its necessity, the answer to it will be nearly self-evident.

His point about the need to properly understand Marx's theoretical questions may itself be self-evident. Yet it is certainly easier said than done. One barrier to this understanding is that Marx at the beginning of *Capital* does not offer us the sort of cut-and-dried definitions of economic terms that we might find in an economics textbook. Rather than quickly defining an economic form and then treating it as a fixed premise, Marx subjects each form to a multi-angled analysis and considers its relation to other forms and concepts. There is a need, therefore, to be aware of the angle from which Marx is carrying out his analysis and grasp why he poses the

---

[1] For information on Kuruma's life and career, see the short biographical article on the Samezō Kuruma Archive of the Marxist Internet Archive (marxists.org/archive/kuruma/index) or my longer article, "Samezō Kuruma's Life as a Marxist Economist," published in the 2007 issue of *Research in Political Economy*.

sort of theoretical questions that economists have tended to overlook or deem unworthy of attention.

For the reader who lacks that sort of understanding, the beginning of *Capital* will probably seem not only difficult but also dull and repetitive. Marx himself recognizes that many readers will find the beginning chapters tedious, warning them in his preface that the analysis of the commodity in Chapter 1 will "seem to turn upon minutiae" to the "superficial observer." He readily admits that his analysis does indeed turn upon minutiae, but underscores the crucial need to subject the commodity to such scrutiny, referring to it as the "economic cell-form" of capitalism. Just as a biologist must examine the cells of a living organism in order to understand it, we need to examine the commodity-form in order to gain a better understanding of capitalism. Our tool in carrying out this analysis – since "neither microscopes nor chemical reagents are of assistance" (Marx, 1976a, p. 90) – is what Marx calls the "power of abstraction" (which I will discuss a bit later). The analysis of the commodity at the beginning of Capital thus presents us with both unfamiliar theoretical questions and a level of analysis on a "microscopic" (= abstract) level, which means that Chapter 1 remains difficult despite Marx's efforts to popularize his presentation.

Paradoxically, though, it may be the disarming "simplicity" of the questions posed at the beginning of *Capital* that contributes to the difficulty. Marx is like an inquisitive child who is always asking *why* things are they way they are. He does not take capitalism or its economic forms for granted. Instead, Marx views capitalism as one *historical* mode of production among others that have existed in the past or will exist in the future. This is the critical perspective from which Marx analyzes capitalistic economic forms; and it informs the theoretical questions that he poses. Having an awareness of Marx's basic approach to the study of capitalism thus facilitates an understanding of *Capital* (and I will conclude this introduction by looking at some of the characteristics of his method).

For the time being, though, we can set aside the general reasons why the beginning of *Capital* is difficult, and focus instead on the theoretical questions themselves. More specifically, we need to look at the theoretical questions that Marx poses in Chapter 1 and 2. And we can get a basic idea of the nature of those questions from the headings below:

- Chapter 1: The Commodity
  - Sec. 1: The Two Factors of the Commodity: Use-value and Value (Substance of Value, Magnitude of Value)
  - Sec. 2: The Twofold Character of the Labor Represented in Commodities
  - Sec. 3: The Value-Form, or Exchange-Value
  - Sec. 4: The Fetish-character of the Commodity and its Secret
- Chapter 2: The Exchange Process

As we can see, Marx is dealing with a number of different theoretical issues, which can be grouped into a number of separate theories. We have the "theory of the substance of value" (or labor theory of value) presented in Section 1 and 2; followed by the "theory of the value-form" in Section 3; the "theory of the fetish-character" in Section 4; and finally the "theory of the exchange process" in Chapter 2. It is only by coming to grips with each of these four theories, and understanding the relation between them, that we can truly overcome the "difficult beginning" of *Capital*.

Kuruma provides us with a detailed examination of three of those four theories in *Marx's Theory of the Genesis of Money*, concentrating on the questions that Marx addresses in Section 3, Section 4, and Chapter 2. In particular, Kuruma offers a detailed explanation of the crucial theory of the value-form, which is at the core of an understanding of money. In this introduction, I will attempt to summarize Kuruma's interpretation of those three theories, while also looking at the theoretical task addressed in Section 1 and 2 and discussing Marx's use of abstraction and his analytical method.

## Labor Theory of Value

The labor theory of value (= theory of the substance of value) is only touched on in passing in *Marx's Theory of the Genesis of Money*, but I want to take a look at it here, given the direct relation that the theory has to the three theories that Kuruma examines and the fact that it has been the target of much criticism by Marx's opponents.

The labor theory of value presents its own difficulties, certainly, but they do not stem from the unfamiliarity of the theoretical question itself. That question, which economists prior to Marx had already pondered, basically comes down to identifying the factor that commodities have in common which determines their "exchange-value" or worth. The Classical school of political economy, starting with Adam Smith, arrived at the answer in asserting that the level at which a commodity will be exchanged is generally determined by the quantity of human labor necessary to produce it.

Marx adhered to this *labor* theory of value, but introduced a far more precise understanding of labor as the "substance" of value: defining it in terms of the quantity of abstract human labor socially necessary to produce a commodity.[2] Yet, perhaps because the merits of the labor theory of value were so clear to him, Marx did not belabor his own explanation of it in Chapter 1 of *Capital*, where he simply writes: "If then we leave out of consideration the use-value of commodities, they have only one common property left, that of being products of labor" (Marx, 1976, p. 128). It is this trait that commodities have in common – as the product of labor – which Marx identifies as the basis of their value.

This matter-of-fact conclusion may seem less than convincing to many readers, given the existence of phenomena that seem to run directly counter to the labor theory of value. There are commodities, for instance, that are the product of little or no labor, yet fetch higher prices than labor-intensive ones. We also know that commodities

---

[2] Unlike the Classical economists, Marx distinguished between various uses of the term "labor," such as the difference between the "concrete labor" that creates a commodity's use-value and the "abstract labor" that creates its value; and the difference between the labor in an active state within the labor process ("living labor") and the labor embodied in the commodity as the result of production ("dead labor"). Furthermore, Marx elucidated the distinction (crucial to the theory of surplus-value) between "labor" in all of those different meanings and the concept of the "labor-power" (or capacity to labor) that the worker sells as a commodity on the labor market in return for a wage and whose value is determined by the value of the commodities that the worker must consume to reproduce that capacity to labor. The Classical economists Smith and Ricardo, in contrast, used the blanket term "labor" to designate all of those separate concepts.

have other factors in common, whether it be their physical attributes or more abstract qualities such as being desired objects. This all contributes to the impression that Marx is engaging in some sort of intellectual sleight of hand, where he limits his discussion to commodities that are the product of labor and then "discovers" that labor determines a commodity's value. Eugen von Böhm-Bawerk, an early critic of Marx, described his intellectual foe as "one who urgently desiring to bring a white ball out of an urn takes care to secure this result by putting in white balls only" (Böhm-Bawerk, 1984, p. 70). Subsequent critics, following Böhm-Bawerk's lead, have seized on this apparent flaw at the basis of the labor theory of value, in an effort to discredit Marx's entire critique of political economy. However, this idea that Marx's logic is circular overlooks important *premises* of the labor theory of value, which are firmly rooted in reality.

One key premise is the vital need, in any form of society, to produce material wealth. It is the continual production of wealth, via human labor, that sustains any society and its members. "Every child knows," Marx wrote to his friend to Ludwig Kugelmann in the summer of 1868, "that any nation that stopped working, not for a year, but let us say, just for a few weeks, would perish" (Marx, 1988, p. 68). We also know that under capitalism the bulk of this crucial material wealth takes the form of "commodities" (i.e., products bought and sold on the market). As Marx points out in the very first sentence of *Capital*: "The wealth of societies in which the capitalist mode of production prevails presents itself as an immense accumulation of commodities" (Marx, 1976a, p. 125). It is the commodity in this *fundamental* sense, as the capitalistic form of material wealth (= products of labor), that Marx analyzes in the first chapter of *Capital*; not the commodity in the purely formal sense as anything with a price. From this perspective, it is quite natural for Marx to identify labor as the factor that commodities have in common which determines their value.

Marx raises a second important premise of the labor theory of value in that same letter, telling Kugelmann that "every child knows, too, that the amounts of products corresponding to the differing amounts of needs demand differing and quantitatively determined amounts of society's aggregate labor" (Marx, 1988, p. 68). What

Marx means – for it is doubtful that even the most precocious child would use those exact terms – is that there is an obvious need, in any social form, to allocate the total labor of society to the various spheres of production in line with the products required (just as there is a need to then distribute those products throughout society in one way or another). The labor theory of value takes this reality as its starting point and seeks to explain the distinctive manner in which labor is allocated (and products distributed) in a capitalist society. Specifically, the theory explains what regulates the commodity exchange that mediates this allocation of labor. Here, just as in the case of the commodity in the "fundamental" sense, the reality of labor and its foundational role in *any* form of society is premised.

Those who overlook these two important premises are likely to view the idea of labor as the "substance" of value as a circular argument, an empty assertion. Not surprisingly, Marx's opponents have aimed much of their criticism at the supposed inadequacy of his "proof" of the labor theory of value in Chapter 1. In his own day, Marx encountered similar criticism and derisively wrote of how the "chatter about the need to prove the concept of value arises only from complete ignorance both of the subject under discussion and of the method of science" (Marx, 1988 p. 68). The "subject under discussion" Marx is referring to is the need in any society for labor allocation and product distribution; while the "method of science" involves explaining the specific way this is carried out in the case of capitalism. Thus, the "proof" of the labor theory of value – although the term seems somewhat inappropriate – is to be found in part within the aforementioned premises, which is why Marx says that "even if there were no chapter on 'value' at all in my book [*Capital*], the analysis I give of the real relations would contain the proof and demonstration of the real value relation" (Marx, 1988, p. 68). We need, then, to understand the nature of the commodity analyzed and appreciate what the labor theory of value actual sets out to explain, in order to properly understand that theory.

Once equipped with this basic understanding, it should be clear that the labor theory of value cannot be refuted by simply noting the existence of other "commodities" that are *not* the product of labor. Not only is such criticism entirely beside the (theoretical) point, it does not adequately acknowledge that Marx was well aware of the existence of such "formal" commodities. Already in Chapter 3 of *Capital*, for instance, he mentions that "things which in and for themselves are not commodities, such as conscience, honor, etc., can be offered for sale by their holders, and thus acquire the form of commodities through their price" so that "a thing can, formally speaking, have a price without a value" (Marx, 1976a, p. 197). And later Marx analyzes commodities that lack intrinsic value (such as land and interest-bearing capital). However, in the case of such "formal commodities" there is often an *indirect* relation to the concept of value, which means that they cannot not be adequately explained until value has first been elucidated through the analysis of the commodity in the fundamental sense.

Marx ridiculed those who expected him to explain everything at the same time, noting that, "if one wanted to 'explain' from the outset all phenomena that apparently contradict the law, one would have to provide the science *before* the science" (Marx, 1988, p. 68). Many of the doubts of Marx's impatient critics – who he described as "clinging to appearances and believing them to be the ultimate" – are answered later in *Capital*, at a different stage in his analysis of capitalism. If Marx had followed his critics' advice by attempting to explain every sort of commodity at once, rather than drawing a distinction between the commodity in its formal sense and in its fundamental sense, his analysis would not have advanced very far. Marx would never have been able to explain how commodity exchange is regulated (so as to mediate the allocation of labor and distribution of goods); nor would he have been able to elucidate the concept of money. We would have been left with nothing more than a *description* of the commodity as "anything with a price."

A quick look at some of the alternatives to the labor theory of value, to conclude this section, further underscores the strength of Marx's position. There is, for instance, the common view that the value of a commodity is determined by supply and demand. This factor does of course account for fluctuations in the prices of commodities, as Marx recognized, but it does not explain why the price of a given commodity will tend to fluctuate around a certain level.[3]

---

[3] Marx offers the following insight on supply in demand in his pamphlet *Wages, Prices and Profit*:

Another erroneous theory of value is based on the idea that that a commodity's value is the sum of the value of the materials and wages expended on its production plus average profit. This is clearly a tautological theory that fails to explain what originally determines the value of those component elements. Finally, there have been theories where value is in the eye of the beholder, so that it is explained as the outcome of subjective evaluations on the part of buyers and sellers. Fanciful scenarios have concocted to "prove" this assertion, such as the story of a man dying of thirst in the desert who would gladly exchange a fistful of diamonds for a glass of water. However, even if this factor accounts for the high price of some rare item or work of art, it does not tell us much about the continual production (= reproduction) that is the basis for the continued existence of any society; nor does it elucidate the specific reality of capitalist commodity production. – In short, none of these "alternatives" to the labor theory of value adequately addresses the theoretical question at hand concerning how commodity exchange is regulated.

## "How, Why and Through What"

We may be in a better position, after that excursion into the labor theory of value, to now look at the three theories that Kuruma examines in detail in this book, namely: the theory of the value-form, the theory of the fetish-character, and the theory of the exchange process.

One guiding thread for Kuruma in seeking to understand these three theories, and grasp the relation and distinction between them, is the issue of how money is discussed in each one. Kuruma was in-

---

"Supply and demand regulate nothing but the temporary *fluctuations* of market prices. They will explain to you why the market price of a commodity rises above or sinks below its *value*, but they will never account for that *value* itself. Suppose supply and demand to equilibrate, or, as the economists call it, to cover each other. Why, the very moment these opposite forces become equal they paralyze each other, and cease to work in the one or the other direction. At the moment when supply and demand equilibrate each other, and therefore cease to act, the market price of a commodity coincides with its real value, with the standard price round which its market prices oscillate. In inquiring into the nature of that value, we have, therefore, nothing at all to do with the temporary effects on market prices of supply and demand." (Marx, 1996, pp. 26–27 – Marx's emphasis)

trigued by the fact that Marx deals with the topic of money in all three of the chapters that make up Part 1, even though money only first appears in a heading in the case of Chapter 3 ("Money, or the Circulation of Commodities). Kuruma felt that Marx provided us with a useful hint, in the following sentence, regarding how money is discussed prior to Chapter 3: "The difficulty lies not in comprehending that money is a commodity, but in discovering *how*, *why*, and *through what* a commodity is money" (Marx, 1976a, p. 186). According to Kuruma, Marx is referring in that sentence to the discussion of money in Section 3, Section 4, and in Chapter 2, respectively, where he arrives at a profound understanding of money through his analysis of the commodity (prior to the theory of money *proper* in Chapter 3). That analysis, in short, reveals the essence of money, its necessity under capitalism, and the specific factor that turns one commodity into money *qua* general equivalent. – But let me elaborate somewhat on each of those three issues.

First, there is the theoretical question regarding the "how of money" in Section 3. The question here centers on how the value of a commodity is expressed. We already know, of course, that the value of a commodity is expressed in the tangible form of money; and Marx's inquiry begins from the money-form ($x$ commodity A $= y$ money commodity). He discovers that the money-form is nothing more than the developed form of the simple value-form ($x$ commodity A $= y$ commodity B). It becomes clear, in the case of the simple value-form, that the commodity on the left of the equation (relative value-form) expresses its own value in the use-value of the commodity on the right (equivalent form). But Marx does more than simply note this fact. He seeks to elucidate the mechanism of value-expression, wherein the commodity in the relative form of value equates the commodity in the equivalent form to itself as a thing of value (*Wertding*), thus positing that commodity as the embodiment of value (*Wertkörper*). In this way, the use-value of the commodity in the equivalent form comes to serve as the material for the commodity in the relative form to express its own value. At first glance this "detour" of value-expression that Kuruma describes may seem inconsequential; but an understanding of it effectively demystifies money, revealing that the peculiar power of gold (or silver) stems from the relation of value expression – not from some intrinsic power *qua* metallic object.[4] It is only within this relationship that the commodity in the equivalent form – and then gold as the "general equivalent" – becomes the embodiment of value or direct incarnation of human labor.

Next, in Section 4, Marx deals with the "why of money" by considering the reason why money exists in the first place under capitalism. This can in turn be reduced to the question of why products of labor must take the commodity-form (and human labor the form of value) in a capitalist society. Marx goes about answering this question by presenting situations or societies where money is not necessary and has no room to exist. His examples include feudal production in the Middle Ages, a peasant family producing for its own consumption, and a future society that he describes as an "association of free men." In each case, the consumption goals are clear from the outset, as are the relations between the producers, so the labor of each individual is expended *directly* as one part of the total labor of the group or society. There is no need, therefore, for production or distribution to be mediated by commodity exchange, and hence no need for money. Under capitalism, however, the situation is quite different. In this form of society, the starting point of production is the labor expended by "private individuals who work independently of each other" (Marx, 1976a, p. 165), and the products are destined to first pass through the market rather than directly meeting specific consumption needs. The private labor expended under capitalism only first becomes one part of the total social labor if and when the products are successfully exchanged. It is only through this act of commodity exchange that the various producers first come into a social relation with each other, thus generating the "fetish-character" unique to capitalist commodity production where so-

---

[4] Marx of course recognizes that the natural qualities of gold (or silver and other metals) make it perfectly suited to the money-role *qua* embodiment of value, because gold is "a material whose every sample possesses the same uniform quality" and it is "divisible at will" and can be "assembl[ed] again from its component parts" (Marx, 1976a, p. 185). But noting this fact is quite different from saying that gold inherently has the power as money outside of the commodity-exchange or value-expression relation. Marx summed up this distinction nicely in *Capital*: "Although gold and silver are not by nature money, money is by nature gold and silver" (Marx, 1976a, p. 184).

cial relations between human beings are manifested as relations between "things" (= money and commodities). Kuruma thus describes value as the "peculiar form assumed by the private labor of commodity owners in order to become social labor" (Kuruma, 1954, p. 88). When labor is instead expended directly as social labor, to meet specific consumption needs, there is no need for it to take an "objectified" form as the substance of value, and so there is no room for the existence of the money- or commodity-form.

Finally, Marx turns his attention to the "through what of money" in Chapter 2. He sets out to elucidate the specific factor that turns one commodity into the general equivalent (= money). That factor can be found, as the chapter's title indicates, within the process of exchange. More specifically, the issue concerns the *contradiction* of the exchange process, where commodities "must be realized as values before they can be realized as use-values" yet also "must stand the test as use-values before they can be realized as values" (Marx. 1976a, p. 179).[5] Consider the perspective of an individual commodity owner. Marx says that the owner only wants to part with a commodity in exchange for a use-value that "satisfies his own need," but at the same time "desires to realize his commodity, as a value, in any other suitable commodity of the same value" regardless of "whether his commodity has any use-value for the owner of the other commodity or not" (Marx 1976a, p. 180). For instance, if a woman owns a copy of *Capital* and wants to exchange it for a six-pack of beer, while the owner of the beer wants to exchange his six-pack for a Che Guevara t-shirt (even while recognizing that *Capital* has an exchange-value about equal to his beer), then exchange could not be

---

[5] Marx explains this "vicious circle" in *A Contribution to the Critique of Political Economy* in the following way:

"One and the same relation must therefore be simultaneously a relation of essentially equal commodities which differ only in magnitude, i.e., a relation which expresses their equality as materializations of universal labor-time, and at the same time it must be their relation as qualitatively different things, as distinct use-values for distinct needs, in short a relation which differentiates them as actual use-values. But equality and inequality thus posited are mutually exclusive. The result is not simply a vicious circle of problems, where the solution of one problem presupposes the solution of the other, but a whole complex of contradictory premises, since the fulfillment of one condition depends directly upon the fulfillment of its opposite." (Marx, 1987a, p. 285)

carried out. This contradiction – between a commodity's realization as use-value and its realization as value – must somehow be mediated in order for the exchange of products to be smoothly carried out and for the products to actually "confront each other as commodities" rather than "as products or use-values only" (Marx, 1976a, p. 180). What actually mediates this contradiction, of course, is money, whose intercession splits the exchange process into a sale and a purchase. This makes it possible for a commodity owner to first exchange a commodity for money, and then use its power of direct exchangeability to purchase whatever commodity is desired. The point emphasized by Marx in Chapter 2 is that money emerges, not as the result of some conscious human act or invention, but rather from the contradiction of the exchange process itself.

* * * * *

The summary above, for all its inadequacy, may at least provide some idea of the characteristics of the three theoretical questions that Kuruma examines. His interpretation is not groundbreaking in itself, as it is simply based on a careful reading of what Marx actually wrote, but explanations of *Capital* do not always (or even often) adequately explain the theoretical tasks that Marx addresses in Part 1.

Consider, for example, two common approaches to the theory of the value-form in Section 3. Some have viewed it from a *historical* perspective, so that the development of the value-form is thought to be a chronological development that begins with primitive barter (= simple value-form) and progresses up to the appearance of money. It is easy enough to slip into this historical approach, given the points of correspondence between the value-forms discussed in Section 3 and the course of real historical development. Nevertheless, it is an approach that hinders the elucidation of the mechanism of value-expression, which is the theoretical task at hand. Meanwhile, often as a reaction against such historical interpretations, some have approached the theory of the value-form from a *logical* perspective, so that the development of the value-form is seen as the logical self-development of forms or concepts. From this perspective, the theoretical task seems to involve explaining (or identifying the motive force that determines) the transition from one form to the next.

The result, again, is that we lose sight of theoretical question specific to the theory of the value-form. The focus in each of the two approaches is on the development of forms, at the expense of elucidating the given theoretical task.

In contrast, Kuruma bears in mind the key question to be solved. He understands that the development of the value-form presented in Section 3 retraces the path of Marx's analysis, which descended from the money-form to the simple value-form in order to clarify the exact mechanism of value-expression. It would thus be pointless (and misleading), Kuruma felt, to sever the development of the value-form from this analysis of value-expression, so as to depict it as a purely historical or logical development. This is one cogent example of how adhering to Kuruma's seemingly obvious advice about bearing the theoretical task in mind results in a more profound understanding of *Capital*.

## The "Power of Abstraction"

The fundamental point emphasized by Kuruma about the need for Marx to pose each theoretical question in a "pure" form, so that it can be properly answered, is intertwined with the issue of abstraction.

We have already seen some examples of how Marx uses abstraction as his analytical tool in Chapter 1 and 2 of *Capital*. His analysis of the commodity at the outset, for instance, is based on abstracting from those purely "formal commodities" that lack intrinsic value. And in this analysis, even though the commodity is the unity of use-value and value, Marx quickly abstracts from the former aspect in order to concentrate on the latter. This abstraction from use-value also involves the abstraction from the particular type of human labor that produces a given use-value, in order to focus instead on the labor that creates the value of a commodity.

These are all examples of how Marx, for the sake of posing a theoretical question in an answerable form, sets aside or "abstracts from" those elements not directly relevant to the task at hand (often the elements that can be easily understood without any close analysis). It is through this use of abstraction that Marx was able to uncover or extract important abstract concepts (such as the concept of value or abstract human labor). Abstraction can thus be simply described as the double-sided cognitive act of temporarily placing out of consideration whatever is not pertinent to the given theoretical question, in order to concentrate on what is.[6]

Those without an appreciation of this need to temporarily set aside irrelevant elements will probably find the beginning of *Capital* "too abstract" in the sense of being detached from reality. That impression is not entirely mistaken, of course, because abstraction does indeed involve taking a step back from concrete reality, as just described. Yet this is a step that must be taken in order to better understand reality, by means of elucidating the elements that constitute it. It is simply not possible to explain every element at the same time. Moreover, even though elements are set aside if they are not relevant to a given theoretical task, it is not the case that they are simply banished forever: those same elements can be examined at a separate stage. Thus, critics who imagine that they can refute Marx by pointing out that a particular abstract concept does not directly correspond to this or that economic phenomenon encountered in daily life, only end up exposing their own poor grasp of the general meaning of abstraction and of the specific theoretical questions addressed in *Capital*.

One such critic in Japan was Kōzō Uno (1897–1977). It was in response to his criticism of Marx that Kuruma offered some observations on the meaning and role of abstraction. Kuruma encountered Uno's criticism in the late 1940s at a series of study meetings on *Capital* that they both participated in. (His encounter with Uno's ideas led Kuruma to later write the series of articles entitled "Theory of the Value-Form & Theory of the Exchange Process" that is in-

---

[6] This meaning of abstraction is reflected in the etymology of the verb "to abstract," which comes from the Latin *abstrahere*, meaning "to draw away, remove something (from something else)" (Inwood, 1992, p. 29). (The noun "concrete" can meanwhile be traced to the past participle of the Latin verb *concrescere*, which means "to grow together, condense.") The Japanese language, incidentally, has two related terms that clarify the meaning of abstraction: *shashō* is the "setting aside" or "abstracting from" those elements within concrete reality not directly pertinent to the theoretical problem at hand; while *chūshō* (as the reverse side of the act of abstraction) is the "extracting" of the element to be examined.

cluded as Part One of this book.) In order to better understand the comments Kuruma made on abstraction at those meetings, we need to first look at some of the points Uno raised there concerning the use of abstraction in *Capital*.

Uno's criticism basically comes down to the idea that Marx abstracted too far, too soon, at the beginning of *Capital*. The debate between Uno and Kuruma centered, in particular, on whether Marx had been correct, in his analysis of the simple value-form, to abstract from the existence of the commodity owner and his desire for a particular use-value. Uno felt it was premature to abstract in this way (at least at that particular stage); and that the outcome is that Marx overlooked the factor that determines which commodity is in the equivalent form. Uno also objected to how Marx abstracts from use-value at the outset to examine value; how he sets aside concrete labor to elucidate abstract human labor; and how he seeks in Section 1 to elucidate the concept of labor as the substance of value.

The basis for Uno's criticism is the idea that such abstraction can only be properly carried out by taking into consideration other processes that have yet to be elucidated in Chapter 1. Marx thus erred, according to Uno, in only carrying out such abstraction within his own mind, while overlooking related processes. This notion was not fully elaborated by Uno at the time, so it is difficult to summarize, but his general view is reflected in the following sorts of comments he made at the study meetings: "Abstraction from use-value takes place in the course of the process of the development of the value-form" (Sakisaka & Uno, 1948, p. 93); "The overall process from the development of the value-form and appearance of money up to the transformation of that money into capital should be understood as the process of the abstraction from use-value" (Sakisaka & Uno, 1948, p. 89); "The basis for clarifying the two-fold nature of labor also emerges in the course of the process from the appearance of money to the appearance of capital" (Sakisaka & Uno, 1948, p. 93).

Uno's view at the time seems to have been that abstraction, rather than solely being a cognitive act, must rather be based on or take into consideration those sorts of processes that unfold separately from the human mind. And he described the processes as a "historical development that we grasp theoretically" (Sakisaka & Uno, 1948, p. 89). It may be more accurate, in fact, to say that Uno thought that abstraction itself takes place *through* such processes. He said, for instance, that abstraction from use-value (and from the commodity owner's desire for a certain use-value) takes place through the appearance of money, which is no longer desired for its specific use-value.

Kuruma, in response to Uno's criticism of Marx, began by pointing out the string of problems that would ensue if Uno's advice of not abstracting from use-value at the outset were followed. Kuruma noted that if the analysis of the commodity does not proceed up to the clarification of the substance of value, then "the twofold character of labor could not be clarified, which in turn would mean that the value-form could not be clarified, so that the necessity of money would likewise remain unclear" (Sakisaka & Uno, 1948, p. 91). With these problems in mind, Kuruma insisted that the criticism of Marx's use of abstraction to analyze the commodity in Chapter 1 amounts to a rejection of his "fundamental thinking regarding the method of his critique of political economy" (Sakisaka & Uno, 1948, p. 91).

On a more fundamental level, Kuruma dissected the confused understanding of the meaning of abstraction that was at the basis of Uno's criticism of Marx. Countering Uno's view that Marx had been wrong to only abstract within his own mind (thereby overlooking objective processes), Kuruma emphasized that abstraction is *necessarily* a cognitive act, noting that "to analyze something is, to begin with, precisely the act of abstraction within human thought, so there is no question that the discovery of abstract labor, or of the concept of abstract labor, is the outcome of mental abstraction through the analysis of the commodity, the product of the workings of the human mind (Sakisaka & Uno, 1948, p. 96). There is a crucial distinction between this cognitive act of abstraction that uncovers an abstract concept, on the one hand, and the process through which that abstract concept *qua* objective entity comes to acquire its abstract character. The latter process clearly unfolds separately from human cognition, so it would be a terrible mistake, Kuruma insisted, to confuse that process with the cognitive process of abstraction.

The distinction and relation between the process of cognition and the process of real development is easier to grasp, I think, if we look at the specific example of abstract human labor (or human labor in general), which Uno and Kuruma addressed at the study meetings.

There is no question that it is the human mind that uncovers the concept of abstract human labor. This is by nature a cognitive act. Yet the mind is able to uncover the concept of abstract labor through analysis precisely because it exists objectively. And it was necessary for labor to have developed up to a certain point before human beings were able to grasp that concept.

The same is true in the case of other abstract concepts. Kuruma pointed out that "abstraction, generally speaking, will only be carried out once a given thing has developed and differentiated itself so as to exist as a rich totality with manifold aspects" – just as, conversely, "abstraction will obviously not be carried out when a thing only exists in a single form" (Kuruma, 1954, p. 16). Those processes of development, which are closely connected to the ability to unearth abstract concepts, unfold separately from the human mind. So there is both a close relation and an important distinction between the processes of real development and the cognitive act of abstraction.

It was not until human labor had "developed and differentiated itself so as to exist as a rich totality with manifold aspects" that the concept of human labor in general – as opposed to labor in its concrete manifestations – could be understood, starting with Adam Smith. This development of labor was closely connected to the expansion of capitalism, which was accompanied by the development of the social division of labor and the increasing mobility of labor between spheres of production, generating an "indifference towards the specific type of labor" (Kuruma, 1954, p. 17). Thus, without the benefit of this historical development of capitalism and the clearer perspective it opened up, even a thinker as acute as Smith would not have been unable to arrive at the concept of human labor in general.[7] This close relationship between objective processes of development and the cognitive act of abstraction does not mean, however, that the importance of the latter should be downplayed; nor that its role should be dissolved within the former. Indeed, Uno's error, according to Kuruma, was to have confused the mental act of abstraction with

---

[7] Marx mentions the interesting case of Aristotle, who came tantalizingly close to a labor theory of value in noting that the equation "5 beds = 1 house" must contain some quality common to both sides" but ultimately could not arrive at the answer because of the "historical limitation inherent in the society in which he lived." (Marx, 1976a, pp. 151–152)

the processes that unfold separately from the human mind and contribute to the ability to arrive at an abstract concept.

\* \* \* \* \*

Marx's use of abstraction might come into clearer view if we consider a specific theoretical question from *Capital*. I think that here, again, the theory of the value-form in Section 3, which was at the heart of the debate between Uno and Kuruma, provides us with the most instructive case.

Uno insisted that Marx had been wrong to abstract from the commodity owner in his analysis of the simple value-form because that abstraction from the want of the commodity owner is only carried out later via other processes (such as the appearance of money, which is no longer desired as a specific use-value). It is only by taking the desire for a specific use-value into consideration, Uno added, that we can understand why a particular commodity (e.g., a coat) is in the equivalent form:

> I think it would instead be clearer to take the commodity owner into consideration from the beginning of the value-form through to the money-form. For example, in seeking to express the value of the linen within the relation between the linen and the coat, I think that we can first understand the expression of value using the coat's use-value by considering the want of the linen owner for the coat. (Sakisaka & Uno, 1948, p. 142)

Uno said that the value-form that Marx examines, 20 yards of linen = 1 coat, "is not possible without the commodity owner" (Sakisaka & Uno, 1948, p. 142). That is to say, without taking into consideration the owner of the linen (relative value-form), we cannot account for why the coat is in the equivalent form. Moreover, according to Uno's logic, this abstraction from the commodity owner of the relative value-form would mean that "anything" could be in the equivalent form so that "it would already be the expanded form of value" (Sakisaka & Uno, 1948, p. 160).

At first glance, Uno's criticism of Marx may seem plausible enough. On a basic level there is a temptation to "hold on" to the commodity owner and not abstract from the role played by the owner's desire for a certain use-value. We know, for instance, that commodities (even livestock) are not in the habit of transporting themselves to the marketplace and haggling over their own prices. So it seems odd for Marx to position an inanimate object, such as linen, as the "subject" of value-expression instead of the living and breathing commodity owner. Translators of *Capital* have found this idea so strange, apparently, that they felt the need to replace "linen" with "commodity owners" (Ben Fowkes) or "we" (Samuel Moore / Edward Aveling) in some sentences.[8]

Kuruma readily conceded that it is the commodity owner's desire for a specific use-value that determines which commodity will be posited in the equivalent form. But he also pointed out that such knowledge does not bring us even one step closer to accomplishing the task of the theory of the value-form, which is to elucidate the mechanism of value-expression. That task remains even *after* we have established why a particular commodity is in the equivalent form. Consequently, we must take a certain value-equation as the given premise and proceed to analyze it, setting aside the role played by the commodity owner in establishing the equation. It is only by taking a particular equation as a given, Kuruma argued, and thus posing the question in a "pure" form, that we are able to precisely clarify how the value of one commodity is expressed in the use-value of another commodity.

In contrast, Uno introduced an element foreign to the question at hand by concentrating on the role of the commodity owner, thus hindering its solution. This is one example of the sort of confusion that can arise from an inadequate awareness of the specific theoretical questions that Marx poses in *Capital*.

---

[8] The introduction of a human subject into the relation of value-expression creates the impression that value emerges from the act of exchange itself – rather than value existing prior to exchange (as determined by the expenditure of labor). Value, in other words, is seen as nothing more than a subjective thing determined through the process of haggling between buyer and seller. This view, needless to say, runs completely counter to the labor theory of value and effectively dissolves the conceptual distinction between value and price.

## Marx's Method of Inquiry

I want to conclude this introduction by looking at some of the characteristics of the overall analytical approach or method that we encounter in *Capital*. This may contribute to a better awareness of how the various analyses of economic forms fit together within Marx's overall investigation of capitalism.

Samezō Kuruma had a keen interest in Marx's method, dedicating two volumes of his *Marx-Lexikon zur Politischen Ökonomie* to that topic.[9] Yet Kuruma had little interest in discussions of Marx's method from a purely philosophical perspective if it meant overlooking the concrete application of that method to analyze capitalism. Kuruma reacted against the Hegelian tendency prevalent in postwar Japan among Marxian philosophers and economists, who often sought points of *direct* correspondence between *Capital* and Hegel's *Science of Logic*.[10] Kuruma of course recognized Marx's enormous intellectual debt to Hegel, and that "familiarizing ourselves with Hegel is obviously very beneficial to an understanding of Marx," but at the same time he stressed the fact that "Marx incorporated Hegel's ideas on the basis of a fundamental criticism" (Kuruma, 1969, p. 1), rather than swallowing those ideas whole. Instead of viewing Marx's method through the prism of Hegelian thought, Kuruma recommended that we go straight to the source, emphasizing that the "surest way to become familiar with Marx's method is to straightforwardly and carefully read *Capital*" because that is where "his method is rendered concrete" (Kuruma, 1969, p. 1).

Marx himself hints at this need for readers to grasp method through an engagement with his actual analysis of capitalism by placing his own brief methodological remarks in the introductions, prefaces, and afterwords to *Capital* (and to other economic works). Yet Marx's inclusion of such methodological comments at all, and their placement outside of the main body, at the same time suggests

---

[9] See the footnote at the beginning of Part Two of this book for a brief explanation of Kuruma's *Marx-Lexikon zur Politischen Ökonomie.*

[10] Many Marxian scholars in Japan took to heart Lenin's aphorism in *Philosophical Notebooks* about how it is "impossible to completely understand Marx's *Capital,* and especially its first chapter, without having thoroughly studied and understood the *whole* of Hegel's *Logic.*" (Lenin, 1976, p. 180)

that readers can benefit from having a basic grasp of his approach to the study of capitalism; and that it may be advantageous to possess such knowledge *before* jumping into the first chapter and struggling with the "difficult beginning." Kuruma paid close attention to such methodological comments, and here I want to draw on some of his observations in order to sketch some of the characteristics of Marx's method.

The passage most often quoted to explain Marx's method is his introduction to *Grundrisse*. In it Marx says that political economy, in its investigation of capitalism, starts out from the "real and the concrete" (e.g., the "population" of a country), but that it soon becomes clear that this concrete reality is actually the "concentration of many determinations, hence the unity of the diverse." Therefore, we will only have a "chaotic conception [*Vorstellung*] of the whole" until we are able to grasp the essential determinations. Marx describes the *descending journey* that moves "analytically towards ever more simple concepts [*Begriff*], from the imagined concrete towards ever thinner abstractions until [we arrive] at the simplest determinations." Once the essential determinations have been elucidated, political economy must then "retrace" that path, taking the *ascending journey* back to the level of the real and the concrete, now understood not as chaos but as a "rich totality of many determinations and relations" (Marx 1973, p. 100).[11] We can see in this passage, once again, the need to step back from reality as it exist in its concrete totality, using the power of abstraction, in order to eventually arrive at a more profound understanding of reality by means of grasping its component elements.

In interpreting Marx's comments, however, it is important to be aware of the overall context of his argument. Kuruma reminds us that Marx is not attempting to explain his own method, but rather sketching the historical development of political economy towards becoming a science. Marx clearly says, for instance, that the descent "from the imagined concrete towards ever thinner abstractions" is the "path

---

[11] Marx in his introduction to *Grundrisse* summarizes the two "journeys" thusly: "Along the first path the full conception was evaporated to yield an abstract determination; along the second, the abstract determinations lead towards a reproduction of the concrete by way of thought." (Marx 1973, p. 100)

historically followed by economics at the time of its origins":

> The economists of the seventeenth century, e.g., always begin with the living whole, with population, nation, state, several states, etc.; but they always conclude by discovering through analysis a small number of determinant, abstract, general relations such as division of labor, money, value, etc. (Marx 1973, p. 100)

Once "these individual moments had been more or less firmly established and abstracted," Marx adds, there "began the economic systems, which ascended from the simple relations, such as labor, division of labor, need, exchange value, to reach the level of the state, exchange between nations and the world market" (i.e., the "ascending journey"). This gradual ascent of political economy towards becoming a *system* of thought is the key point Marx is emphasizing in his introduction.

Marx describes that ascending journey as "obviously the scientifically [*wissenschaftlich*] correct method." In other words, political economy only first approached the level of science when economists began to erect economic *systems* upon the basis of the abstract concepts and determinations they had elucidated. Kuruma is quick to note, however, that Marx is not suggesting that the descent towards the essential determinations is somehow *un*-scientific, because the analytical descent is in fact the indispensable premise for the subsequent ascent towards a systematic understanding of capitalist society. The point is simply that the ascending journey is "scientifically correct" in the sense that the various pieces of knowledge (*Wissen*) regarding economic forms and concepts are organized into a system of knowledge, thus rising to the level of science (*Wissenschaft*).[12]

---

[12] In a discussion on the topic of Marx's method, Kuruma pointed to the following two passages, from Hegel's *Phenomenology of Spirit* and *The Encyclopaedia Logic*, to illustrate the close relation between "scientific" and "systematic":

"The systematic development of truth in scientific form can alone be the true shape in which truth exists. To help to bring philosophy nearer to the form of science – that goal where it can lay aside the name of love of knowledge and be actual knowledge – that is what I have set before me. The inner necessity that knowledge should be science lies in its very nature; and the adequate and sufficient explanation for this lies simply and solely in the systematic exposition of philosophy itself." (Hegel, 1977, p. 3)

We can see, then, that Marx was not unique in making the descent towards "thinner abstractions"; nor was he the first to erect a system of thought upon that basis. The Classical economists Smith and Ricardo (as well as the earlier Physiocrats led by Quesnay) had gradually moved towards simpler or more essential economic concepts in their analyses, and then attempted to present a system of thought that could encompass and explain the capitalist mode of production as a whole. This approach set them apart from earlier thinkers who had been primarily engrossed in this or that economic problem, often in direct relation to state policy.

In contrast to the introduction to *Grundrisse*, Kuruma thought that the following passage from Marx's afterword to *Capital* better explains the characteristics of his method:

> Of course the method of presentation must differ in form from that of inquiry. The latter has to appropriate the material in detail, to analyze its different forms of development, to trace out their inner connection. Only after this work is done, can the actual movement be adequately described. If this is done successfully, if the life of the subject-matter is ideally reflected as in a mirror, then it may appear as if we had before us a mere *a priori* construction. (Marx, 1976a, p. 102)

Setting aside the method of presentation for the moment, we can see from this brief passage that Marx describes the need for the process of inquiry "to appropriate the material in detail, to analyze its different forms of development, [and] to trace out their inner connection." This is precisely what the Classical economists had failed to adequately accomplish. They had moved towards the essential determinations of economic forms, but did not manage to fully understand the connections between determinations and forms or elucidate the development (or genesis) of forms. Smith and Ricardo found it difficult to fill in all of the points separating an abstract concept from its concrete or phenomenal manifestations, often directly and mechani-

---

"A philosophizing without system cannot be scientific at all; apart from the fact that philosophizing of this kind expresses on its own account a more subjective disposition, it is contingent with regard to its content. A content has its justification only as a moment of the whole, outside of which it is only an unfounded presupposition or a subjective certainty." (Hegel, 1991, p. 39)

cally applying the abstract concept to "explain" this or that economic fact. Marx, in contrast, succeeded in filling in the points of mediation connecting a given economic phenomenon or form to its essential determinations. Unlike his predecessors, Marx thus managed to appropriate the material in detail.[13]

One important reason why the Classical economists failed to adequately "analyze its [the material's] different forms of development" or "trace out their inner connection" is that they viewed capitalism as somehow being a natural state of affairs that reflects an unchanging human nature. From this perspective, they took capitalistic economic forms for granted, rather than pondering the genesis of those forms. Marx notes that Classical political economy "is not interested in elaborating how the various forms come into being, but seeks to reduce them to their unity by means of analysis, because it starts from them as given premises" (Marx, 1989a, p. 500). This contrasts sharply with Marx's own view of capitalism as one historical mode of production.

The inadequacy of the method or approach of Smith and Ricardo, particularly the lack of development in their thought, is reflected in the presentation of their ideas. Marx describes the "faulty architectonics" of Ricardo's *Principles of Political Economy*, where the "entire Ricardian contribution is contained in the first two chapters." In those initial chapters Ricardo provides "great theoretical satisfac-

---

[13] The relation between "value" and "price" highlights the methodological difference between Marx and the Classical economists. Both started from the exchange-value of commodities to arrive at an understanding of the concept of value (and labor as the "substance" of value) as the underlying essence of that phenomenal form. And it is upon the basis of this labor theory of value that both Marx and the Classical economists erected their respective systems of economic thought. Yet the Classical economists did not adequately analyze the different forms of development or trace out their inner connection: they did not examine the form of value itself or consider why that form (or the commodity- and money-form) must exist in the first place. Marx, meanwhile, examined the forms themselves (not only their essential content) and pondered their necessity under capitalism. Moreover, through his theory of production price, Marx elucidated the points connecting the concept of value to the concrete level of the actual prices we encounter in everyday life. The Classical economists, lacking all such knowledge, attempted to directly apply the concept of value to explain prices, which ended in bewilderment and the collapse of their school of thought.

tion," Marx says, by presenting "the whole bourgeois system of economy as subject to one fundamental law, and extract[ing] the quintessence out of the divergence and diversity of the various phenomena." Yet there is no subsequent development. Ricardo merely regards the "phenomenal form as the immediate or direct proof or exposition of the general laws" (Marx, 1989a, p. 394), and in a mechanical fashion he *directly* applies the concept of value in an attempt to explain actual commodity prices.

Marx contrasts the static presentation in the works of Classical economists with a presentation based upon a successful method of inquiry, where the "life of the subject-matter is ideally reflected as in a mirror" so that "it may appear as if we had before us a mere *a priori* construction." This is precisely what Marx succeeds in doing: reconstructing within his own mind the capitalist mode of production in its complexity. Those unaware of his method of inquiry might mistake the theoretical edifice presented in *Capital* for a castle of the imagination, but in fact Marx's seemingly *a priori* presentation reflects the success of his inquiry, which not only descends to the simplest determinations but also appropriates the material in detail, analyzes its different forms of development, and traces out their inner connection, so as to arrive at a systematic (= scientific) understanding of capitalism as a concrete whole.

If we combine the insights from the two passages discussed thus far, I think that we can get a basic image of Marx's overall approach to the investigation of capitalism. We need to keep in mind, in other words, both the description of the descending and ascending journeys in the introduction to *Grundrisse*, as well as the emphasis on the effort to "appropriate the material in detail, to analyze its different forms of development, [and] to trace out their inner connection" in the afterword to *Capital*.

Certainly, Marx descends towards the simplest determinations by means of abstraction, from the starting point of reality in its concrete appearance. But it would be wrong, or at least overly simplistic, to envisage that analytical descent as a single sweeping journey that heads more or less in a straight line. There is in fact an analytical descent – from the phenomenal to the essential level – for the analysis of *each* economic form. We have already seen how Marx starts from the price- or money-form, and then descends to the essential level of the concept of value. The overall analytical descent, of the sort described in the introduction to *Grundrisse*, is thus made up of the analyses of various economic forms. Indeed, it is the pursuit of each form's essential determinations, and the tracing out of the connections between forms and determinations, that drives the overall downward movement towards the simplest concepts, leading eventually to the key concept of value uncovered in the analysis of the commodity.[14]

The same can be said of the journey back to the level of the concrete. It does not follow a straight trajectory along the well-worn path taken on the way down; nor does it begin at the exact moment when the downward descent uncovers the simplest of simple concepts. Rather, we can already see movements back towards the "surface" reality in the various analyses of economic forms For instance, after elucidating the fundamental concept of value through the analysis of the value-form of the commodity, Marx returns to examine that form in Section 3 in order to elucidate the mechanism of value-expression, and then in Section 4 he considers why the value- or money-form is necessary at all under capitalism. Likewise, the organizing of knowledge into a system of thought, which is the ascent towards political economy as a science, is an ongoing process (rather than one that begins the moment the descending journey of abstraction reaches its end). Having said all of that, it is also important to note that the relations between forms and determinations can only be fully elucidated on the basis of an understanding of the most fundamental concepts (most notably the concept of value). So there is an important distinction between the analytical descent towards the simplest determinations and the ascent upon that basis towards a systematic understanding of capitalism in its concrete totality.

The main point I wish to make, in any event, is that there is a great deal of overlap between the analytical descent via abstraction

---

[14] Marx in his introduction to *Grundrisse* touches on how the analysis of one form or concept leads to other analyses, as we discover how things are inter-related and inter-determined. He notes that if we begin with the "population" of a country, we will soon discover that the population itself is made up of "classes," which can only be understood on the basis of the concepts of wage-labor and capital that are themselves based on other concepts such as "exchange, division of labor, prices" etc., etc. (Marx, 1973, p. 100)

and the ascent back to the concrete through systematization; and that neither journey follows a straight path. This is where it helps, I think, to bear in mind the brief comments made by Marx in the afterword to *Capital* about how the process of inquiry involves appropriating the material in detail by means of clarifying the development of forms and the connections between forms and determinations.

The short passage in the afterword also draws a clear line between the method of inquiry and the *presentation* of the knowledge gained through that analytical process. Marx says that it is only after the work of appropriating the material in detail has been completed, so that we have arrived at a systematic understanding of capitalism in its concrete totality, that it is then possible to present the system of thought. This point is worth emphasizing because some have mistaken the ascending journey spoken of in the introduction to *Grundrisse* for a description of Marx's method of presentation. According to this view, the presentation begins once the analytical descent has uncovered the most essential concepts. It is true, of course, that the presentation in *Capital* begins with the concept of value, which is the most essential concept uncovered through Marx's analysis, but he is only in a position to begin that explanation once his theoretical system is fully in place within his own mind, which involves more than merely arriving at the simplest determinations. Indeed, it would have been strange for Marx to describe the ascending journey as being "scientifically correct" in his introduction if he had been referring narrowly to the method of presentation.

* * * * *

Delving too much further into these methodological issues might generate more confusion than clarification. It is sufficient, I think, for readers of *Capital* to have a basic image of Marx's approach to the study of capitalism, as a means of better orienting themselves at times. My own image of Marx's method came into clearer focus upon reading an explanation by Kuruma's younger colleague Teinosuke Otani, included in his recently published book *Zukai shakai keizaigaku* (An Illustrated Guide to Political Economy). In this book, Dr. Otani compares the approach we must take when investigating capitalism to the process of examining a clock – as I will attempt to explain here to bring this introduction to a close.

If our aim is to understand, literally, what makes a clock tick, we obviously need to take the clock apart and examine its parts. It would be laughable to suggest we could understand how a clock functions by simply staring at its "surface reality" and watching the minute and second hands go around. Of course, even a child (or a chimpanzee) can "dismantle" a clock by removing – or ripping out – one part after another. But that one-directional process would not lead to a much clearer understanding of its internal mechanism. Rather than simply removing one part after another, we need to dismantle the clock while examining each individual part and considering how the parts fit back together. In other words, the overall downward process of disassembly naturally involves upward movements where certain parts are reassembled. It is through this process of carefully dismantling and examining the parts of the clock, and grasping their inner connection, that we can mentally reproduce the overall mechanism of the clock within our minds; and then, upon that basis, reassemble the whole clock, starting from the individual pieces.

Similarly, in Marx's investigation of capitalism, there is a general downward process of analysis, where he starts from the reality of capitalism as it presents itself phenomenally, and then abstracts to examine the various determinations or "parts" that make up this reality. This general analytical descent towards the simplest concepts includes the analyses of various economic forms, and those analyses involve movements back up towards the surface reality. It is through this process of analyzing individual forms, and sorting out their determinations and interrelations, that an understanding of capitalism in its concrete totality can emerge within Marx's mind. And once he has arrived at this systematic understanding of capitalism, the task simply becomes how to adequately present his knowledge so that "the life of the subject-matter is ideally reflected as in a mirror." This is the system of thought encountered in the pages of *Capital* – which we can make our own.

# A NOTE ON THE TEXT

*Marx's Theory of the Genesis of Money* contains the full text of Kuruma's book *Kachikeitai-ron to kōkan-kate-ron* (Theory of the Value-Form & Theory of the Exchange Process), published in 1957 by Iwanami Shoten; and a slightly abridged version of Part 1 of his book *Kahei-ron* (Theory of Money), published in 1979 by Otsuki Shoten. I have made a number of changes to the passages quoted from Marx, which ranged from altering spelling or hyphenation and making stylistic changes to correcting apparent errors. In making such changes, I have referred to the Japanese translations that appear in Kuruma's two books, the original German texts, translations by Hans Ehrbar, Mike Roth and Wal Suchting's translation of the appendix of the first German edition of *Capital*, and most importantly the advice of Dr. Teinosuke Otani. Given these various sources, and the large number of changes made, I have not inserted footnotes to explain the exact reason for each change. Also note that unless otherwise indicated italicized words and expressions reflect the emphasis of Kuruma, rather than Marx. My own footnotes (apart from those in the introduction) are placed in brackets to distinguish them from Kuruma's footnotes. Finally, to avoid possible confusion, Japanese names that appear are written with the surname last.

# PART ONE

*Theory of the Value-Form &*
*Theory of the Exchange Process*

# PREFACE

This is a collection of four articles published in the Hosei University journal *Keizai shirin* (The Hosei Economic Review) as a series entitled: "Theory of the Value-Form & Theory of the Exchange Process." The first article appeared in Vol. 18, No. 1 (January 1950), the second in Vol. 18, No. 3 (July 1950), and the third in Vol. 19, No.1 (January 1951). Up to that third article the series was proceeding as planned, but in the spring of 1951 I suddenly fell ill before completing the planned fourth article. Even though I recovered in a few months, it seemed too much of a chore to complete that article (perhaps owing to my laziness), and it remained unfinished for a long time although still in the back of my mind. The first three articles had dealt with the three main objections Kōzō Uno raised against the view, held by me and others, that it was natural for Marx to abstract from the role played by the want of the commodity owner in the theory of the value-form (unlike the case in the theory of the exchange process).

My intention for the fourth article was to then advance my own ideas regarding the difference and relation between the theory of the value-form and the theory of the exchange process. I had already formed my basic view on the relation between those two theories some time earlier, so the difficulty was merely how to express it effectively in writing. I had discussed my view with colleagues on a number of occasions and also presented my ideas at a symposium of the Japanese Society for the History of Economic Thought held in 1954 at Yokohama University, so I felt that someone else would eventually pursue this issue even if I did not go to the trouble of doing it myself. I did end up tackling it again in the autumn of 1955, however, when the editors of the journal *Hosei* asked me to contribute to a symposium they were planning. Unlike the earlier symposium at Yokohama University, where I had not been able to fully express my views given the limited time available, I was to be allotted three hours to speak and a stenographer would also be present. I hoped to take advantage of the opportunity in order to complete the article that had remained unfinished for so long. After my presentation, I revised the written transcript of it in the summer of 1956, which was necessary in part because I had delivered it without relying on notes; and this revised version was published in *Keizai shirin*, Vol. 24, No. 4 (October 1956) as the fourth article in the series.

The content of the fourth article overlaps with that of the previous three articles to some extent because it was based on a separate presentation. Despite its different style, which may seem out of place compared to the other three articles, the fourth article has a systematic structure that may make it easier to understand than if it had been rewritten entirely as a new article. Here I have reversed the original order of the articles, with the fourth article positioned as Part 1 and the three earlier articles as Part 2. One reason for reversing the order is that each of the first three articles begins by presenting the ideas of Kōzō Uno before then responding to his criticism, whereas it seems more appropriate to begin the book by first presenting my views first and then addressing Uno's criticism.

In editing the book, some revisions and additions have been made to the earlier articles – along with "technical" revisions such as correcting typographical errors, altering inappropriate expressions, and incorporating footnoted material into the main body – but none of the changes made altered the gist of the subject matter, as they mainly involved adding passages from Marx's writings to elaborate a particular point or provide a point of reference.

February 17, 1957

# Theory of the Value-Form &
# Theory of the Exchange Process

A quick look at Part 1 of *Capital* reveals that Chapter 1 is divided into four sections: "The Two Factors of the Commodity: Use-Value and Value (Substance of Value, Magnitude of Value)"; "The Twofold Character of the Labor Represented in Commodities"; "The Value-Form, or Exchange-Value"; and "The Fetish-Character of the Commodity and its Secret." This is followed by Chapter 2 and Chapter 3, respectively entitled "The Exchange Process" and "Money, or the Circulation of Commodities." In looking at this structure, a number of questions arise.

First of all, the term "money" only first appears in a heading in Chapter 3, where Marx presents his theory of money, but even prior to that chapter money is analyzed. The term is first discussed in the theory of the value-form, appears again in the theory of fetish-character of the commodity, and is dealt with a third time in the theory of the exchange process. What is the exact relation between those three analyses of money and the theory of money presented in Chapter 3? That sort of question naturally arises, I think. It may seem obvious that Chapter 3 presents the fundamental theory of money, whereas Marx's earlier analyses are an introduction of some sort to that theory, but we still need clarify the essential distinction between the two.

Second, assuming that the analyses of money prior to Chapter 3 are indeed introductory, what is the significance of each of the three theories just mentioned? A sense of frustration would be unavoidable, I think, unless we can elucidate this question.

A third point to consider is that, of the three theories thought to play an introductory role, the theory of the value-form and the theory of fetish-character are positioned as sections within Chapter 1 on the commodity, whereas the theory of the exchange process is positioned as the separate Chapter 2 placed parallel to the entire theory of the commodity. Moreover, that second chapter is placed on such equal footing despite being shorter than either of those two sections. We need to consider why this is the case.

These are the sorts of questions that will certainly arise if a person sets out to thoroughly understand the structure of Part 1 – or at least it was so in my case. In particular, the relation between the theory of the value-form and the theory of the exchange process is an issue that I struggled with over a very long period of time, starting shortly after reading *Capital* for the first time about thirty-five years ago. In each of those theories, the analysis seems to revolve around how money is generated; but the manner in which Marx carries out his analysis is completely different. Elucidating the essential difference between the two is actually quite difficult. Related to the difficulty is the fact that the theory of the value-form is one section within the chapter on the commodity, whereas the theory of the exchange process constitutes an independent chapter. Considering why this is the case was at the source of questions that I long struggled with.

When I first began studying *Capital* no detailed explanations were available in Japanese. Later I read *Shihon-ron chūkai* (Commentary on *Capital*) by [the Soviet scholar] D.I. Rozenberg and *Shihon-ron nyūmon* (An Introduction to *Capital*) by Hajime Kawakami, when those books were published; but neither provided what I felt was a fully convincing argument regarding the relation between the theory of the value-form and theory of the exchange process. After giving the matter considerable thought on my own, I eventually arrived at a view that seemed fundamentally correct. It was around that time, in 1947, that I participated in a series of monthly study meetings on *Capital* sponsored by the journal *Hyōron*, during which the question of the difference between the two theories was raised. The person leading that particular discussion explained the difference on the basis of the idea that the theory of the exchange process takes into consideration the role played by the commodity owner as a desiring agent (or the role played by the want of the commodity owner), whereas that role is abstracted from in the theory of the value-form. The discussion thus centered on whether it is possible to understand the value-form if the want of the commodity owner is abstracted from. The majority of the participants, myself included, sided with the view of that presenter, insisting that it is indeed possible. On the other side stood Kōzō Uno, who steadfastly maintained that the value-form cannot be understood if the want of commodity owner is set aside. Various arguments were raised by each side, but neither backed down. Ultimately the discussion broke down because of this disagreement, leaving us with no definitive answer regarding the essential difference between those two theories in *Capital*.

A transcript of the study meetings was published in the pages of *Hyōron* and later as a book. Carefully reading that transcript helped me to clarify my own ideas and thus arrive at a position that seemed fairly secure. I first presented my ideas in a series of articles entitled, "Theory of the Value-Form & the Theory of Exchange Process," published in the journal *Keizai shirin*. The first article appeared in the January 1950 issue, followed by two others. I was in the process of writing a fourth article when I fell ill and that article was not completed.

Here I want to take up this topic again, drawing on the incomplete fourth article. I should note that the first three articles, which are grouped together in Part 2, respond to the three basic theoretical grounds of Uno's view that the value-form cannot be understood if the want of the commodity owner is set aside. What remained to be done was to present my own positive views on the various questions that I raised earlier, particularly the distinction between the theory of the value-form and the theory of the exchange process. The three earlier articles, in responding to the theoretical basis of Uno's argument, already naturally touched on the theory of the value-form because the issue of whether it is correct to abstract from the want of the commodity owner essentially concerns a methodological question determined according to the theoretical task of that theory. However, it is necessary to touch on the matter further here, as it is crucial to an understanding of the difference between the theory of the value-form and the theory of the exchange process.

In the theory of the value-form, Marx sets out to unravel the riddle of a commodity's price (i.e., the riddle of the money-form), while at the same time untangling the riddle of money. The riddle of the money-form concerns the fact that the value of a commodity is generally expressed in the form of a certain quantity of a particular use-value: gold. The riddle of money concerns how, in that case, gold's use-value – which is the element in opposition to its value – has general validity in its given state as value. Not only had no one prior to Marx solved those riddles, there was not even an awareness that they are in fact riddles. Marx became the first to thoroughly clarify these problems by raising the theoretical question in *Capital* pertaining to the value-form. Marx perceived, first of all, that the money-form is the developed value-form. This means that the riddle of the money-form is nothing more than an extension of the fundamental riddle of the value-form. By tracing the money-form to its source, thereby reducing it to its elemental form, which is the simple value-form, Marx locates the core of the riddle of the money-form and of money: the fact that a commodity expresses its own value in the use-value of another commodity that it equates to itself, thereby making the use-value of that other commodity the form of its own value. This is precisely the riddle of the value-form, which is the basis of the riddle of the money-form and the riddle of money. Without unraveling the first riddle, it is quite impossible to unravel the latter two; whereas those riddles are easily unraveled once the former has been elucidated.

The problem does not appear in such a simple shape, however, if the money-form is directly observed. This is because in the money-form the values of all commodities are only expressed in one particular commodity, gold, so that the riddle pushed to the forefront concerns the distinctive and mysterious character of gold based upon its privileged position. It is through the examination of the simple value-form that it first becomes apparent that the value of a commodity is expressed in the use-value of another commodity that is equated to it, and thus the fundamental problem regarding how this is possible comes to be posed in a pure form. Here we have the central question that Marx considers when analyzing the simple form of value. This is the reason he does not ponder why the coat, rather than some other commodity, is posited as the equivalent form of the linen. Granted, it is the action of the linen owner that posits the coat in the equivalent form, and this occurs because the owner wants a coat. But analyzing that factor is of no use when seeking to elucidate the question just posed. In fact, concentrating on it actually hinders the discovery of the answer by raising an unrelated question that blurs the problem at hand. This point becomes clear if we consider the fact that for the coat to be the value-form of the linen it must be equal to the linen, whereas for the owner of the linen to want the coat it must be different from the linen – the former is a relation of equality, the latter a relation of inequality. It is simply not possible to elucidate the *how* of a relation of equality by considering the *why* of positing different things. The question particular to the value-form is one that remains even after the role played by the individual want of the commodity owner has been clarified. It can only be posed as an independent problem by taking the value-equation, which is created by the commodity owner on the basis of his want, as a given. Naturally, a problem can only be thoroughly solved once it has been posed in a pure, independent form. Marx, in his theory of the value-form, analyzes the equation 20 yards of linen = 1 coat, without concerning himself with why the coat (rather than some other commodity) has been posited as the equivalent vis-à-vis the linen. He does this in order to pose the question of how the natural form of one commodity, a coat, becomes the form of value for the linen so that the value of linen can be expressed using the natural form of the coat. Marx thus uncovers the "detour" that constitutes the secret of value-expression, and upon that basis he became the first to thoroughly unravel the riddle of the money-form and the riddle of money.

In addition to the overview just provided regarding the theoretical task and method of the theory of the value-form (also discussed in Part 2), I want to offer an additional explanation for those who might find the overview too sketchy or difficult to understand or who may be unfamiliar with the "detour" of value-expression explained in detail in the first article of Part 2.

Generally speaking, the value of a commodity is always expressed using the use-value of another commodity that is posited as equal to it. In other words, it is expressed in the form of a thing. Developed further we arrive at the money-form, which is the form of price that is actually visible to us, where the values of all commodities are expressed in the form of a certain quantity of gold. The values of all commodities are expressed as gold of such-and-such *yen*. The term "yen" itself was originally the unit-name for the weight of a certain amount of gold *qua* money; under the Coinage Law in Japan it was the name given to 2 *fun* (.750g) of gold money. In other words, the term "yen" (in terms of gold of such-and-such yen) is nothing more than a quantity of gold expressed in a unit of weight that is solely used for money, replacing the usual weight unit names such as *fun* (.375g) or *momme* (3.75g) that were formerly used in Japan. It is through this quantity of gold that the value of a commodity – its value-character and its magnitude of value – is expressed in reality. Here we have the riddle of money. We see that the value of a commodity is expressed by a quantity of gold *qua* thing. But what makes this possible?

That is the question that Marx was the first to raise. And he goes on to brilliantly solve it. Marx perceives, first of all, that the expression of value in money (20 yards of linen = gold of £2; or 20 yards of linen = gold of such-and-such yen) is nothing more than the developed version of the simple value-form (20 yards of linen = 1 coat). Thus, the fundamental mystery of value-expression can be traced to that simple form of value. It is through his analysis of the simple value-form that Marx discovers the "detour" that constitutes the fundamental secret of value-expression. The detour concerns how, in the case of the equation "20 yards of linen = 1 coat," in order for the value of linen to be expressed in the form of a coat, the coat itself must be the embodiment of value, which is to say the value-body [*Wertkörper*].[1] Otherwise, the quantity of the coat as a thing would not be able to express a magnitude of value. Because the coat is equated to the linen, its natural form in that given state is able to become something that expresses value. It becomes the embodiment of value. The coat thus attains the competence just mentioned, which is a definite economic form, thus coming to bear a social relation of production. The labor that makes the coat, of course, is itself specific

---

[1] [Here and elsewhere Kuruma originally used the term "value-thing" (*ka-chi-butsu; Wertding*), rather than "value-body" (*kachi-tai; Wertkörper*); however, in his 1979 conversation with Teinosuke Otani, published as Part 1 of Kuruma's book *Kahei-ron* (Theory of Money), he recognized that it "was an oversight" on his part to use the term "value-thing" in this case to refer to what should be called the "value-body" or "a thing that counts as a value-thing" (Kuruma, 1979, pp. 99–100). (That part of their conversation is not included in Part Two of this book.) In line with Kuruma's comment, I have replaced "value-thing" with "value-body" when it is used inappropriately. – EMS]

concrete labor, not abstract labor. When the coat is equated to the linen, the tailoring labor that makes the coat is equated to the weaving labor that makes the linen, so that the coat-making labor is reduced to abstract human labor, which both types of labor have in common. Meanwhile, the coat is the embodiment of this abstract human labor. It takes on significance as the value-body, or embodiment of value, acquiring that formal determination. The linen, by positing the coat with that formal determination, expresses its own value in the body of the coat *qua* value-thing. Marx says that it is from this perspective that the riddle of value-expression can be unraveled for the first time. Here we need to pay special attention to the fact that the linen, in the value-expression 20 yards of linen = 1 coat, does not immediately turn itself into the form of value by saying that it is equal to the coat. Rather, the linen posits the coat as the form of value by saying that the coat is equal to itself, so that the natural form of the coat, in its given state, expresses value. The value of linen is thus expressed for the first time (in distinction from its use-value) in the natural form of a coat. This is what Marx calls the "detour" of value-expression. It is generally thought, and Marx himself concurred, that the theory of the value-form is the most difficult part of *Capital*. When Marx explains the detour of value-expression in the first German edition of *Capital*, he describes it as "the point where all the difficulties originate which hinder an understanding of the value-form" (Marx, 1976b, p. 21). Not only is the issue itself quite difficult to grasp, there has been a general lack of understanding regarding why it is necessary to ponder this issue at all (despite the explanations offered by Marx). The fact is, however, that the issue is at the core of the secret of value-expression. Without understanding the detour of value-expression, it is impossible to unravel the riddle of the money-form and the riddle of money; whereas those riddles can be easily grasped once the detour has been properly understood. The riddle of the money-form, as noted already, deals with the strangeness of a commodity's value being generally expressed in the form of a certain quantity of gold. The riddle of money, meanwhile, involves the peculiarity in this case of the natural form of gold – its given bodily form – having general validity as value. This is the problem of the value-form posed in *Capital*, and it was by clarifying the detour of value-expression that Marx became the first to thoroughly solve it.

\* \* \* \* \*

Next, I want to look at the theory of the exchange process in contrast to the theory of the value-form. I will begin by considering the characteristics of the theory of the exchange process in comparison to the entirety of Chapter 1 on the commodity. My reason for doing so is that the theory of the exchange process also constitutes an entire chapter and because I think it will be an easy-to-understand approach. We can find clues regarding those different chapters in passages from *A Contribution to the Critique of Political Economy*) [hereafter: *Contribution*] and the first German edition of *Capital*. Those passages, which appear in both of Marx's books prior to the analysis of the exchange process,[2] can be referred to as his "transition definition." Marx offers one clue in the following passage from *Contribution*:

> So far, the two aspects of the commodity – use-value and exchange-value – have been examined, but each time one-sidedly. The commodity as commodity however is the unity of use-value and exchange-value immediately; and at the same time it is a commodity only in relation to other commodities. The actual relation between commodities is their exchange process. (Marx, 1987, pp. 282–283)

Marx offers a similar description at the end of the analysis of the commodity in the first German edition of *Capital*, prior to examining the exchange process:

> The commodity is an immediate unity of use-value and exchange-value, i.e., of two opposite moments. It is therefore an immediate contradiction. This contradiction must develop itself as soon as the commodity is not, as it has been so far, analytically considered (at one time from the viewpoint of use-value and at another from the viewpoint of exchange-value), but rather placed as a totality into an actual relation with other commodities. The actual relation of commodities with each other, however, is their exchange process. (Marx, 1976b, p. 40)

---

[2] In *Contribution*, those parts corresponding to Chapter 1 on the commodity and Chapter 2 on the exchange process in *Capital* are all included within Chapter 1, without any separating headings; but if we look at the actual content it is obvious which part in *Contribution* corresponds to the theory of the exchange process in *Capital*.

These descriptions make it clear that Marx – at least in *Contribution* and the first German edition of *Capital* – felt the theory of the exchange process differs essentially from the preceding analysis, with different observational dimensions.[3] Prior to that theory, the commodity is only examined analytically (and thus in a one-dimensional fashion); i.e., at times solely from the perspective of use-value and at other times solely from the perspective of exchange-value. That is not the case, however, in the theory of the exchange process, where a variety of commodities that are each the unity of use-value and value appear and are able as such to enter an actual relationship with each other in that process. I want to consider this point further, as it has significant bearing on the problem we are addressing.

Few would likely disagree that the commodity is considered analytically in *Capital* prior to the analysis of the exchange process (both in Section 1 and Section 2); and that the same can be said of the corresponding parts in the first German edition or *Contribution* which are not divided into those sections. But what about Section 3 where Marx analyzes the value-form? Can that section really be described as analytical? Or should it be said that both value and use-value play an indispensable role in the expression of value? Such questions seem likely but from my perspective they are based on a clear misunderstanding.

What is certain to begin with is that the theory of the value-form, not surprisingly, centers on the commodity's form of value. The commodity, which is a unity of use-value and value, appears exclusively as value in the case of the value-form, which is a form distinct from the commodity's direct existence as a use-value. It is natural in the theory of the value-form, therefore, to set aside the use-value of the commodity whose value-expression is being considered (i.e., the commodity in the relative form of value). Certainly, the commodity in its direct natural appearance, by nature, has the form of use-value. And then, in addition to that form, it comes to have the form of value, thereby acquiring the twofold form in which a commodity is actually manifested. The value-form of the commodity, therefore, is at the same time the "commodity-form of the product," so that the

---

[3] The passage just quoted does not appear in the subsequent editions of *Capital*; and later I will speculate as to why it was removed.

elucidation of the value-form of the commodity is simultaneously the elucidation of the commodity-form of the product. Still, this does not by any means negate the analytical and one-dimensional nature of the theory of the value-form. That theory solely concerns the commodity's form of value: the form in which a commodity expresses its value in distinction from its direct existence as use-value. The task particular to the theory of the value-form is to elucidate this value-form. The fact that the value-form of the commodity is also the commodity-form of the product (so that the elucidation of the value-form is the elucidation of the commodity-form of the product) means that the form of use-value is posited from the outset within the natural form of the commodity, and is therefore premised as such when the value-form is considered. This, to borrow Marx's words, means:

> The labor-product in its natural form brings the form of a use-value along with itself into the world. Thus there is only a need for the value-form in addition in order for it to possess the commodity-form. (Marx, 1976b, p. 61)

The theory of the value-form clarifies how a product, in order to appear as a commodity, obtains the form of value that it must have in addition to its inherent form as a use-value. If use-value can be said to play an indispensable role in the value-expression of a commodity, it is only the use-value of the commodity in the equivalent form, not the commodity in the relative form of value. A commodity's value is clearly expressed using the use-value of another commodity that it is equivalent to it. Use-value, in its given state, thus becomes the form of value. This is precisely the relation that the theory of the value-form seeks to elucidate, its fundamental task; but that does not negate that the theory of the value-form is analytical and one-dimensional.

First of all, the use-value of the commodity in the equivalent form is *not* the use-value of the commodity whose value-expression is at issue, and is therefore not the use-value that is the oppositional factor to the value being expressed. In our familiar example, it is the linen's value that is expressed, with the use-value of the coat playing a role in that expression of value. Even if it can be said that both value and use-value are being considered at the same time, it is the value of the linen and the use-value of the coat, not two oppositional factors within the *same* commodity. Thus, the commodity is not being analyzed as a totality consisting of both use-value and value. The issue revolves around the expression of the linen's value and the perspective is solely that of value. The use-value of the coat is only manifested as the material for the value-expression of the linen. Moreover, as long as the coat is manifested as such, its use-value plays a role solely as the embodiment of abstract human labor, not in terms of its natural quality as a useful article of clothing.[4]

In the theory of the value-form, therefore, Marx solely considers the commodity from the perspective of value, setting aside its use-value. That is not the case in the theory of the exchange process. There, the process of exchange that is examined is first and foremost a process whereby commodities pass from the hands of the person for whom they are not use-values into the hands of the person for whom they are. This is the material content of the exchange process, and the process is unthinkable apart from this content. Marx thus describes the exchange process as, first of all, a process for the realization of the commodity as use-value. It should be noted, however, that the "realization of a commodity *as* use-value" is different from the "realization *of* use-value." The "realization of use-value" concerns the attribute of being useful in satisfying a certain want, and thus involves actually putting a thing to use so as to realize its potential. This realization takes place within the process of consumption. In contrast, the "realization of a commodity as use-value" pertains to the exchange process. In the case of the latter, the use-value of the commodity is not merely use-value as such but a use-value with a certain social determinacy. It is not a use-value for the person who possesses it, but rather for another person. The commodity must therefore pass into the hands of that other person, and by so doing it first becomes truly useful as a use-value. This is what Marx is referring to by the "realization of a commodity as use-value" – which occurs in the exchange process rather than in the consumption process.

However, the exchange process of commodities is not limited to

---

[4] This is a point I make in the first article of Part 2 in relation to the question of abstracting from the want of the linen owner.

the process of realizing a commodity as use-value: it must at the same time be a process for realizing it as value. There are some, though, who have failed to understand what "realization *as* value" means, confusing it with "realization *of* value," thus turning Marx's theory of the exchange process into a complete muddle. The realization of value refers to the transformation of the value of a commodity – which had only existed in what might be called a "latent" state – into real value. In other words, the transformation of value into the shape of objectively valid value: money. This is something that clearly takes place in the process of selling. However, in the theory of the exchange process, where the question centers on the realization of the commodity as value, money has yet to be formed and the process of exchange has not yet been divided into the two processes of sale and purchase. From this point alone, it should be clear that the "realization of a commodity as value" differs from the "realization of a commodity's value." Regarding the former, Marx notes:

> He [the commodity owner] desires to realize his commodity, as a value, in any other commodity of equal value that suits him, regardless of whether his own commodity has any use-value for the owner of the other commodity or not. (Marx, 1976a, p. 180)

As is clear from this passage, the realization of a commodity as value signifies that a commodity counts as something that actually has value, realizing its potential as value. As use-values, commodities come in an infinite variety, and for this reason they can be exchanged for each other; but as value (i.e., as the objectification of abstract human labor) commodities are indistinguishable and should be able to be replaced with any other commodity, at a given proportion. In order for a commodity owner's product to be useful in that latter way, he produces commodities that are not use-values for himself. The owner, as the bearer of one part of the social division of labor, engages in the production of a particular commodity. But in order to do so the particular commodity produced must be exchangeable for a variety of commodities that are necessary to satisfy the owner's various wants. As a simple use-value there is the likelihood that the commodity of a given owner will not be an object desired by the owners of the commodities that the owner himself wants. This would mean that exchange could not be carried out and that commodity owners would be unable to engage in the production of their own particular commodities without anxiety. This in turn would mean that commodity production itself would not be possible as one mode of the social division of labor. In order for commodity production to exist as a mode of the social division of labor, commodity producers must produce objects that are somehow socially desired. And to the extent that a commodity owner produces a socially desired object, he must at the same time be able to procure other commodities through exchange that are the product of the same amount of labor, regardless of whether his own commodity is an object desired by the owners of the particular commodities he wants or not. This is the original requirement of the commodity as value; which is to say, the requirement of the commodity as the objectification of labor that is indiscriminate, uniform and (in that form) social. And this is a requirement that must be realized in the process of exchange. The requirement of the commodity as value is naturally reflected in the consciousness of the commodity owner. As Marx notes in the passage just quoted, the commodity owner "desires to realize his commodity, as a value, in any other commodity of equal value that suits him, regardless of whether his own commodity has any use-value for the owner of the other commodity or not."

The exchange process must thus be a process for the realization of the commodity as use-value, and at the same time a process for its realization as value. Yet the two realizations mutually presuppose and mutually exclude each other. Here a problem arises that is particular to the exchange process. The realization of a commodity as use-value occurs when it is handed over to another person, but the handing over of the commodity clearly presupposes the realization of the commodity as value. Meanwhile, the realization of the commodity as value is premised on its realization as use-value. If the commodity is not a use-value for the other person, it is not a value. However, the commodity is only first demonstrated to be a use-value for the other person when it is handed over as a use-value in the exchange process. This means that the commodity cannot provide itself with validity as value from the outset when it is exchanged. Not only is the realization of a commodity as use-value and as value a vicious circle of mutually presupposition, it is also a contradictory relation of mutual exclusion:

> They [commodities] can be exchanged as use-values only in connection with particular wants. They are, however, exchangeable only as equivalents, and they are equivalents only as equal quantities of materialized labor-time, when their physical properties as use-values, and hence the relations of these commodities to specific wants, are entirely disregarded. A commodity functions as an exchange-value if it can freely take the place of a definite quantity of any other commodity, irrespective of whether or not it constitutes a use-value for the owner of the other commodity. But for the owner of the other commodity it becomes a commodity only in so far as it constitutes a use-value for him, and for the owner in whose hands it is it becomes an exchange-value only in so far as it is a commodity for the other owner. One and the same relation must therefore be simultaneously a relation of essentially equal commodities which differ only in magnitude, i.e., a relation which expresses their equality as materializations of universal labor-time, and at the same time it must be their relation as qualitatively different things, as distinct use-values for distinct wants, in short a relation which differentiates them as actual use-values. But equality and inequality thus posited are mutually exclusive. The result is not simply a vicious circle of problems, where the solution of one problem presupposes the solution of the other, but a whole complex of contradictory premises, since the fulfillment of one condition depends directly upon the fulfillment of its opposite. (Marx, 1987a, pp. 284–285)

The contradiction specific to the exchange process is manifested also as the collision between the various original wants of the commodity owner. That is, there is the want of the commodity owner to realize his commodity as value, which is the need to exchange it for a commodity of the same value regardless of whether his own product is a use-value for the owner of that particular commodity or not. At the same time, if the commodity owner is unable to exchange his own commodity for the other commodity that is a use-value for himself, he is also unable to hand over his own commodity. In other words, the owner wants his own commodity to count as value, but the other person might not recognize it as such. This situation is not limited to the owner of one particular commodity: every commodity owner is in this same position. As long as this is the case, exchange is blocked; and if the exchange process is at a standstill, commodity production also cannot be generally carried out.

This contradiction must somehow be mediated in order for commodity production to be generalized. What mediates it, needless to say, is money. With the appearance of money, exchange is carried out via the two processes of sale and purchase. The commodity owner no longer has to immediately seek to exchange his own commodity for the other commodities he wants. Instead, he can first exchange his commodity for money. This is the sale. In this process the commodity owner, instead of immediately seeking for his commodity to count as use-value, first hands it over as a use-value to transform it into money. By so doing, the labor expended on the production of the commodity is demonstrated to be socially useful labor. The commodity thus becomes the socially current form of value that is accepted throughout the commodity world; i.e., the commodity becomes money. When this happens, the commodity owner is able in the subsequent purchasing process to make this money count as value, exchanging it for the other commodity (or commodities) that he wants. This is objectively possible because his own commodity has become money. That was not the case prior to the appearance of money. Let us suppose that the owner's commodity is linen, which he wants to exchange for a Bible. It would be very fortunate for him if there happened to be an owner of a Bible who is willing to exchange it for linen. But if the person who wants linen is the owner of wheat, while the Bible's owner craves a bottle of whiskey, exchange could not be carried out. In that particular case, the owner of the linen has produced a commodity that is desired by the owner of wheat. This means that it is socially desired and that the labor objectified in the linen, which constitutes its value, is a certain quantity of human labor expended in a socially useful form. Despite this, if the linen cannot be exchanged for the commodity its owner is seeking (a Bible in this case), the linen cannot be realized as value. This contradiction is only mediated, in the manner noted earlier, with the appearance of money.

The exchange process constitutes a particular object of study as the place where the contradiction of the commodity as the immediate unity of use-value and value unfolds, and therefore as the place where the genesis of money becomes necessary to mediate that contradiction. This is precisely why Marx posits the theory of the exchange process as an independent chapter in *Capital*, placing it on the same level as Chapter 1. Yet some have argued that the contradiction of the exchange process is nothing more than the externalization of the contradiction inherent to the commodity between use-value and value at the stage of the value-form, so that it cannot be said that the contradiction first appears in the exchange process. I must say, however, that this view adheres to identity at the expense of distinction. Certainly, the analysis of the commodity is carried out through the analysis of the form in which the product appears as a commodity; but as long as the analysis of the form itself is at issue the commodity is not yet in a process of motion. We are not yet dealing, at this stage, with the process whereby the commodity as use-value passes into the hands of the commodity owner who wants it, nor are we considering the process whereby the commodity as value is actually transformed into another commodity. The realization of the commodity, as use-value or as value, has yet to be considered; therefore, the contradictory relationship between its realizations as that twofold entity has also not yet been examined. Moreover, the need for money to mediate this contradiction has not yet been raised at that point. The genesis of money is examined in the theory of the value-form, but the question revolves around *how* money is generated (not "through what"). In other words, the question centers on how gold, as a particular commodity, becomes the general equivalent, so that its natural form comes to count as value throughout the commodity world. It does not center on what makes this necessary or through what such a thing is formed. Not only is it possible to draw a distinction between these issues, it is only by actually setting them apart that we can thoroughly elucidate each as a distinct problem.

I do not mean to suggest, however, that the theory of the value-form and the theory of the exchange process are totally distinct from each other. There is in fact an extremely close organic relationship between the two, which I will consider. But we need to be aware of the significant difference between *Capital* and *Contribution* on this point. In *Capital*, prior to presenting his theory of the exchange process, Marx develops the theory of the value-form. In the theory of the exchange process, therefore, after Marx has traced the development of the contradiction of the commodity in that process and clarified the necessity for its mediation, when the question becomes what mediates the contradiction he can state that it was already clarified in the theory of the value-form. Marx pursues the issue further in *Capital*, after his examination of the relation of mutual presupposition and exclusion between the realization of the commodity as use-value and its realization as value, by posing the following problem:

> Let us take a closer look. The owner of a commodity considers every other commodity as the particular equivalent of his own commodity, which makes his own commodity the general equivalent for all the others. But since every owner does the same thing, none of the commodities is general equivalent, and the commodities do not possess a general relative form of value in order to equate each other as values and compare the magnitudes of their values. Therefore they do not even confront each other as commodities, but as products or use-values. (Marx, 1976a, p. 180)

Marx is saying that as long as all of the commodity owners want their own commodities to count as value immediately, not only does this requirement confront the contradiction that unfolded at the previous stage, but also the formation of the general equivalent to mediate the contradiction becomes impossible. Thus, taking his argument one step further, Marx writes:

> In their dilemma our commodity owners think like Faust: "In the beginning was the deed." They have therefore already acted before thinking. The laws of the commodity nature [*Warennatur*] come to fruition in the natural instinct of the commodities owners. They can only relate their commodities to each other as values, and therefore as commodities, if they place them in a polar relationship with a third commodity that serves as the general equivalent. *We concluded this from our analysis of the commodity*. But only a social deed can turn a specific commodity into the general equivalent. The social action of all other commodities, therefore, excludes one specific commodity, in which all others represent their values. The natural form of this commodity thereby becomes the socially recognized equivalent form. Through the agency of the social process it becomes the specific social function of the excluded commodity to be the general equivalent. It thus becomes: money. (Marx, 1976a, pp. 180–181)

This passage clearly shows both the distinction and relation between the theory of the value-form and the theory of the exchange process. When Marx says that the commodity owners "can only relate their commodities to each other as values, and therefore as commodities, if they place them in a polar relationship with a third commodity that serves as the general equivalent," and that we "concluded this from our analysis of the commodity," he is clearly referring to the theory of the value-form or, more precisely, the examination of the general value-form. In *Capital*, as we have seen, prior to the theory of the exchange process the theory of the value-form is developed, where Marx elucidates how the general equivalent is formed and how the relation between commodities as value (and therefore as commodities) is mediated. Thus, in the theory of the exchange process, when Marx – having traced back the unfolding of the contradiction of the commodity within that process – arrives at the conclusion that, as long as the commodity owners immediately seek for their commodities to count as value, ultimately no commodity can count as such, making it impossible for them to come into a relationship as commodities, he is then able to say that the path towards breaking through the deadlock was already elucidated in the theory of the value-form. However, even though that was clarified, it is the joint action (or "social deed") of the commodity world that actually sets apart a particular commodity that becomes the general equivalent in reality. This joint action is made necessary by the deadlock of the unmediated exchange process and the contradictions that arise from that process which necessitate some sort of mediation. The task particular to the theory of the exchange process, along with tracing back the contradictions, is to analyze the necessity of the general equivalent for mediating the exchange process – i.e., the discussion of the necessity of the genesis of money – which is a task that falls outside of the realm of the theory of the value-form.

Incidentally, in the passage just quoted, Marx, in the literary style of expression he was fond of, writes:

> In their dilemma our commodity owners think like Faust: "In the beginning was the deed." They have therefore already acted before thinking. The laws of the commodity nature [*Warennatur*] come to fruition in the natural instinct of the commodities owners. (Marx, 1976a, p. 180)

Some have suggested that Marx in this passage is saying that the action of the commodity owners solves a problem that is theoretically unsolvable. On the basis of that view a unique explanation regarding the relationship between the theory of the value-form and the theory of the exchange process has been offered, which is then used to criticize Marx's supposed theoretical bankruptcy. However, if we read a bit further on from the passage in question, it becomes clear that he is not arguing that an unsolvable theoretical problem is resolved through praxis. In fact, quite to the contrary, Marx notes that commodity owners act precisely in the manner elucidated by theory:

> The laws of the commodity nature [*Warennatur*] come to fruition in the natural instinct of the commodities owners. They can only relate their commodities to each other as values, and therefore as commodities, if they place them in a polar relationship with a third commodity that serves as the general equivalent. We concluded this from our analysis of the commodity. (Marx, 1976a, p. 180)

Why, then, does Marx say that the commodity owners are somehow perplexed? Prior to the appearance of money the contradiction we have looked at must be confronted. But the commodity owners act in accordance with what theory has demarcated. In this way, they generate money, which is indispensable to the meditation of the contradiction. Marx describes the owners as having "already acted before thinking." This is a wittier way, I think, of saying that money – like all other relations of commodity production – is something *spontaneously* generated, not the product of examination or some "discovery" as bourgeois economists often claim. There would be little point in using any witty turn of phrase if one ends up being misconstrued in the manner that Marx has. If he is to be blamed, it is not for leaving to praxis what his theory could not explain (and thus exposing his own theoretical impotence), but for not anticipating that he might be misconstrued in such a way.

My comments, however, pertain to *Capital*, because the matter is not presented in the same way in *Contribution*. In that earlier book, the theory of the value-form does not yet exist as an independent section or in terms of content (at least not as we find it in *Capital*). The same sorts of forms appear in *Contribution* (simple value-form, developed value-form, and general value-form), and they are developed in the same order. But when Marx analyzes the simple value-form in *Capital* he poses and elucidates the fundamental question of the value-form, whereas no such analysis exists in the earlier book. In *Contribution*, Marx simply writes:

> The exchange-value of a commodity is not expressed in its own use-value. But as materialization [*Vergegenständlichung*] of universal social labor-time, the use-value of one commodity is brought into relation with the use-values of other commodities. The exchange-value of one commodity thus manifests itself in the use-values of other commodities. (Marx, 1987a, p. 279)

In *Contribution*, crucial matters to be elucidated in the theory of the value-form are not dealt with at all, including the oppositional relationship between the relative value-form and the equivalent form, the detour of value-expression, and the particularities of the equivalent form. Without solving such fundamental problems, Marx discusses a development of form that is similar to the discussion in *Capital* in appearance only. Marx then examines what in *Capital* is called the "quantitative determinacy of the relative form of value," followed by his analysis of the exchange process, where – upon sequentially unfolding the contradictions of that process – he poses the ultimate question that the issue comes down to:

> It is through the alienation of its use-value, that is of its original form of existence, that every commodity has to acquire its corresponding existence as exchange-value. The commodity must therefore assume a double existence in the exchange process. On the other hand, its second existence as exchange-value itself can only be another commodity, because it is only commodities which confront one another in the exchange process. *How does one represent a particular commodity directly as* materialized universal labor-time, *or – which amounts to the same thing – how does one give the individual labor-time materialized in a particular commodity directly a general character?* (Marx, 1987a, pp. 286–287)

When the problem concerning the exchange process is ultimately posed by reducing it to the form above, Marx can respond in *Capital* by saying that the solution was already provided in the theory of the value-form. That is not possible in *Contribution*, however. In that earlier book, something similar to the theory of the value-form is developed prior to the analysis of the exchange process, but it does not answer the problem that is posed in the passage quoted above. After posing that problem in *Contribution*, and then introducing a series of equations for the developed value-form of linen, Marx offers the following response:

> This is a theoretical statement since the commodity is merely regarded as a definite quantity of materialized universal labor-time. A particular commodity as a general equivalent is transformed from a pure abstraction into a social result of the exchange process, if one simply reverses the above series of equations. (Marx, 1987a, p. 287)

This can be said to occur by reversing the equations because the linen, which had been in the relative form, comes to be posited in the equivalent form. As for why this occurs when linen is placed in the equivalent form, that is a problem pertaining to the equivalent form in general, and therefore to the value-form in general, preceding not only the reversal of the equation but the developed value-form as well. It is thus a problem that must be solved when analyzing the simple form of value. In *Contribution*, however, there is no such examination. There is the passage above, where Marx explains the effect of the reversal of the equation, but that is merely confirmed as a fact and the theoretical elucidation is far less thorough than in *Capital*.

Further light can be shed on this issue by consulting letters Marx exchanged with Engels after sending him the revised proofs for the first German edition of *Capital* to solicit his opinions. Engels responded to Marx's request in a letter dated June 16, 1867, noting his impressions regarding the analysis of the value-form. In that letter, after saying that divisions and headings should be added, Engels offers the following comment:

> Compared with your earlier presentation [*Contribution*], the dialectic of the argument has been greatly sharpened, but with regard to the actual exposition there are a number of things I like better in the first version. (Marx, 1987b, p. 382)

Marx responded in a June 22 letter:

> With regard to the development of the form of value, I have both fol-
> lowed and **not** followed your advice, thus striking a dialectical attitude
> in this matter, too. That is to say, (1) I have written an appendix in
> which I set out the same subject again as simply and as much in the
> manner of a school textbook as possible, and (2) I have divided each
> successive proposition into paragraphs etc., each with its own heading,
> as you advised. In the preface I then tell the "non-dialectical" reader to
> skip page x-y and instead read the appendix. It is not only the philis-
> tines that I have in mind here, but young people, etc., who are thirsting
> for knowledge. Anyway, the issue is crucial for the whole book. These
> gentry, the economists, have hitherto overlooked the extremely simple
> point that the form 20 yards of linen = 1 coat is but the undeveloped
> basis form of 20 yards of linen = gold of £2, and thus that the simplest
> form of a commodity, in which its value is not yet expressed as its re-
> lation to all other commodities but only as something differentiated
> from its own natural form, contains the whole secret of the
> money-form and thereby, *in nuce*, of all bourgeois forms of the prod-
> uct of labor. In my first presentation [*Contribution*], I avoided the dif-
> ficulty of the development by providing an actual analysis of the
> expression of value only when it appears already developed and ex-
> pressed in money. (Marx, 1987b, pp. 384-385)

Marx points out that in his earlier work he did "not actually analyz[e]
the *way value is expressed* until it appears as its developed form, as
expressed in money." And we have noted that even this analysis of
value-expression is certainly not carried out to a full extent in that
book. In *Capital*, Marx does thoroughly examine this problem in a
pure form, separate from the theory of the exchange process, as an
independent problem that intrinsically belongs to the analysis of the
commodity (along with the other theories that constitute Chapter 1).

* * * * *

My interpretation presented thus far regarding the relationship between the theory of the value-form and the theory of the exchange
process is one that I arrived at after a long struggle, and I think that it
grasps some fundamental points. However, one question I noted at
the outset remains: Why was the "transition definition" that Marx

placed between the theory of the value-form and the theory of the exchange process in the first German edition of *Capital* (and in *Contribution*) removed from the second edition of *Capital*? I am not so confident that I have the definitive answer to that question, however, because it is not something that can be answered on a purely theoretical basis. Moreover, Marx leaves us no comment anywhere related to this matter. What I can provide, then, is only conjecture.

One possibility is related to the changes Marx made to the theory of the value-form. Already we have looked at the nature of the theory of the value-form in *Contribution*, but in the main text of the first German edition of *Capital* as well the development of the value-form comes to an end with the rather peculiar form IV[5] instead of progressing to the money-form. In the case of form IV, what can be said of linen can also be said of any one of a multitude of commodities. Marx lists a number of equations expressing the developed value-form that include commodities such as coffee, tea, etc., in addition to linen, from which he deduces that "each of these equations *read backwards* gives coat, coffee, tea, etc. as general equivalent, therefore the expression of their value in coat, coffee, tea, etc. as the general relative form of value of all other commodities" (Marx, 1976b, p. 33). Marx also notes:

> The general equivalent form always falls only on one commodity as opposed to all other commodities, but it falls on each commodity as opposed to all other commodities. If therefore each commodity opposes its own natural form to all other commodities as the general equivalent form, all commodities exclude all others from the general equivalent form, and therefore exclude themselves from the socially valid representation of their magnitudes of value. (Marx, 1976b, p. 33)

This is Marx's examination of form IV and questions directly related to it in the main body of the first German edition of *Capital*. At first glance, though, it may seem that he is suggesting that the formation of a general equivalent is not possible; and since the formation of the general equivalent was already explained in form III, it may be dif-

---

[5] [I have used roman numerals (I, II, III and IV) to indicate the four forms of value in the first German edition of *Capital* and capital letters (A, B, C and D) to refer to the forms that appear in the second edition of *Capital*. – EMS]

ficult to see why such an analysis needs to be pursued. That is a view
that has been advanced at times to criticize Marx, but from my perspective it is founded upon a clear misunderstanding. Marx is certainly not arguing that the formation of a general equivalent is
impossible. Rather, he is indicating, from a more concrete perspective, the boundary between the earlier theory of the value-form and
the theory of the exchange process, by means of reflecting on the
outcome of the theory of the value-form developed up to that point
and clarifying the limitations of an understanding based on abstraction from that earlier perspective. In the theory of the value-form,
taking linen as his example, Marx clarifies how that commodity becomes the general equivalent through the process of a development
of form. If linen has become the general equivalent, it must be
thought to have passed through that process. However, as long as
Marx is using the method of demonstrating the genesis of the general
equivalent, any other commodity could pass through the same process (not just the linen); and to that extent any commodity could become the general equivalent. At the same time, however, no two
commodities can become the general equivalent at the same time. If
every single commodity simultaneously became the general equivalent, and developed into the specific relative value-form *qua* general
equivalent, then "all commodities [would] exclude all others from
the general equivalent form." In short, the general equivalent must be
limited to a specific commodity. Yet for this to occur, the operation
of another factor – not mentioned in the analysis up to that point – is
necessary so that the general equivalent can adhere to that specific
commodity. What is that factor? This is an issue that does not belong
within Marx's analysis of the commodity (which includes the theory
of the value-form as one of its parts). This, at any rate, is my understanding of the gist of what Marx is saying in that passage quoted
from the first German edition of *Capital*.[6]

---

[6] After that passage, Marx goes on, in addressing the same fundamental point, to
write:

"As one sees, the analysis of the commodity yields all essential determinations
of the form of value. It yields the form of value itself, in its opposite moments, the
general relative form of value, the general equivalent form, finally the
never-ending series of simple relative value expressions, which first constitute a
transitional phase in the development of the form of value, in order to eventually

The following passage from the theory of the exchange process (quoted earlier with regard to the difference and relation between that theory and the theory of the value-form) corresponds exactly to the passage above:

They [commodity owners] can only relate their commodities to each other as values, and therefore as commodities, if they place them in a polar relationship with a third commodity that serves as the general equivalent. We concluded this from our analysis of the commodity. But only a social deed can turn a specific commodity into the general equivalent. The social action of all other commodities, therefore, excludes one specific commodity, in which all others represent their values. The natural form of this commodity thereby becomes the socially recognized equivalent form. Through the agency of the social process it becomes the specific social function of the excluded commodity to be the general equivalent. It thus becomes: money. (Marx, 1976a, pp. 180–181)

We have already seen that Marx subsequently altered the content of form IV completely, inserting the money-form in its place. He also eliminated the description appended to form IV indicating the nature of abstraction in the theory of the value-form. I want to consider why Marx made such changes.

It seems likely that the money-form was inserted because the value-form reaches completion with the money-form and because it is the money-form that is posited in front of our eyes. It would have thus been insufficient had the value-form not advanced up to the

---

turn into the specific relative form of value of the general equivalent. However, the analysis of the commodity yielded these forms as forms of the commodity in general, which can therefore be taken on by every commodity – although in a polar manner, so that when commodity A finds itself in one form determination, then commodities B, C, etc. assume the other in relation to it." (Marx, 1976b, pp. 33–34)

If it is the case that the discussion of form IV itself and issues related to it are a reflection on form III and that, in relation to the determination of the general equivalent posited there, the abstract character of the theory of the value-form is elucidated and the limitations of such cognition suggested, then I think it could be said that the passage above looks back on the entirety of the value-form developed up to that point and more generally clarifies its abstract character, while suggesting the limitations of that level of cognition.

money-form.[7] It also seems likely that Marx removed form IV and the description added to it because he thought that the previous limitations of the theory of the value-form had been superceded through the introduction of the money-form, rendering invalid the earlier reflection on the abstract character of the theory, because the advance from the general value-form to the money-form solely concerns the fact that "the form of direct and general exchangeability, in other words the general equivalent form, has now by social custom irrevocably become entwined with the specific bodily form of the commodity gold" (Marx. 1976b, p. 69).

The same situation may account for why Marx removed the "transition definition" from the second edition of *Capital*. If the advance from the general value-form to the money-form is simply a matter of the fact that "the form of direct and general exchangeability, in other words the general equivalent form, has now by social custom irrevocably become entwined once with the specific bodily form of the commodity gold" – and if it is true that "form D [the money-form] does not differ at all from form C [the general value-form] except that now instead of linen gold has assumed the general equivalent form" (Marx. 1976a, p. 162) – then the distinction between the two forms is not a difference in form, but rather concerns the real attributes of the general value-form. Hence, the question cannot be posed merely as an analysis of form. It can only posed for the first time on the premise of the real process that posits a specific commodity with the attribute of being the general value-form. This means that the transition definition, which includes the determination of the abstract character of the standpoint in Chapter 1, is no longer relevant. It is from this basic perspective that we can de-

---

[7] Marx writes in the second edition of *Capital*:

"Every one knows, if he knows nothing else, that commodities have a value-form common to them all which presents a marked contrast to the varied bodily forms of the use-values – i.e., their money-form. Here, however, a task is set to us, which bourgeois economics never even tried to accomplish; namely, to trace the genesis of this money-form, i.e., to pursue the development of the expression of value contained in the value-relation of commodities, from its simplest, almost imperceptible shape, to the blinding money-form. When this is done, the riddle of money will also disappear at the same time." (Marx, 1976a, p. 139)

As a matter of course, no description of this sort can be found in the first edition of *Capital*.

duce why Marx removed the transition definition; or at least I can think of no other convincing explanation. Still, I do not necessarily think that introducing the money-form made it necessary for Marx to remove that passage. It is true that the issue regarding what specific commodity comes to acquire the attribute of the general equivalent form is quite different from the question of how the general equivalent itself is formed, as the latter can be examined abstractly (unlike the former). For the moment, though, we can set aside the conditions and reasons for the general equivalent form ultimately being affixed to gold[8] and instead treat the adhesion to gold as a fact, in order to

---

[8] In the theory of the exchange process this issue is discussed in the following way:

"In the direct exchange of products, each commodity is a direct means of exchange to its owner, and an equivalent to those who do not possess it, although only in so far as it has use-value for them. At this stage, therefore, the articles exchanged do not acquire a value-form independent of their own use-value, or of the individual wants of the exchangers. The need for this form first develops with the increase in the number and variety of the commodities entering into the process of exchange. The problem and the means for its solution arise simultaneously. Commercial intercourse, in which the owners of commodities exchange and compare their own articles with various other articles, never takes place unless different kinds of commodities belonging to different owners are exchanged for, and equated as values with, one single further kind of commodity. This further commodity, by becoming the equivalent of various other commodities, directly acquires the form of a general or social equivalent, if only within narrow limits. The general equivalent form comes and goes with the momentary social contacts which call it into existence. It is transiently attached to this or that commodity in alternation. But with the development of exchange it fixes itself firmly and exclusively onto particular kinds of commodity, i.e., it crystallizes out into the money-form. The particular kind of commodity to which it sticks is at first a matter of accident. Nevertheless there are two circumstances which are by and large decisive. The money-form comes to be attached either to the most important articles of exchange from outside, which are in fact the primitive and spontaneous forms of manifestation of the exchange-value of local products, or to the object of utility which forms the chief element of indigenous alienable wealth, for example cattle. ... In the same proportion as exchange bursts its local bonds, and the value of commodities accordingly expands more and more into the material embodiment of human labor as such, in that proportion does the money-form become transferred to commodities which are by nature fitted to perform the social function of a general equivalent. Those commodities are the precious metals. The truth of the statement that 'although gold and silver are not by nature money, money is by nature gold and silver,' is shown by the congruence between the natural properties of gold and sil-

examine the value-form solely from the aspect of form. This is indeed what Marx does in analyzing the money-form in the theory of the value-form.[9] Thus, even if the money-form is added, it is not

ver and the functions of money. ... Only a material whose every sample possesses the same uniform quality can be an adequate form of appearance of value, that is a material embodiment of abstract and therefore equal human labor. On the other hand, since the difference between the magnitudes of value is purely quantitative, the money commodity must be capable of purely quantitative differentiation, it must therefore be divisible at will, and it must also be possible to assemble it again from its component parts. Gold and silver possess these properties by nature." (Marx, 1976a, pp. 182–184)

[9] In carrying out his analysis, Marx notes:

"The specific kind of commodity with whose natural form the equivalent form is socially interwoven now becomes the money commodity, or serves as money. It becomes its specific social function, and consequently its social monopoly, to play the part of universal equivalent within the commodity world. Among the commodities which in form B figure as particular equivalents of the linen, and in form C express in common their relative values in linen, there is one in particular which has historically conquered this advantageous position: gold. If, then, in form C, we replace the linen with gold, we get ... " (Marx, 1976a, p. 162)

At that point, Marx shows us form D (money-form), featuring an equation with an infinite number of commodities on the left-hand side and gold placed on the right, and then writes:

"Fundamental changes have taken place in the course of the transition from form A to form B, and from form B to form C. As against this, form D differs not at all from form C, except that gold instead of linen, gold has now assumed the general equivalent form. Gold is in form D what linen was in form C: the general equivalent. The advance consists only in that the form of direct and general exchangeability, in other words the general equivalent form, has now by social custom irrevocably become entwined with the specific bodily form of the commodity gold." (Marx, 1976a, p. 162)

But the money-form does not stop at this alone. Immediately following the passage above, Marx adds:

"The simple relative expression of the value of some commodity, such as linen, in the commodity which already functions as the money commodity, such as gold, is the price form. The 'price form' of the linen is therefore: 20 yards of linen = 2 ounces of gold, or, if 2 ounces of gold when coined are £2, 20 yards of linen = £2." (Marx, 1976a, p. 163)

Marx explains this point in greater detail in his discussion of the function of money as the measure of value in the Section 1 of Chapter 3:

"The expression of the value of a commodity in gold – $x$ commodity A = $y$ money commodity – is its money-form or its price. A single equation, such as 1 ton of iron = 2 ounces of gold, now suffices to express the value of the iron in a socially valid manner. There is no longer any need for this equation to line up to-

necessarily imperative to also eliminate the transition definition. This is my reason for saying earlier that I am not convinced that I have arrived at *the* definitive answer.

*  *  *  *  *

The preceding has covered all of the points that I had planned to address with regard to the topic indicated in the title. However, there is still the issue noted at the outset regarding the fact that money is dealt with even prior to the theory of money proper in Chapter 3, not only in the theory of the value-form and the theory of the exchange process but also in the theory of the fetish-character in Section 4 of Chapter 1. Here I want to comment briefly on Section 4, beginning with the question of why the theory of the fetish-character is included in Chapter 1 on the commodity (along with Section 3 on the value-form) and how Section 4 differs from the other sections in that chapter (particularly Section 3).

We have seen that Marx examines the commodity in Chapter 1, which naturally involves an analysis of the commodity-form in which products appear. He elucidates, first of all, that the commodity is a twofold entity: both a use-value and an exchange-value. After noting this fact, however, Marx sets aside use-value because it does not express any social relation, despite being the "bearer" of social

---

gether with all other equations that express the value of the other commodities, because the equivalent commodity, gold, already possesses the character of money. The commodities' general relative value-form has thus the same shape as their original relative value-form: the simple or individual relative value." (Marx, 1976a, p. 189)

In other words, although it can be said that the money-form is inherently the same shape as the general value-form, it certainly does not remain at this level. Rather, it is completed upon the general equivalent form adhering to gold, so that it is gold's "specific social function, and consequently its social monopoly, to play the part of universal equivalent within the commodity world." Thus, the list of commodities on the left side of the equation that characterizes the general relative form of value is dissolved to bring about the price-form, which has the same appearance as the initial simple value-form. This is also the form of commodity-value that presents itself to us in reality: the completed appearance of the value-form. The discussion of this form is therefore the natural task for the theory of the value-form. Not only is it possible, from a purely formal perspective, to discuss the money-form separately from the general value-form, it is in fact necessary to do so.

relations of production. Marx's subsequent analysis focuses on ex-change-value, whose simplest form is: $x$ quantity of commodity $A = y$ quantity of commodity B. Marx advances his analysis of that form by noting that the commodities on both sides of the equation have something in common even though they differ as use-values. He then elucidates what that thing in common is and what determines its magnitude. This is his inquiry in Section 1, which is entitled "The Two Factors of the Commodity: Use-Value and Value (Substance of Value, Magnitude of Value)." That first section already clarifies the distinction between the two elements (use-value and value) that make up the commodity, as well as the abstract character of the labor that forms value. In Section 2 ("The Twofold Character of the Labor Represented in Commodities"), Marx then clarifies the twofold character of the labor that produces a commodity, in terms of being an oppositional relationship between the labor that forms use-value and the labor that forms value. In this sense, Section 2 basically deepens the analysis from Section 1. The same equation is again ana-lyzed in Section 3 ("The Value-Form, or Exchange-Value"), but from a different perspective. Whereas earlier he had examined the equa-tion from the perspective of both commodities having something in common of the same magnitude, and then clarified what that is, in Section 3 Marx concentrates on how the commodity on each side of the equation plays a different role. He analyzes the fact that the commodity on the left has its value expressed in the use-value of the commodity on the right, clarifying how the value of a commodity is expressed in the use-value of another commodity and how value is ultimately expressed in a certain quantity of the money-commodity.

Marx also analyzes the equation in the theory of the fet-ish-character in Section 4 (or more specifically: "The Fet-ish-Character of the Commodity and its Secret"), but from a perspective that again differs. Having already pondered *what* is ex-pressed in the equation in Section 1 and 2, and *how* it is expressed in Section 3, Marx turns his attention in Section 4 to the question of *why*:

> Political Economy has indeed, however incompletely, analyzed value and its magnitude, and has uncovered the content concealed within these forms. But it has never once asked *why* this content takes that

form, that is to say, *why* labor is expressed in value, and *why* the measurement of labor by its duration is expressed in the magnitude of the value of the product. (Marx, 1976a, p. 174)

Marx is raising a theoretical question not posed before. The question involves examining why the value of a commodity appears in the form of a quantity of another commodity that is equated to it (and ultimately in a quantity of the money-commodity gold that we encounter as "such-and-such" yen), rather than being directly expressed as a certain quantity of labor-time. In relation to money in particular, the theory of the fetish-character analyzes the *why* of money, whereas the theory of the value-form looks at the *how* of money.

In contrast to Section 4, the characteristics of the theory of the exchange process should be clear if we recall the difference between the theory of the value-form and the theory of the exchange process. Simply put, the investigation in Chapter 1 concerns the analysis of the commodity. This analysis is naturally carried out by examining the form in which products appear as commodities. However, as long as the problem is approached in this manner, the commodity has yet to enter a process of motion. The commodity is not in a process of motion as use-value, in terms of passing into the hands of another commodity owner who wants it; nor is it in a process of motion as value, in terms of being actually transformed into the commodity its owner wants. Marx has yet to examine the realization of the commodity as use-value or as value. Therefore, he has not yet analyzed the real contradiction that exists between the realizations *qua* those two elements; nor has he examined money as the mediator of that contradiction. All of those issues are first raised in the analysis of the exchange process. The genesis of money is discussed in the theory of the value-form, but the problem centers on "how" money is generated, not "through what." In other words: *How* does a particular commodity (gold) become the general equivalent so as to count as value in its given natural form? The question does not concern *through what* money is made necessary and generated. These points have already basically been dealt with, but I want to add a further explanation here.

Marx analyzes the *how* of money in the theory of the value-form and the *why* of money in the theory of the fetish-character, whereas in the theory of the exchange process he examines the question of *through what*. Near the end of Chapter 2, as the final consideration of money prior to Chapter 3 (where he presents the theory of money proper), Marx writes: "The difficulty lies, not in comprehending that money is a commodity, but in discovering how, why, and through what [*wie, warum, wodurch*] a commodity is money" (Marx, 1976a, p. 186). Marx's indication of these three difficulties clearly suggests that he managed to brilliantly overcome them, but no hint is provided regarding where this is carried out. My view is that Marx answered the questions *how*, *why*, and *through what* in Section 3 and 4 of Chapter 1 and in Chapter 2, respectively. In other words, the three problems are listed in the order that he solves them in *Capital*.

I should note, incidentally, that Marx does not pose the three problems as a sort of logical schema or in some frivolous manner. They are realistic problems. Without solving each one an adequate understanding of money is not possible. Indeed, earlier political economy slipped into a variety of errors by failing to solve these problems. One must begin with the realistic problem to be solved. Then the issue becomes how to solve the problem, in terms of where and how it should be examined. Therefore, it would be a waste of time, like casting pearls before swine, to present the solution to someone who has not yet grasped the problem. Yet some imagine that Marx is engaging in a frivolous discussion by posing those three questions, while others focus their attention on his statement as the penetration of some sort of Hegelian process of logic. Given the existence of such views, I think we can relish the following observations Marx made in a letter to Engels regarding the ideas of Ferdinand Lassalle:

> *Heraclitus, the Dark Philosopher*, is quoted as saying in an attempt to elucidate the transformation of all things into their opposite: "Thus gold changeth into all things, and all things change into gold." Here, Lassalle says, gold means money (*c'est juste*) and money is value. Thus the Ideal, Universality, the One (value), and things, the Real, Particularity, the Many. He makes use of this surprising insight to give, in a lengthy note, an earnest of his discoveries in the science of political economy. Every other word a howler, but set forth with remarkable pretentiousness. It is plain to me from this one note that, in his second grand opus, the fellow intends to expound political econ-

omy in the manner of Hegel. He will discover to his cost that it is one thing for a critique to take a science to the point at which it admits of a dialectical presentation, and quite another to apply an abstract, ready-made system of logic to vague presentiments of just such a system. (Marx, 1983a, pp. 260–261)

Finally, I want to touch very simply on the relationship between the three theories in *Capital* examined thus far and Chapter 3 ("Money, or the Circulation of Commodities"). Even if it is natural to view Chapter 3 as the *fundamental* theory of money, compared to the preceding introductory ideas, there is still the question of where to draw the essential distinction between the two. That particular question falls outside the framework of the present work, but I would like to simply note my view that money only first appears as the *subject* carrying out certain functions in Chapter 3. In contrast, the subject in the first two chapters is not money but the commodity. In those two chapters, money only appears as something necessary that the commodity brings forth to mediate its own contradiction; whereas in Chapter 3 the money thus created now appears as the subject that performs a number of functions. Here I think we have the essential difference, in very simple terms, between Chapter 3 and the first two chapters.

## Why is the Want of the Commodity Owner
## Abstracted from in the Theory of the Value-Form?
### (A Response to the View of Kōzō Uno)

What is the relationship in *Capital* between the theory of the value-form in Section 3 of Chapter 1 and the theory of the exchange process in Chapter 2? At first sight both seem to demonstrate the necessity of money. So why did Marx go to the trouble of discussing that in two separate places? Or we might pose the question more generally: What is the particular significance of each theory in terms of the descriptive method that Marx employs?

These are questions that anyone who has studied *Capital* to some extent has probably pondered, but understanding the relationship between the two theories is in fact quite difficult. Or, at least in my own case, the issue was a problem that I struggled with for a long time. In order to better understand this relationship I read a number of explanations of *Capital*, but all seemed somewhat beside the point, not offering a fully satisfactory answer. Finally, not so long ago, I arrived at an explanation of my own that seemed reasonable – although from my current perspective even that explanation was somewhat unclear.

My view took on more definite shape as a result of participating in a series of study meetings on *Capital* sponsored by the journal *Hyōron*, where I had the opportunity to come into contact with the polar opposite view held by Kōzō Uno. In responding to Uno's arguments, I came to realize that his perspective was one that I had yet to consider; and this encounter with a new perspective helped me to gradually clarify my own thinking. The transcript of the study meetings, published in the pages of *Hyōron*,[1] gives an idea of my basic

---

[1] [The transcript was later published by Kawade Shobō in 1949 as a two-volume

position at the time. But I did not carefully or systematically express my views and many points were inadequately discussed at the meetings. My view seemed to come together somewhat as a result of closely re-reading the comments Uno made at the meetings and examining the ideas he expressed in his subsequently published books: *Kachi-ron* (Theory of Value) and *Shihon-ron nyūmon* (Introduction to *Capital*). So the main aim of these articles, which I completed thanks to the persistence of the *Keizai shirin* editors, is to present my current view on the subject.

When considering the significance of the theory of value-form and the theory of the exchange process, it is natural (and I think convenient) to begin by looking at the essential difference between them. One point immediately apparent to anyone is that the beginning of the theory of the exchange process has a description of the *commodity owner*. Marx thus posits the fundamental role played by the commodity owner and his desire for a certain thing. Careful readers will notice that this role played by the want of the commodity owner is abstracted from in the theory of the value-form. However, the question really *begins* from this point. First of all, even though it appears from the passage at the beginning of Chapter 2 that the role of the want of the commodity owner was abstracted from in the theory of the value-form, one needs to determine whether this is in fact true. Also, there is the question of whether it is indeed possible to understand the value-form in isolation from the role played by the owner's want.[2] And there is the question of why the role played by the commodity owner is abstracted from in the theory of the value-form even though a commodity cannot exist in reality without an owner. If these questions are thoroughly clarified, the particular significance of each of the two theories will become clear in turn – or at least the effort will provide us with the key to elucidating the issue at hand. Once this has been accomplished the significance of the theory of value-form and the theory of exchange process with regard

---

book entitled *Shihon-ron kenkyū* (Study of *Das Kapital*), and then issued in a single volume under the same title by Shiseido Shoten in 1958. – EMS]

[2] Uno said that it is *not* possible to understand the value-form apart from the role played by the owner's want, and in insisting on that position he provided those of us on the other side of the debate with material for reflection and a valuable opportunity to better formulate our ideas.

to our understanding of money should also be self-evident.

At the *Hyōron* study meetings, however, the discussion did not develop in that particular manner. The participants very quickly became deadlocked over the question of whether or not one should abstract from the commodity owner in the analysis of the value-form. Kōzō Uno confidently asserted that the want of the commodity owner should *not* be abstracted from, while I argued to the contrary along with several others. In the end, though, our side did not manage to convince Uno. Even though there was a discussion, which I participated very little in, regarding the significance of the theory of the value-form and the theory of the exchange process to an understanding of the necessity of money, no definitive consensus resulted from the discussion because it was not based on an adequate understanding of the fundamental questions at hand. Here I want examine the issue once again, beginning with the first question noted above, even if it will overlap somewhat with points I made at the study meetings.

Uno raised various arguments to support his idea that the role played by the want of the commodity owner should *not* be abstracted from in the theory of the value-form, but it seems to me that the following three points are the theoretical basis for his view:

1.  In the simple form of value, the question of why a particular commodity is in the equivalent form cannot be understood without taking into account the want of the owner of the commodity in the relative form of value. In the case of the equation, 20 yards of linen = 1 coat, for example, the coat is in the equivalent form because it is an object that the linen owner wants.

2.  Without considering the commodity owner, it is not possible to understand why the commodity in the relative form of value and the commodity in the equivalent form are each in their respective forms, which would mean that it is all the same whether one of the commodities is in one form as opposed to the other. The demand for the active expression of value is the demand of the commodity owner, and a certain commodity is in the relative form of value because of the ex-

istence of that commodity owner. In contrast, as the commodity in the equivalent form is ideal, the owner has yet to appear in reality. It is by thinking in this manner that a subjective understanding of the value-form becomes possible.

3. The essential difference between the general equivalent form and the money-form first becomes clear when we consider the want of the commodity owner. That is, when the general equivalent becomes money it is no longer limited to the relation where it is desired for its original use-value, and thus it expresses the value of a commodity. If we set aside this characteristic, there would be no essential distinction established between the general equivalent form and the money-form.

I will criticize each of these three arguments, in sequential order. But to avoid any misunderstanding that might arise from the points above being my summary of Uno's position (rather than a detailed account of his main thesis), and because I do not necessarily employ his exact terminology, each of the three articles begins with quotations from Uno himself, followed by the presentation of my own view in direct relation to his position.

# 1.

---

## Uno's First Argument:

*I*n the simple form of value, the question of why a particular *commodity is in the equivalent form cannot be understood without taking into account the want of the owner of the com-modity in the relative form. It is thus mistaken to think that the role played by the want of the commodity owner is abstracted from in the theory of the value-form.*

Uno's first argument against abstracting from the want of the commodity owner, summarized above, is expressed in the following comments that he made at the *Hyōron* study meetings:

> It is somewhat understandable why the exchange process and the value-form are divided in that particular manner, but I think it is problematic as a method. That is, in the examination of the exchange process, Marx seems to be offering a concrete and historical explanation as a supplement to the previous development of the value-form. Although I do not think that the sort of historical process explained in the chapter on the exchange process should be inserted, as is, within the section on the value-form, it does seem somewhat hard to understand, from a methodological standpoint, how one could think that an explanation corresponding to the content of Chapter 2 should not be inserted there. Use-value cannot be understood if it becomes abstract use-value in general that is set apart from the wants of individuals; and I think it would instead be clearer to take the commodity owner into consideration from the beginning of the value-form through to the money-form. For example, in seeking to express the value of the linen within the relation between the linen and the coat, I think that we can first understand the expression of value using the coat's use-value by considering the want of the linen owner for the coat. (Sakisaka & Uno, 1948, p. 142)

I want to pose the fundamental question. In considering the fact that the linen is in the relative form of value and the coat in the equivalent form, is it really satisfactory to not consider why the linen has taken the coat for its equivalent form, and to not premise the linen owner's desire for the coat? Would this form even be possible apart from that relation? (Sakisaka & Uno, 1948, p. 157)

The question is whether it is acceptable, even in the expression of value, to abstract from the commodity owner. For example, the expression "20 yards of linen is worth 1 coat" is not possible without the commodity owner. Is it really satisfactory to abstract that far? The commodity originally appears upon becoming the property of some person. (Sakisaka & Uno, 1948, p. 159)

Of course, in *Capital* the value-form and the exchange process are explained separately, and even assuming them separated as such, if we abstract from the owner of linen, to consider linen itself, we will not be able to understand why the linen in the relative form of value brings in the coat to the equivalent form; and if this is abstracted from anything could be in that form, so it would already be the expanded form of value. (Sakisaka & Uno, 1948, p. 160)

Uno's ideas were expressed in the course of the particular discussions at the study meetings, so heterogeneous problems are intertwined in the passages quoted and we can see his view stated in various forms. I want to begin, therefore, by considering the points in common among the passages. For example, after noting that he wants to "pose the fundamental question," Uno says:

> In considering the fact that the linen is in the relative form of value and the coat in the equivalent form, is it really satisfactory to not consider why the linen has taken the coat for its equivalent form, and to not premise the linen owner's desire for the coat? Would this form even be possible apart from that relation? (Sakisaka & Uno, 1948, p. 157)

This view, in itself, is reasonable. I certainly do not claim that the form exists "apart from this relation." Still, that is not the essential question, but rather an issue that precedes it. Even if it is obvious that we cannot understand "why the linen has taken the coat for its equivalent form" without considering the want of the linen owner, there is still the question of whether it is indeed necessary to consider that issue, given the particular aim of the theory of the value-form. My difference of opinion with Uno concerns the latter question, not the former. And it is the understanding of the latter that should be the basis of discussion. It is thus convenient, I think, to begin by clarifying my fundamental view on that question.

The aim of the theory of the value-form is to clarify the form in which the value of a commodity is manifested. We do this by analyzing the value-equation, which is the form in which a commodity's value is always manifested in reality. In that analysis the value-equation is taken as a given, which is natural considering the scientific method of political economy. The approach of taking the equation as a given and then proceeding to analyze it is not unique to the theory of the value-form. Indeed, the same is true for the entirety of Chapter 1 where the commodity is analyzed. In Section 1 and 2 of that chapter, however, Marx concentrates on the fact that there must be some quantitatively equal element in common between the commodities on each side of the equation. Section 3, in contrast, examines how the commodity on the left of the equation and the commodity on the right play different roles. Thus, in the theory of the value-form, Marx takes the equation 20 yards of linen = 1 coat as his given premise and through an analysis from this point of view recognizes, from the very structure of the equation, that the linen expresses its own value using the coat and that the coat serves as the material for the value-expression of the linen. The linen is therefore playing an active role, while the coat is in a passive role. With this as his starting point, Marx goes on to reveal the *mechanism* whereby the value of a commodity is expressed in the use-value of another commodity, as well as the necessary developmental process of value-expression that is restricted by this mechanism of value-expression.

This is my understanding of the gist of the theory of the value-form in *Capital*. Accordingly, even though we can only know why the coat (rather than some other commodity) is in the equivalent form by considering the want of the linen owner, pondering that issue is not a task pertinent to the theory of the value-form. It is quite sufficient, in analyzing the value-form, to take a certain equation as a given and then clarify the relation of value-expression within it, showing how the value of the commodity on the left is expressed in the use-value of the commodity on the right, so that the value of the commodity on the left assumes a form separate from its own use-value form. What we need to do, in short, is to analyze and clarify this relationship between the two commodities. Not only is it unnecessary to consider any other factor, to do so would significantly hinder our ability to pose the question in a pure form so that it can be answered.

In response to my basic view, sketched above, I imagine that various sorts of criticism might be voiced. Some may argue, for instance, that according to my view there is no need to consider why a certain commodity is on the right of the equation (e.g., a coat rather than wheat), because it is sufficient to analyze and clarify the relation wherein the value of the commodity on the left (relative value-form) is expressed using the use-value of the commodity on the right (equivalent form); whereas in fact, contrary to my view, it is impossible to understand that precise relation apart from the want of the owner of the commodity in the relative form. According to this criticism, the use-value of the commodity in the equivalent form is able to express the value of the commodity in the relative form because it is an object desired by the owner of the relative-form commodity. In other words, there is no way for the relation of value-expression to be clarified without taking into consideration this other relation. Therefore, far from being irrelevant, considering the want of the commodity owner is at the essence of the theory of the value-form.

Our everyday experience teaches us that the value of a commodity is expressed in the use-value of some other commodity. But how, exactly, is this expression of *value* through *use-value* possible? Is it because the owner of the commodity in the relative form wants the other commodity? Or is some other explanation needed? Here we have the crux of the issue.

We can begin by making a clear distinction between the question of *why* a specific commodity is positioned in the equivalent form, and the question of *how* the use-value of a commodity in the equivalent form is able to express the value of the commodity in the relative form. These are two different questions that must be considered separately. The former concerns the want of the owner of the commodity in the relative value-form; and it can be easily answered by considering that factor. But that is not the case for the latter. It remains to be solved even after we have assumed that a specific commodity is posited in the equivalent form on the basis of the want of the owner of the commodity in the relative value-form. It is only by taking an equation as a given that we can independently pose the latter question. And the elucidation of that question, in my view, is fundamental to the theory of the value-form. This is the reason why, as noted earlier, Marx takes a value-equation as a given in the theory of the value-form and sets himself the task of analyzing the equation in order to clarify the expression of value within it. How do we carry out this task? How should we explain the fact that the value of a commodity is expressed in the use-value of some other commodity that is equivalent to it? Marx offers us the following:

> In order to decipher how the simple expression of the value of a commodity is embedded in the value-relation between two commodities, we must, for now, look at the value-relation independently of its quantitative aspect. The usual procedure is the precise opposite of this: one sees in the value-relation only the proportion in which definite quantities of two sorts of commodity count as equal to each other. One overlooks that the magnitudes of different things only become comparable in quantitative terms when they have been reduced to the same unit. It is only as expressions of such a common unit that they are of the same denomination, and are therefore commensurable magnitudes.
>
> But these two qualitatively equated commodities do not play the same role. Only the value of the linen is expressed. And how? By relating itself with the coat as its "equivalent," or the "thing exchangeable" for it. In this relation the coat counts as the form of existence of value, as the thing representing value – for only as such is it the same as the linen. On the other hand, it is also revealed here, or obtains an independent expression, that linen itself is value – for only as value can the linen relate itself to the coat as something equivalent with the linen or exchangeable for linen. ...
>
> If we say that, as values, commodities are simply congealed masses of human labor, our analysis reduces them to the abstraction "value," but does not give them a form of value distinct from their natural forms. It is otherwise in the value-relation of one commodity to another. The first commodity's value character steps forward here through its own relationship with the second commodity.
>
> For example, through the coat *qua* value-thing being equated to the linen, the labor embedded in the coat is equated to the labor embedded in the linen. It is true that the tailoring which makes the coat is concrete labor of a different sort than the weaving which makes the linen.

But by being equated to the weaving the tailoring is in fact reduced to what is actually equal between the two kinds of labor, which is the characteristic they have in common as human labor. Through this detour, weaving too, in so far as it weaves value, has nothing to distinguish it from tailoring, and, consequently, is abstract human labor. Only the different sorts of commodities as equivalents makes the specific character of value-creating labor apparent, by in fact reducing the different kinds of labor embedded in the different kinds of commodities to their general quality of being human labor in general. (Marx, 1976a, pp. 140–142)

Here we need to pay particular attention to the fact that, in the value-equation 20 yards of linen = 1 coat (or 20 yards of linen are worth one coat), the linen does not immediately posit itself as equivalent to the coat to obtain the form of value. Rather, it first *posits the coat as equivalent to itself*, thus giving the coat the formal character as the direct embodiment of abstract human labor, as the "value-body" [*Wertkörper*], and it is upon this basis that the linen can first express its own value through the natural form of the coat that is this existence *qua* embodiment of value. Without such a "detour" the commodity cannot acquire the form of value. The linen cannot become the value-body by immediately equating itself to the coat, thereby declaring itself to be equal to the coat, which would be nothing but a "self-complacent" or "presumptuous" [*hitoriyogari*] act, so to speak. For the linen to be able to express its own value in the natural form of the coat, with the natural form of the coat being the form of the linen's own value, the coat must first be posited with determinate being as the embodiment of value. In other words, the natural form of the coat, in its given state, must become a thing that has significance as the embodiment of abstract human labor. This occurs through the *linen positing the coat as equal to itself*. While the linen cannot become the value-body by declaring itself equal to the coat, it can make the coat the embodiment of value by declaring the coat to be equal to itself (although the coat only counts as such vis-à-vis the linen, not in relation to other commodities). By thus declaring itself identical with the coat – in terms of being value – and thereby making the coat the value-body, the linen expresses its own value-character in the form of a coat. In other words, the linen comes to have a value-form in distinction from its natural form as a use-value, which is its tangible form as a useful article of clothing.

The commodity only obtains the form of value through a detour, but this does not mean that the detour involves passing through two acts that follow each other temporally. It is instead achieved at once, through a *single* act. For the linen to express its value in the form of a coat, it only has to posit the coat as equal to itself, and through this same action of equating the linen makes the coat the value-body, thus simultaneously coming into a relationship with this coat *qua* value-body. This is how the linen comes to express its own value in the form of a coat.

The great amount of attention directed towards how the *linen equates the coat to itself* (thus making the coat the value-body) – rather than the linen equating itself to the coat – must seem "to the superficial observer," to borrow Marx's expression, an analysis of forms that "turns upon minutiae." Indeed, the issue *does* center on minutiae. Marx in fact compares his analysis of economic forms to the study of "microscopic anatomy" and notes that "in the analysis of economic forms neither microscopes nor chemical agents are of assistance" so the "power of abstraction must replace both" (Marx, 1976a, p. 90). Precisely for this reason, the discussion of the above distinction must seem a mere scholarly pastime at first glance.

The crucial significance of the distinction Marx draws has been overlooked not only by the "superficial observer" but even by supposed authorities on *Capital*. This is reflected in the Japanese translations of Marx's writings, such as the two different versions of the first German edition of *Capital* translated, respectively, by Fumio Hasebe and Minoru Miyakawa. Both of them end up, for example, conveying the opposite meaning of the following passage in which Marx explains the detour of value-expression:

> Qualitativ *setzt sie sich den Rock gleich*, indem sie sich auf ihn bezieht als Vergegenständlichung gleichartiger menschlicher Arbeit, d.h. ihrer eignen Werthsubstanz, und *sie setzt sich* nur *einen Rock gleich* statt x Röcke, weil sie nicht nur Werth überhaupt, sondern Werth von bestimmter Größe ist, ein Rock aber grade soviel Arbeit enthält als 20 Ellen Leinwand. (Marx, 1983b, p. 29)

Hasebe offers the following version:

> Qualitatively the *linen posits itself as equal to the coat* by relating it-
> self with the coat as the objectification of human labor of the same
> species, i.e., of its own value-substance, and the *linen posits itself as
> equal to one coat*, instead of *x* quantity of coats, because the linen is
> not just value in general, but value of a determined magnitude, and
> moreover because one coat contains just as much labor as 20 yards of
> linen.

Miyakawa, for his part, translates the passage as follows:

> The *linen posits itself as* qualitatively *equal to the coat* by coming into
> relation with the coat as the objectification of an identical type of hu-
> man labor, i.e., of the value-substance of the linen itself, and the *linen
> posits itself as equal to one coat*, instead of *x* coats, because the linen
> is not just value in general, but value of a certain magnitude, and
> moreover because one coat contains exactly as much labor as 20 yards
> of linen.

We can also consider their translations of another passage from the
first German edition:

> Indem *sie ihn als Werth sich gleichsetzt,* während sie sich zugleich als
> Gebrauchsgegenstand von ihm unterscheidet, wird der Rock die Er-
> scheinungsform des Leinwand-Werths im Gegensatz zum Lein-
> wand-Körper, ihre Werthform im Unterschied von ihrer Naturalform.
> (Marx, 1983b, p. 30)

In Hasebe's translation, it reads:

> By the linen's *equating itself to the coat as value* – and by the linen at
> the same time distinguishing itself from the coat as a useful object –
> the coat becomes the phenomenal form of linen-value, which opposes
> the linen-body, becoming the value-form of the linen distinguished
> from its natural form.

Miyakawa translates the passage along the following lines:

> By the linen's *equating itself to this coat as value,* and at the same
> time by distinguishing itself from the coat as a useful object. ...

It should be immediately clear, however, that because "*den Rock*" is in the accusative case in the phrase "*setzt sich den Rock gleich*," it should be translated in terms of the linen *equating the coat to itself* (rather than "equating itself to the coat" or "making itself equal to the coat"). Likewise, because the "*ihn*" in "*ihn als Werth sich gleich-setzt*" is in the accusative case, it should be translated as *equates the coat to itself as value* (rather than "equates itself to the coat as value" or "makes itself equal to the coat as value").

What does it suggest, then, that two translators chose expressions that convey a meaning directly opposite to the original German? Considering the fact that both are extremely conscientious and meticulous translators, it seems likely that it was not the result of simple carelessness but rather was a case where each sought to correct a supposed oversight or error on the part of Marx. It must be said, though, that if the translators were attempting to make a correction, their attempt was based upon a fundamental misunderstanding (and even if they were simply careless, their error concerns a matter of crucial importance).

Kōzō Uno commits a similar error (albeit not in such a clear form); or at the very least he seems to lack a sufficient understanding of the importance of Marx's distinction. In Uno's book *Kachi-ron* (Theory of Value), for instance, he writes the following in a section entitled "The Value-Form of the Commodity":

> The "objectivity" [of the value of linen] cannot be grasped as is. The linen owner must express the value of linen through another use-value that he wants to exchange the linen for, such as a coat for example. In this case, *for the linen owner*, the commodity coat has already come to have the same quality as the linen. This means that "as a use-value, the linen is something palpably different from the coat; as value, it is equal to the coat, and therefore looks like a coat" (Marx, 1976a, p. 143), and thus the value of the linen, by being given expression in the coat, is able to express itself apart from its use-value.
>
> This occurs, of course, not because the *labor that makes the linen* is simply the useful labor of weaving labor, but rather by means of it *being reduced to human labor* as a *thing equal to the labor that makes the coat*, or at least as the thing in common between the two different types of concrete labor; but this is certainly not immediately carried out as the abstract human labor the two have in common, being rather an abstraction carried out via the *"detour" of the weaving labor of the*

81

*linen being equated to the concrete tailoring labor of the coat. ...*
  For the linen's value to be able to be expressed in the coat, *the premise to begin with, as mentioned above, is that the linen must make itself equal to the coat,* but if this is carried out we enter into the issue of the owner of the linen offering the linen for the certain amount of coats that he desires. (Uno, 1947, pp. 142–144)

Uno's explanation, from the perspective of my own position, contains a number of unsatisfactory aspects. For instance, when he says that, *"for the linen owner,* the commodity coat has already come to have the same quality as the linen," it would be more appropriate to say "linen" (instead of "linen owner") because the coat is still a desired object for the linen's owner, who views it as being qualitatively different, rather than having "the same quality as the linen." From the perspective of the linen, meanwhile, which has no need to keep warm or strike a fashionable pose, the coat exists solely as value. Still, if we replace "linen owner" with "linen" the matter is exactly as Uno indicates. However, instead of explaining how the coat comes to have "the same quality as the linen," Uno writes:

This occurs, of course, [because] the *labor that makes the linen ...* [is] *reduced to human labor* as a *thing equal to the labor that makes the coat,* or at least as the thing in common between the two different types of concrete labor; but this is certainly not immediately as the abstract human labor the two have in common, being rather an abstraction carried out via the *"detour" of the weaving labor of the linen being equated to the concrete tailoring labor of the coat.* (Uno, 1947, p. 142)

This "detour" differs greatly from the one I described earlier – or rather it is not a detour at all. If the weaving labor to make the linen is reduced to abstract human labor, by being directly equated to the concrete tailoring labor of the coat, then the linen could on its own accord become the direct embodiment of abstract human labor through this act, i.e., it could become the value-body, which would constitute a "self-complacent" act, as noted earlier. So here we have the real necessity of the "detour" of value-expression. Instead of a commodity declaring itself to be value by directly equating itself to another commodity, it first equates the other commodity to itself, positing that other commodity with determinate being as the value-body, and upon this basis it expresses its own value in the natural form of the other commodity. This is the true meaning of the "detour" and it is also precisely the manner in which Marx spoke of it. For instance, in a passage that I quoted earlier, Marx writes:

> For example, *through the coat qua value-thing being equated to the linen, the labor embedded in the coat is equated to the labor embedded in the linen.* It is true that the tailoring which makes the coat is concrete labor of a different sort than the weaving which makes the linen. But *by being equated to the weaving the tailoring* is in fact reduced to what is actually equal between the two kinds of labor, which is *the characteristic they have in common as human labor. Through this detour,* weaving too, in so far as it weaves value, has nothing to distinguish it from tailoring, and, consequently, is abstract human labor. Only the expression of different sorts of commodities as equivalents makes the specific character of value-creating labor apparent, by in fact reducing the different kinds of labor embedded in the different kinds of commodities to their general quality of being human labor in general. (Marx, 1976a, p. 142)

Marx describes the detour of value-expression in the following way in the first German edition of *Capital*:

> The commodity is, since the moment it is born, something twofold, use-value and value, the product of useful labor and the congelation of abstract labor. In order to represent itself as what it is, it must therefore duplicate its form. The form of a use-value it possesses by nature; it is its natural form. The value-form it can acquire only in intercourse with other commodities. But this value-form must itself be an objective form. The only objective forms of the commodities are their useful shapes, their natural forms. However, since the natural form of a commodity, of the linen, for instance, is the diametrical opposite of its value-form, it must turn a different natural form, the natural form of a different commodity, into its value-form. *That which it cannot do immediately vis-à-vis itself, it can do immediately vis-à-vis another commodity, thus doing it vis-à-vis itself via a detour.* It cannot express its value in its own body or in its own useful shape, but it can relate itself to a different use-value or commodity-body as the immediate determinate being of value. It cannot relate itself to the concrete labor contained in itself as the mere form of realization of abstract human labor, but it can relate itself to that contained in other commodity

kinds. *All it has to do is to equate the other commodity to itself as the equivalent. Generally, the use-value of a commodity exists only for a different commodity[1] so far as it serves, in this way, as the form of appearance of its value.* (Marx, 1976b, p. 22)

If the detour of value-expression is not correctly understood, the meaning of the coat, in its given state, becoming the shape of value for the linen will not be correctly grasped. The use-value (or natural form) of the coat is able, in its given state, to be the shape of value for the linen because the linen has equated the coat to itself, positing the coat with the formal determination as value-body. The linen is first able to express its own value in the existence *qua* value-body that the coat is posited as. That is, *in the relation where the linen expresses its own value using a coat, the coat functions only as this existence, whereas its own intrinsic utility (as a thing that satisfies the want of the linen owner) plays no role at all.* For the owner of the linen, the use-value of the coat is not merely useful as the phenomenal form of the value of his linen (as the linen's equivalent), and therefore the coat does not merely exist for the owner as the embodiment of value. Rather, the coat at the same time exists as the object that the owner wants. That is not the case for the commodity linen, however. The linen is not a person and thus lacks human wants. As far as the linen is concerned, the natural body of the coat cannot be of any use as a means of staying warm or looking fashionable. The natural body of the coat is only useful for the linen as a mirror that reflects its own value. Here the coat's natural body only plays a role as the embodiment of abstract human labor. However, even though the natural form of the coat is only functioning as the embodiment of abstract human labor, the labor that is expressed in the natural form (or specific use-value) of the coat is the specific *concrete* labor of tailoring, not human labor as such.

Human labor pure and simple, the expenditure of human labor-power, although capable of every determination, is in and for itself indeterminate. It can only realize itself, objectify itself, if the human labor-power is expended in a determinate form, as determinate labor,

---

[1] For the owner of the "different commodity," the "use-value of a commodity" exists *not only* as such but also as the object he wants.

since only the determinate labor is confronted with a natural matter, an exterior material, in which it objectifies itself. Only the Hegelian "concept" manages to objectify itself without an exterior matter. (Marx, 1976b, p. 20)

It is the concrete labor of tailoring that creates the specific use-value of a coat, and that specific use-value, in its given state, then becomes the shape of value for the linen. This certainly does not mean, however, that concrete labor ceases to be concrete labor. Rather, specific concrete labor, as such, comes to have significance as a certain mode in which human labor is realized or human labor-power is expended:

> Linen cannot relate itself to the coat as value or incarnated human labor without relating itself to tailoring labor as the immediate form of the realization of human labor. However what interests the linen in the use-value coat is neither its woolen comfort nor its buttoned-up character, nor any other useful quality that stamps it as a use-value. The coat only serves for the linen to represent its value-objectivity as opposed to its starched use-value objectivity. The linen would have reached the same purpose, had it represented its value in Assa Fötida or Poudrette, or shoe polish. The tailoring labor, therefore, does not count for the linen, so far as it is purposeful productive activity, useful labor, but so far as it, as determinate labor, is the form of realization, mode of objectification, of human labor pure and simple. Were the linen to express its value in shoe polish, instead of a coat, then the making of polish, instead of tailoring, would count for it as the immediate form of realization of abstract labor. A use-value or commodity-body becomes therefore a form of appearance of value, or an equivalent, only by the fact that the other commodity relates itself to the concrete, useful kind of labor contained in it as the immediate form of realization of abstract human labor. (Marx, 1976b, pp. 20–21)

Grasping this point is the greatest difficulty concerning the understanding of the value-form; therefore, the failure to even perceive the need to grasp this point is the greatest barrier to a correct understanding of the value-form. The fact that the use-value of the coat, in its given state, becomes the form of value for the linen can, if not carefully reflected on, foster the illusion that the coat as a useful thing is capable in that given state of expressing the value of the linen by being an object that the linen owner wants. However, even if a child has some spare playing cards that he wants to trade for a spinning top and then asks if anyone would be willing to give him a top in exchange for ten cards, because this is not a value-relation between commodities the top does not become the phenomenal form of the cards' value. What characterizes a value-relation between commodities is the relation of equivalence between commodities as objectified human labor:

> As values, commodities are expressions of the same unity, of abstract human labor. In the form of exchange-value they appear to each other as values and relate themselves to each other as values. With this, they relate themselves at the same time to abstract human labor as their joint social substance. Their social relation consists exclusively in counting for each other as only quantitatively different, but qualitatively equal (and therefore replaceable by one another and exchangeable with one another), expressions of that social substance which is theirs. As a useful thing, a commodity possesses social determinateness as far as it is use-value for others than its possessor, thus satisfying social wants. But regardless of whose wants the commodity's useful properties establish a relationship with, by these it always only becomes an object placed in a relation to human wants, not a commodity for other commodities. Only that which turns mere useful objects into commodities can relate them as commodities with each other and therefore place them into a social connection. That is exactly the value of commodities. (Marx, 1976b, p. 28)

In the case of the value-expression of one commodity using the use-value of another commodity, there is no reason for it to change that the relation of equivalence between commodities as objectified human is what characterizes the value-relation between commodities; but in such a case an inversion takes place that is inevitable in the fetishized commodity world:

> In tailoring, as well as in weaving, human labor-power is expended. Both, therefore, possess the general property of being human labor, and there may be cases, such as the production of value, in which they must be considered only under this aspect. There is nothing mysterious in this. But in the value-expression of the commodity the matter is stood on its head. In order to express the fact that weaving, for instance, creates the value of linen through its general property of being human labor, rather than in its concrete form as weaving, the concrete labor that produces the equivalent of the linen, namely tailoring, is

placed in relation to it as the tangible form in which abstract labor is realized. (Marx, 1976a, p. 150)

It is here that misinterpretations may arise, however, because matters become complicated and difficult to understand.

> Within the value-relation, and in the expression of value included therein, the abstract and general does not count as the property of the concrete and the sensibly-real, but rather it is the opposite: the sensibly-concrete counts as the mere appearance-form or determinate realization-form of the abstract and general. For example, in the value-expression of linen, the tailoring-labor of the equivalent coat does not possess the general property of also being human labor. It is the opposite case, where being human labor counts as the essence of the tailoring labor, and being tailoring labor only counts as the appearance-form or determinate realization-form of this essence of tailoring labor. This *quid pro quo* is unavoidable because the labor manifested in the labor-product only forms value insofar as it is indiscriminate human labor, and therefore insofar as the labor objectified in a product is indistinguishable from the labor objectified in a different sort of commodity.
>
> The inversion whereby the sensibly-concrete counts only as the appearance-form of the abstractly-general, rather than the abstractly-general counting as a property of the concrete, characterizes value-expression. At the same time, this makes it difficult to understand value-expression. If I say: Roman Law and German Law are both laws, that is obvious. But if I say, on the other hand, the Law, this abstract entity, realizes itself in Roman Law and German Law, in these concrete laws, then the connection becomes mystical. (Marx, 1976b, pp. 56–57)

To say that the role played by the want of the commodity owner is abstracted from in the theory of the value-form certainly does not deny the significance of the role played by the use-value of the commodity in the equivalent form nor negate in any way the role played by the commodity in the equivalent form as a specific use-value. It is only as a specific use-value that the coat expresses the value of the linen. But the coat is not playing a role, in this case, as a useful item that clothes the linen owner: it is only in its existence as something with significance as a certain realization-form of human labor (or mode of the expenditure of human labor-power) that the tailoring labor of the coat is able to express the value of the linen.

Uno, however, in rejecting Marx's view that the role played by the want of the commodity owner is abstracted from in the theory of the value-form, does not seem to grasp this point adequately. For instance, in a passage that I quoted earlier, Uno makes the following comment:

> It is somewhat understandable why the exchange process and the value-form are divided in that particular manner, but I think it is problematic as a method. That is, in the examination of the exchange process Marx seems to be offering a concrete and historical explanation as a supplement to the previous development of the value-form. Although I do not think that the sort of historical process explained in the chapter on the exchange process should be inserted, as is, within the section on the value-form, it does seem somewhat hard to understand, from a methodological standpoint, how one could think that an explanation corresponding to the content of Chapter 2 should not be inserted there. Use-value cannot be understood if it becomes abstract use-value in general that is set apart from the wants of individuals. (Sakisaka & Uno, 1948, p. 142)

As long as the role played by the want of the commodity owner is abstracted from, the role of use-value as a desired object is likewise set aside. This certainly does not mean, however, that the abstraction from the role played by use-value as a desired object should be thought of in terms of "abstract use-value in general that is set apart from the wants of individuals." First of all, it is not at all clear what is meant by "abstract use-value in general." If Uno is defining this in a manner similar to "use-value in general," as understood by the theory of marginal utility, that is certainly not my own understanding, nor is it the view of Marx.[2] It is not as "use-value in general" that

---

[2] Marx, in a letter to Engels, derisively commented (parenthetically) on the following criticism made by the "critical genius of professorial political economy," Karl Knies:

"Not even great perspicacity such as is at the command of Marx is able to solve the task of 'reducing use values' (the idiot forgets that the subject under discussion is 'commodities') i.e., vehicles for enjoyment, etc. to their opposite, to amounts of effort, to sacrifices etc. (*The idiot believes that in the value-equation I wish to 'reduce' use-values to value.*) That is to substitute a foreign element. The *equation of disparate* use values is only explicable by the reduction of the same to a common

the coat expresses the value of the linen. Rather, the coat consistently plays the role of equivalent as a *specific* use-value. As long as the coat is posited as the equivalent form, its natural form is ultimately the form of value. Certainly the coat is posited as the equivalent form because it is an object that the linen owner wants; but the reason the coat is able to express the value of the linen is not because it is a desired object. The coat is able to express the value of the linen because the tailoring labor objectified in the coat is equated to the weaving labor objectified in the linen by means of the coat being equated to the linen. Thus, the tailoring labor in its existence as specific concrete labor becomes the realization-form of human labor in common with the weaving labor. The coat, as a specific use-value, takes on significance as the direct embodiment of human labor, becoming the value-body; and it is in its existence as such that the coat can express the value of the linen. Use-value in this case, therefore, is not abstracted from to arrive at use-value in general. Rather, a specific use-value in its given state appears in an existence separate from its existence as a useful thing, and it is in this existence that it plays the role of equivalent. We do not abstract from the specific qualities of a use-value to arrive at use-value in general. Instead we abstract from the commodity's character as a useful article, where it only has significance in connection to some human want, so that the commodity is purified as the embodiment of human labor. Within this existence, as the purified embodiment of value, it for the first time becomes a value-mirror that selectively and purely reflects the value-character of another commodity.

In speaking of "use-value in general that is set apart from the wants of individuals," perhaps Uno instead has in mind the "general use-value" of money as a "general means of exchange" (i.e., money's capability of purchasing anything, which makes it an object that everyone wants); and it could also be that Uno believes the specific use-value is overlooked if we abstract from the role of desire in the analysis of the value-form, so that we think in terms of use-value in general, and that the simple form of value "cannot be understood" if the equivalent form within it is viewed in that manner. If that is indeed Uno's view, it should be clear from the points made thus far that

---

factor of use value. (Why not simply to – *weight*?)." (Marx, 1991, p. 252)

it is based on a misunderstanding. Even if the "general use-value" of money can be said to be the object of general desire (rather than some specific want), this does not change the fact that it *is* a use-value and must be thought of in relation to some want. Therefore, even if we were to think of the specific use-value as a general use-value, it would of no use at all in elucidating the fundamental issue of the theory of the value-form, which centers on how the value of a commodity can be expressed in the use-value of another commodity. It would only be useful in elucidating why all commodities, including all newly emerging ones, express their value in a particular commodity: gold. Moreover, even in the case of gold, which has that "general use-value," the ability of its natural form to express the value of another commodity is not the result of it being the "general object of desire" but rather – in quite the same way as in the case of the coat – because other commodities equate the gold to themselves,[3] thus positing it with the formal determination as the embodiment of value or "value-body." The fundamental riddle of value-expression – concerning why the value of a commodity can be expressed in the use-value of another commodity – cannot be elucidated by viewing the use-value of the commodity in the equivalent form as "general use-value" (i.e., by viewing it as a problem related to a want). Rather, the very general use-value of money can only be first understood upon elucidating the riddle of value-expression. This is precisely why Marx elucidates the fundamental relation of value-expression in the simple form of value, instead of the money-form.

Finally, there is the criticism made by Uno in the following passage, which I quoted earlier:

> Of course, in *Capital* the value-form and the exchange process are explained separately, and even assuming them separated as such, if we abstract from the owner of linen, to consider linen itself, we will not be able to understand why the linen in the relative form of value brings in the coat to the equivalent form; and if this is abstracted from anything could be in that form, so it would already be the expanded form of value. (Sakisaka & Uno, 1948, p. 160)

---

[3] It is not only a single commodity (such as linen) that equates gold to itself, of course, but all of the other commodities that constitute the commodity world.

First of all, to repeat a point made already, it is certainly not possible to understand why the linen posits the coat as its equivalent without considering the want of the linen owner. If we are dealing here, quite literally, with the question of "why the *linen* in the relative form of value *brings in* the coat to the equivalent form," as Uno says, this is not the action of the commodity owner, so the why pertaining to it can be understood even apart from the owner. However, what actually brings the coat into the equivalent form is the linen *owner*, not the linen, so the why of the action cannot be understood apart from the owner. Despite being the action of the linen owner (and of no concern to the commodity linen), in order to carry out a pure analysis of the value-relation between two commodities it is no hindrance, and in fact a necessity, to set aside the want of the commodity owner. We do this by first treating a certain value-equation as a given, and then solely analyzing the relation of value-expression within it. Thus, the person carrying out the analysis must play two roles. He begins by proposing a certain equation as the sample. In establishing the equation, he acts as what might be called a "proxy" for the commodity owner. In place of the commodity owner, who in reality posits in the equivalent form the commodity that he wants to exchange his own commodity for, the person analyzing the equation posits whichever single commodity he wishes to have on the right of the equation. As long as the simple value-form is at issue, only a single commodity is needed, and there is no particular type of commodity that must be selected. Regardless of the commodity chosen, simply by being placed in the equivalent form, the concrete labor embodied in that commodity is equated to the labor of the commodity in the relative form of value, thus becoming the phenomenal form of abstract human labor that the two commodities have in common. By means of this, the commodity in the equivalent form becomes the phenomenal form of value for the commodity in the relative form. Thus, in setting up the equation, the person carrying out the analysis is perfectly free to choose whichever commodity he likes. In this sense, and only in this sense, "anything" could be in the equivalent form, as Uno says. But this is only the case for setting up the equation. Once a certain equation has been posited, such as 20 yards of linen = 1 coat, it is treated as a given and then analyzed. At that point, it is not acceptable for the commodity on either the left or the right of the equation to be randomly substituted. In terms of our example above, it is the coat, and not some other commodity, that is in the equivalent form, with the natural form of the coat becoming the form of value for the linen. In short, it is certainly not true that "anything" can be brought into the process of analysis.

This all seems obvious to me. I have a hard time understanding how Uno could say that, "if this is abstracted from anything could be in that form, so it would already be the expanded form of value." In the case of a given equation, there is only one commodity in the equivalent form (as long as we are dealing with the simple value-form), and that single commodity is fixed in place. In setting up the equation, it is a random matter what sort of commodity is placed in the equivalent form, but it must be a *single* commodity rather than several commodities. Saying that any commodity can be placed in that form is merely a reflection, on the level of method, of the actual fact that it is unclear what sort of commodity the commodity owner himself will actually choose. Regardless of what commodity is chosen, that commodity, simply by being placed in the equivalent form, becomes the form of value of the owner's commodity.

Given all of this, it is unclear (at least according to my way of thinking) how Uno could think that the simple value-form "would already be the expanded value-form." And this makes it quite difficult to respond to his criticism. If forced to speculate, however, I would interpret his statement as follows. In the relation of the value-expression of the linen, where the coat is the equivalent of the linen, we abstract from the coat as a useful item that the linen owner wants, to concentrate solely on its existence as the embodiment of abstract human labor.[4] We think in terms of the value of the linen only first being able to be expressed in the existence of this value-body. Uno, however, may have interpreted the idea of abstracting from the aspect of a commodity as a useful thing to concentrate exclusively on its existence as the value-body, as an abstraction from the particularity of use-value to arrive at use-value in general. At the same time, he may have mistaken the fact that the linen is first

---

[4] In this case, needless to say, we are dealing with "abstract human labor" in common solely between the labor that makes the linen and the labor that makes the coat.

able to express its value in that existence *qua* "value-body" as signifying that the coat becomes the value-form as use-value in general, instead of as a particular use-value. Perhaps based on that sort of misinterpretation, Uno says that because the particularity of concrete use-values is abstracted from to arrive at use-value in general, this must involve abstraction from various types of use-values to end up with the expanded value-form. If indeed this is Uno's logic, it is similar to his mistaken idea, dealt with earlier, that "use-value cannot be understood if it becomes abstract use-value in general that is set apart from the wants of individuals"; so my earlier comments would be applicable here as well.

All of this, however, is speculation on my part regarding the meaning of Uno's statements, after having struggled to understand what he is trying to say. I may be completely off the mark, but at present I can think of no other plausible explanation.

# Uno's Second Argument:

Without considering the commodity owner, it is not possible to understand why the commodity in the relative form of value and the commodity in the equivalent form are each in their respective forms, which would mean that it is all the same whether one of the commodities is in one form as opposed to the other. The demand for the active expression of value is the demand of the commodity owner, and a certain commodity is in the relative form of value because of the existence of that commodity owner. In contrast, as the commodity in the equivalent form is ideal, the owner has yet to appear in reality. It is by thinking in this manner that a subjective understanding of the value-form becomes possible.

As in the previous article, in addressing the argument summarized above, I will begin with Uno's own words to avoid misunderstandings and then develop my views in direct relation to the passages quoted:

> I want to clearly consider the relation of opposition between the relative value-form and the equivalent form. If this could be reversed at any time the oppositional relation would have no great meaning. ... The question posed here is how much of a difference there is between the relative value-form and the equivalent form if the commodity owner is not considered; this is the point that should be clarified. (Sakisaka & Uno., 1948, p. 164)

> What is the actual significance of the linen and the coat being in opposite positions, with the linen actively seeking to express its value? I think that unless the owner of the linen wanted the coat, the linen would not be able to express its value in the use-value of the coat. If this want is also abstracted from, the coat itself could express its value in the linen as well, so that the "relative" form would become recipro-

cal. But I do not believe that that is the sense of "relative" in this case. (Sakisaka & Uno, 1948, p. 162)

If there were no owner of the linen, for example, there would also not be any desire for the use-value of the commodity in the equivalent form, which is the coat. Both the linen and the coat would then express their respective value in each other. With the existence of the owner, the linen for the first time assumes the relative value-form, and the linen owner, as such, comes to desire that the linen's value be actively expressed. The coat in the equivalent form has yet to appear in a material form, so it does not become active. Which particular commodity is in the equivalent form is something decided by the owner of the commodity in the relative form. (Sakisaka & Uno, 1948, p. 166)

I also want to say that the commodity in the equivalent form is an ideal existence, so the commodity owner as well is not actually in a relation of opposition. If the two commodities are both thought of as actual commodities it would be the same as barter. Value-expression is naturally thinkable because the commodity owner has been presupposed. One might deal with the value-expression in a third-person manner, in terms of attempting to express value by positing one of the two given commodities in the relative form, but in that case it would be easy to fall into the error of Hilferding. ... Even in the case of the simple value-form, the commodity in the relative value-form and the commodity in the equivalent form are not in a relation of simple equality. ... If indeed the two commodities were equated because of being equal, then I think we would be dealing with a relationship where the commodity in the relative value-form and in the equivalent form could be on either side of the equation. ... When the owner of the commodity is taken into consideration, it becomes clear that the equation cannot easily be reversed. ... I would like it to be understood that, in the relation of equating for the commodity, it is not the case that equal things are premised from the beginning so that the equating is the outcome of this. If value-expression is thought of as preceding exchange, then the question of something equal between the two commodities existing will be clarified subsequently. That is to say, the commodity in the relative value-form is in the form for expressing its own value, but we do not know whether this will be actually realized. The commodity in the equivalent form, for its part, is not yet actually provided for exchange. (Sakisaka & Uno, 1948, pp. 233–235)

In the first passage quoted above, Uno poses the question in terms of wanting to "clearly consider the relation of opposition between the relative value-form and the equivalent form" and clarify "how much of a difference there is between the relative value-form and the equivalent form if the commodity owner is not considered." From my perspective, however, Marx in the theory of the value-form – without giving any consideration to the commodity owner – managed to thoroughly elucidate the "relation of opposition between the relative value-form and equivalent form" (and thus explain "how much of a difference there is between the relative value-form and the equivalent form") through his analysis of the value-equation as the form of value-expression. Moreover, this is something that anyone who has carefully read Marx's analysis of the value-form should be able to perceive; and there is no reason to imagine that Uno is unaware of this. So when Uno says that the difference between the two forms is not clear without considering the commodity owner, he must be referring to some other issue. Basically, I think that Uno is trying to say the following. If we look at the structure of the value-equation itself, the meaning of the commodity on the left and on the right side of the equation, and their oppositional relationship, is clear even without considering the commodity owner. But it is only by taking the commodity owner into consideration that we can know why a particular commodity (linen) is in the relative value-form on the left of the equation, while another commodity (a coat) is in the equivalent form on the right. If this is not understood, no distinction between a given equation and its opposite could be arrived at, so it could be thought that each is merely a different way of expressing the same fact. This would result in an inability to subjectively grasp the value-form or understand the crux of that form. As for why that would be the case, Uno first offers the following argument:

> What is the actual significance of the linen and the coat being in opposite positions, with the linen actively seeking to express its value? I think that unless the owner of the linen wanted the coat, the linen would not be able to express its value in the use-value of the coat. If this want is also abstracted from, the coat itself could express its value in the linen as well, so that the "relative" form would become reciprocal. (Sakisaka & Uno, 1948, p. 162)

As I discussed in detail in my earlier article, the value of the linen happens to be expressed in a coat because the coat is an object that the linen owner wants, but this is not an issue relevant to the theory of the value-form. The aim of that theory is to unravel both the riddle of a commodity's price (i.e., money-form) and the riddle of money. Upon deeper reflection, however, we find that the riddle of the money-form is ultimately rooted in the peculiar fact that the value of a commodity is expressed in the oppositional element to *value*: a commodity's *use-value*. In order to solve the riddle of the money-form, therefore, we must first answer the fundamental question of how it is possible, exactly, for a commodity's value to be expressed in the use-value of another commodity. The problem does not present itself in that manner when we directly consider the money-form. For in the case of the money-form, the value of every commodity is expressed in a single independent commodity (gold), so the issue pushed to the forefront is the mysterious nature of gold that stems from this special privilege. Only in the case of the simple value-form does it becomes vividly apparent that the value of a commodity is expressed in the use-value of another commodity equated to it, thus making it possible to first pose, in a pure form, the key question of how this is possible.[1] This is the fundamental issue that Marx examines in his analysis of the simple form of value. Therefore, he does not raise the question of why the coat is posited as the equivalent form for the linen. There is no question that the owner of the linen is the one who posits the coat as the equivalent form, and that he does so because he wants the coat. Yet no matter how long we might dwell on this fact, it is of no use in elucidating the fundamental problem at hand. That problem remains even after the role of the commodity owner has been clarified. It is first posed in an independent form when the process through which a certain value-equation is created (according to the want of a commodity owner) is set aside and the equation is taken as a given. We have two separate is-

---

[1] Marx writes:

"Bailey's reasoning is of the most superficial description. Its starting point is his concept of value. The value of the commodity is the expression of its value in a certain quantity of other values in use (the use-value of other commodities). ... [*The real problem, how it is possible to express the value in exchange of A in the value in use of B does not even occur to him.*]" (Marx, 1989a, p. 335)

sues, belonging to what might be called two different dimensions. It is an intentional act on the part of the commodity owner that posits a specific commodity in the equivalent form. This is a point that can be grasped easily by normal human cognition. In contrast, the process whereby the use-value of the commodity in the equivalent form becomes the value-form for the commodity in the relative value-form takes place independently of the consciousness of the commodity owner. The subject is the commodity, not a human being, and in place of human language we have a fetishistic world where the "language of commodities" is spoken.[2] This is precisely why – when

---

[2] "If we say that, as values, commodities are simply congealed quantities of human labor, our analysis reduces them to the abstraction 'value,' but does not give them a form of value distinct from their natural forms. It is otherwise in the value-relation of one commodity to another. The first commodity's value character steps forward here through its own relationship with the second commodity.

"For example, through the coat *qua* value-thing being equated to the linen, the labor embedded in the coat is equated to the labor embedded in the linen. It is true that the tailoring which makes the coat is concrete labor of a different sort than the weaving which makes the linen. But by being equated to the weaving the tailoring is in fact reduced to what is actually equal between the two kinds of labor, which is the characteristic they have in common as human labor. Through this detour, weaving too, in so far as it weaves value, has nothing to distinguish it from tailoring, and, consequently, is abstract human labor. Only the different sorts of commodities as equivalents makes the specific character of value-creating labor apparent, by in fact reducing the different kinds of labor embedded in the different kinds of commodities to their general quality of being human labor in general. ...

"*We see, then, that everything our analysis of the value of commodities previously told us is repeated by the linen itself, as soon as it interacts with another commodity, the coat. Only it reveals its thoughts in a language with which it alone is familiar, the language of commodities.* In order to say that its own value has been created by labor in its abstract quality of being human labor, it says that the coat, in so far as it counts as its equal, i.e., in so far as it is value, consists of the same labor as it does itself. In order to say that the sublime objectivity which makes up its value differs from its starched body, it says that value has the appearance of a coat, and therefore that in so far as the linen itself is a value-thing, it and the coat are as alike as two peas." (Marx, 1976a, pp. 142–144)

"If I say: The linen *qua* commodity is use-value and exchange-value, then this is the judgment concerning the nature of the commodity obtained through analysis. On the other hand, in the expression 20 yards of linen = 1 coat or 20 yards of linen is worth 1 coat, *the linen itself says* that it is (1) use-value (linen), (2) exchange-value differing from that use-value (a thing equal to a coat), and (3) a unity of both these differences, therefore a commodity." (Marx, 1976b, p. 61)

considering this issue that is the core of the riddle of the value-form – the commodity owner must be abstracted from, by taking a certain equation as a given. Marx thus takes the equation 20 yards of linen = 1 coat as his premise, and then sets about clarifying the relation of value-expression within it solely by analyzing the form of the equation. Through this analysis Marx discovers the "detour" of value-expression – not perceived by earlier economists – and thereby unravels the fundamental riddle of the value-form.

If these points are adequately understood it becomes apparent how misguided it is, in terms of the aim of the analysis of the simple value-form, to think in the manner of Uno that "unless the owner of the linen wanted the coat, the linen would not be able to express its value in the use-value of the coat." It also becomes clear that there is no need for Uno's concern that "if this want is also abstracted from, the coat itself could express its value in the linen, so that the 'relative' form would become reciprocal." Once we take the equation 20 yards of linen = 1 coat as a given, it is clear even without considering the want of the linen owner that the *linen* (not the coat) is in the position of expressing its own value as the commodity in the relative form of value. There is no reason, then, to imagine that "the coat itself could express its value in the linen as well."

If, along with the equation above, the opposite equation (1 coat = 20 yards of linen) is posited at the same time, then indeed "the coat itself could express its value in the linen as well" and the value-expression would be carried out "reciprocally." This is a premise that would naturally exist in an actual case where 20 yards of linen and 1 coat are exchanged as commodities. Furthermore, if we presuppose that the exchange between the linen and coat is repeatedly carried out, rather than being an isolated incident, then the rate of exchange between 20 yards of linen and 1 coat is not the simple expression of the want of the owner of linen, but has instead been established objectively as the regular rate of exchange. This means that included in reality as the premise, along with the expression 20 yards of linen = 1 coat, is the opposite value-expression: 1 coat = 20 yards of linen. Marx points out, for instance, that "the expression 20 yards of linen = 1 coat, or 20 yards of linen are worth 1 coat, also includes its converse: 1 coat = 20 yards of linen, or 1 coat is worth 20 yards of linen" (Marx, 1976a, p. 140).

That situation is premised by Marx, as is natural from a methodological standpoint. As long as Marx's aim is to elucidate the value-relation by analyzing the value-equation, with a certain equation posited as his premise, he must assume that the equation expresses a relation of equivalent exchange (not merely the want of a commodity owner). When Marx says that "the expression 20 yards of linen = 1 coat ... also includes its converse: 1 coat = 20 yards of linen," this means that the opposite relation of value-expression is simultaneously posited from the outset, which is to say that the opposite value-form is included within the premise itself. This does not mean, however, that a given value-expression naturally includes the opposite value-expression without the aforementioned condition of repeated (rather than isolated) exchange.[3] And it certainly does not mean that the subject-object relationship *in a single value-expression* is unclear. Nor does it mean that, within the value-expression 20 yards of linen = 1 coat, "the coat itself could express its value in the linen as well," as Uno writes. This is precisely why Marx makes the following observation:

> But in this case I must reverse the equation, in order to express the value of the coat relatively; and, if I do that, the linen becomes the equivalent instead of the coat. The same commodity cannot, therefore, simultaneously appear in both forms in the same expression of value. These forms rather exclude each other as polar opposites. Whether a commodity is in the relative form or in its opposite, the equivalent form, exclusively depends on the position it holds in the expression of value. That is, it depends on whether it is the commodity whose value is being expressed, or the commodity in which value is being expressed. (Marx, 1976a, p. 140)

In other words, the subject of value-expression is posited along with the equation. As long as the equation of value-expression is taken as a given, the subject is clear even without considering the commodity owner. If we assume that two equations of value-expression exist at the same time, expressing opposite relations, we can of course choose to examine either one. And depending on our choice one of

---

[3] We are not dealing with value-expression, in the strict sense of the term, without this condition of *repeated* exchange.

the commodities will be the subject of value-expression. This certainly does not mean, however, that "the commodity in the relative value-form and in the equivalent form could be on either side of the equation." If it appears that the subject and object are reversed, this is only because two different value-expressions are posited at the same time; it is not occurring within the *same* value-expression. Within a given expression of value, the commodity posited in each of the two forms is fixed. Those positions certainly cannot be altered. Moreover, the fact that we can observe the value-expression of either of the two commodities does not mean, as Uno suggests, that one is dealing with "value-expression in a third-person manner, in terms of attempting to express value by positing one of the two given commodities in the relative form." We are not merely taking two commodities as givens, but also presuming two expressions of value. Each of the two commodities posits the other as its equivalent. Of course, it would be quite wrong-minded for someone to think that instead of two value-expressions it was simply two commodities that are posited and that we seek to "express value by positing one of the two given commodities in the relative form." Uno refers to this as dealing with the expression of value in a "third-person manner," but from my own perspective it is in fact the opposite. The misunderstanding stems rather from the attempt to play a role in value-expression despite being in a third-person position (as the analyst); i.e., despite not being in the position of the person concerned in value-expression. This is precisely the approach that I am criticizing. Uno also objects to this position, saying that "it would be easy to fall into the error of Hilferding," but the reason he provides for his objection is completely different from my own view. For Uno, the defect in the approach above is that it goes no further than a third-person perspective, from which the truth regarding the value-form cannot be grasped. Uno insists that it is necessary to consider the standpoint of the commodity owner, and that without doing so the subject of value-expression would be unclear. From my perspective, however, the fundamental error is not related to a third-person stance. Indeed, a person analyzing the value-form must take such a stance, with a certain value-equation treated as a given. Once we have taken an equation as the premise, we then solely concern ourselves with elucidating the relation of value-expression within it. When a certain equation is premised, it is perfectly clear which commodity is the subject of value-expression, even without considering the commodity owner. This explanation, however, seems unlikely to satisfy Uno, as he has also made the following claim:

> If there were no owner of the linen, for example, there would also not be any desire for the use-value of the commodity in the equivalent form, which is the coat. Both the linen and the coat would then express their respective value in each other. With the existence of the owner, the linen for the first time assumes the relative value-form, and the linen owner, as such, comes to desire that the linen's value be actively expressed. (Sakisaka & Uno, 1948, p. 166)

The question centers here on the latter half of that comment, as I have already dealt with the first half. I think that the true basis for Uno's way of thinking is the idea he presents here that the subject in value-expression is a human being (and could not be the commodity), so that without considering the commodity owner we are unable to know which commodity is the subject of value-expression. However, can it really be said that a human being is the subject of value-expression? My own view is that it is neither impossible nor a case of forced logic to think of the commodity, rather than the commodity owner, as the subject. Moreover, this is correct from a methodological standpoint.

What is clear first of all is that the equation of value-expression, 20 yards of linen = 1 coat, is created by the owner of the linen. Nevertheless, the value that is being expressed in the equation is that of the linen (not an expression of the linen owner's value). If we then consider what makes the value-expression of linen inherently necessary, we see that it stems from the essential nature of linen as a commodity. That is, a commodity by nature is a twofold thing – as the unity of use-value and value – and its natural form is its form as a use-value, not the value-form. Thus, the form of value must be acquired in addition; otherwise the product could not acquire a form as a commodity. In short, the need for value-expression stems from the nature of the commodity itself. Yet the commodity itself is unable to perceive this necessity and obviously cannot carry out this or that action. It is the commodity owner who "comes to desire that the linen's value be actively expressed." Likewise, it is the owner who places a price tag on a commodity. However, as far as this is an expression of the commodity's value as such, the commodity owner is not carrying out some arbitrary action as a person with some individual want. Rather, the commodity owner has perceived the essential nature of the commodity as his own instinct and is merely acting upon that basis. The commodity is therefore first and foremost the subject, whereas the owner can be viewed as nothing more than its automaton, which is why Marx speaks of "the personification of things and the reification of persons" (Marx, 1976a, p. 209).

I would have thought that anyone familiar with *Capital* would require no further explanation of this point, as Marx explains it in detail. So it is surprising that Uno insists that the subject of value-expression cannot be understood apart from the commodity owner. It would seem, then, that some special circumstance must account for Uno's way of thinking. Here I want to offer my own frank conjecture regarding what that circumstance might be. I hope that my interpretation, even if off target, will at least contribute to our general understanding of the value-form.

The key issue concerning the value-form, as noted earlier, appears vividly for the first time in its most undeveloped form, which is the simple value-form. It is the analysis of this form that Marx concentrates on in *Capital*. However, the simple value-form is also the *undeveloped* form of value, which introduces a separate difficulty to the analysis of it purely as the form of value. This difficulty is connected to the fact that the simple value-form of a commodity is not yet a form independent of the want of its owner. In our example of 20 yards of linen = 1 coat, the coat is the form of value for the 20 yards of linen, with significance as the embodiment of abstract human labor of the same quality as the labor embodied in the linen. *At the same time*, the coat is the particular object that the linen owner wants, with significance as a product of specific concrete labor that differs from the labor that makes the linen. In other words, the coat is simultaneously in two completely different relations: it plays two completely different roles, with two completely different determinations. Without the "rather intense application of our power of abstraction" (Marx 1976b, p. 18), we would not be able to distinguish one relation from the other and those two essentially different relations would be mixed up. The restriction on the commodity's value-form by the want of an individual commodity owner is more than just an inconvenient matter that has confounded economists. It is a serious defect for the value-form, as it runs counter to the essential nature of value itself. Therefore, the value-form, instead of remaining at the simple value-form, must proceed to the money-form, where it is first freed from the connection to the individual want of the commodity owner, thus reaching completion as a form of value.

In order to better appreciate the distinction between two different relations, which seem interconnected in the case of the simple value-form and therefore difficult to separate, we can look at what becomes of them in the case of the money-form. It probably goes without saying that when the value-form develops into the money-form – so that a particular commodity (gold) exclusively plays the role of equivalent *qua* money-commodity within the commodity world – commodities are divided into normal commodities and the money-commodity, so that $C_1$–$C_2$ is divided into the two independent processes of $C_1$–$M$ (sale) and $M$–$C_2$ (purchase). We need to begin by examining the significance of each of the two processes. In the case of $C_1$–$M$, we have the process of the realization of the value-form $C_1$ (i.e., $C_1$=$M$) that expresses its own value ideally in a relation of equivalence to $M$, which is the generally valid figure of value. Meanwhile, the significance of $M$–$C_2$ is completely different. Because $M$ is already a commodity with the formal determination as general equivalent, and its natural form thus has general validity as the figure of value, there is no further need for it to turn the use-value of another commodity into the shape of value, and through this express its own character as value. So $M$ cannot occupy the position of the relative form of value in the original sense. However, if we reverse the list of prices, it would at first glance be the same as the extended value-form (form B), with the value of $M$ indicated in every possible commodity. Marx calls this the "specific relative value-form of the money commodity" [*spezifische relative Wertform der Geldware*],[4] with the term "specific" used to fundamentally dis-

---

[4] "The simple relative value-expression of a commodity in money – *x* commodity A = *y* money-commodity – is the price of this commodity. ... On the other hand, the developed relative expression of value, i.e., the endless row of relative value-expression, becomes the *specific relative value-form of the money-commodity*. But this row is now already given within the various commod-

tinguish it from the relative value-form in the original sense. In other words, despite money being on the left of the equation, and in that sense in the relative form of value, it does not forfeit its status as general equivalent and still maintains general direct exchangeability. Therefore, M–C$_2$ is not a process involving the realization of the value-form of M by transforming M into actual value. Rather, it is a process whereby the formal, general use-value of a commodity, which already has the form of general validity *qua* value-body (and therefore the form of absolute exchangeability), is realized in a particular commodity that is the object of the individual want of the owner of the commodity now in the form of M. *It is within this relation that the want of the commodity owner plays a role.* As far as the

---

ity prices. If we read the price-list backwards, we can see the magnitude of the value of money indicated in every possible sort of commodity. This row also comes to have new significance. Since gold is money, already in its natural form, the general equivalent form, i.e., the form of general direct exchangeability, is rendered independent of these expressions of relative value. Therefore, the row of value expressions now at the same time, in addition to the magnitude of the value of gold, expresses the developed world of the material wealth, i.e., use-values, into which gold is directly convertible." (Marx, 1983b, pp. 59–60)

"The commodity that figures as the general equivalent is … excluded from the uniform and therefore from the general relative form of value of the commodity world. If the linen, or any commodity in the general equivalent form, were, at the same time, to share in the relative form of value, it would have to serve as its own equivalent. We should then have: 20 yards of linen = 20 yards of linen, a tautology in which neither value nor its magnitude is expressed. In order to express the relative value of the general equivalent, we must rather reverse form C. This equivalent has no relative form of value in common with other commodities; its value is, rather, expressed itself relatively in the infinite row of all other commodity-bodies. Thus, the expanded relative form of value, or form B, now appears as *the specific relative form of value of the equivalent commodity.*" (Marx, 1976a, p. 161)

"The expression of the value of a commodity in gold – *x* commodity A = *y* money commodity – is the money-form or price of the commodity. … On the other hand, the expanded relative expression of value, the endless row of equations, has now become *the specific relative form of value of the money commodity.* This row, however, is now already socially given in the prices of the commodities. We only need to read the quotations of a price list backwards to find the magnitude of the value of money expressed in all possible commodities. A price, however, money does not have. This uniform relative form of value of the other commodities is not open to money, because money cannot be brought into relation with itself as its own equivalent." (Marx, 1976a, p. 189)

Cf. Marx, 1976a, pp. 199 and 205.

commodity itself is concerned, being now in the form of M merely signifies that it is in the form of possessing general direct exchangeability, and it is a matter of indifference to this commodity whether that ability is realized through its exchange with this or that commodity type. The decision regarding which commodity it will be exchanged with in order to realize that potential is exclusively made by the owner (in this case, the owner of money). The owner reads backwards from the list of the values of commodities expressed in the form of M, which is made up of an infinite number of individual value-equations, and then chooses the particular $M=C_2$ on the right of which is placed the object of his particular individual want. *This is the only point at which the owner's specific individual want plays a role.* It is in this form that the ideal use-value of his money, as a general means of exchange, is realized.

In the case of $C_1=C_2$ (and therefore $C_1–C_2$ as its realization), what is subsequently differentiated to become independent has yet to split apart; $C_1$ equates $C_2$ to itself, thus positing it with the formal determination as value-body, and then expresses its own value in the natural body of $C_2$ (thus positing that natural body with significance as the embodiment of the abstract human labor within $C_1$). Along with this relative value-expression of $C_1$ in the original sense, there is at the same time the expression of the will of the owner of $C_1$ who seeks to realize the formal use-value of $C_1$ as a potential value-body – and therefore as a potential means of direct exchange[5] – in the concrete use-value of $C_2$ which is the particular object that he happens to want (so that the natural body of $C_2$ comes to have significance as the product of specific concrete labor of a different type than the labor that made $C_1$). The former moment subsequently develops into the independent factor of $C_1=M$, while the latter moment develops into $M=C_2$. In contrast, the two factors have not yet split apart in the case of $C_1=C_2$. But the fact that they are not yet separate at that stage does not mean that they are indistinguishable, nor does it by any means suggest the latter constitutes an essential moment of

---

[5] In the case of $C_1$ as well, as far as it is posited in the equivalent form for another commodity, a potentiality naturally taken into consideration by the producer of $C_1$ from the outset, it comes to be the value-body for the other commodity and thus also has direct exchangeability vis-à-vis that commodity.

the former. The expression of the want of the commodity owner (simultaneously encompassed within $C_1=C_2$) is not what constitutes the value-form as such. In fact, it is a heterogeneous factor that renders the form incomplete as a value-form. Therefore, the value-form cannot remain in the simple value-form: it has to develop to the money-form, where the value-form is first completed by freeing itself from the heterogeneous factor that develops into the separate and independent form of $M=C_2$. If our intention in analyzing $C_1=C_2$ is to elucidate the value-form, we naturally need to uncover and extract the form that becomes independent as $C_1=M$ (i.e., the money-form), not the factor that develops subsequently to become independent as $M=C_2$. This primarily involves uncovering the embryo of the money-form within $C_1=C_2$, thus providing a vital clue for unfolding the theory of the value-form in *Capital*. Marx proudly noted that this was one of his most important original ideas:

> These gentry, the economists, have hitherto overlooked the extremely simple point that the form 20 yards of linen = 1 coat is but the undeveloped basis form of 20 yards of linen = gold of £2, and thus that the simplest form of a commodity, in which its value is not yet expressed as its relation to all other commodities but only as something differentiated from its own natural form, contains the whole secret of the money-form and thereby, *in nuce*, of all bourgeois forms of the product of labor. In my first presentation [*Contribution*], I avoided the difficulty of the development by providing an actual analysis of the expression of value only when it appears already developed and expressed in money. (Marx, 1987b, p. 384)

> Every one knows, if nothing else, that commodities have a common value-form which presents a marked contrast to the varied natural forms of their use-values: the money-form. Here, however, we have to perform a task never even attempted by bourgeois economics; namely, to show the genesis of this money-form, i.e., to pursue the development of the expression of value contained in the value-relation of commodities, from its simplest, almost imperceptible shape, to the dazzling money-form. When this has been done, the riddle of money disappears also at the same time. (Marx, 1976a, p. 139)

> The only difficulty in the comprehension of the money-form is that of grasping the general equivalent form, and hence the general form of value itself, i.e., form C. Form C can be reduced by working back-

wards to form B, the expanded form of value, and its constitutive element is form A: 20 yards of linen = 1 coat or $x$ commodity A = $y$ commodity B. The simple commodity form is therefore the germ of the money-form. (Marx, 1976a, p. 163)

This form [the simple value-form] is somewhat difficult to analyze, because it is simple. ([Footnote:] It is, to a certain extent, the cell-form or, as Hegel would say, the "*an sich*" of money.) The different specifications which are contained in it are veiled, undeveloped, abstract, and consequently only able to be distinguished and grasped through the rather intense application of the power of abstraction. (Marx, 1976b, p. 18)

The value-form of the commodity must itself again be an objective form. The exclusive objective forms of commodities are their use-figures, i.e., their natural forms. Now, since the natural form of a commodity, of the linen, for instance, is the diametrical opposite of its value-form, it must turn a different natural form, the natural form of a different commodity, into its value-form. That which it cannot do immediately vis-à-vis itself, it can do immediately vis-à-vis another commodity, thus doing it vis-à-vis itself via a detour. It cannot express its value in its own body or in its own use-value, but it can relate itself to a different use-value or commodity-body as the immediate existence of value. It cannot relate itself to the concrete labor contained in itself as the mere form of realization of abstract human labor, but it can relate itself to that contained in other commodity kinds. All it has to do is to equate the other commodity to itself as the equivalent. Generally, the use-value of a commodity exists only for a different commodity so far as it serves, in this way, as the form of appearance of its value. If one considers in the simple relative expression of value, $x$ commodity A = $y$ commodity B, only the quantitative relation, one will also only find the laws developed above about the movement of relative value.[6] ... However, if one considers the value-relation of the two commodities according to their qualitative side, one uncovers in every simple value-expression the secret of the value-form, and therefore, *in nuce*, that of money. (Marx, 1976b, p. 22)

In addition to his various arguments that I introduced earlier, Uno also says that "the coat in the equivalent form has yet to appear in a material form, so it does not become active" (Sakisaka & Uno, 1948,

---

[6] Cf. Marx, 1976a, pp. 144–146.

p. 166); that "the commodity in the equivalent form is an ideal existence, so the commodity owner as well is not actually in a relation of opposition"; and that "the commodity in the equivalent form … is not yet actually provided for exchange" (Sakisaka & Uno, 1948, pp. 233–235). These sorts of views, however, are clearly based on a misconception.[7] The fact that the coat is the equivalent form for the value-expression of another commodity certainly does not mean that it does not exist actually as a commodity. The coat itself also actually exists as such, and it is precisely because of the possibility of it being "actually provided for exchange" with the value-expression in which the coat posits the linen in the equivalent form, that the value-expression of the linen (in which it posits the coat in the equivalent form) is also able to be given. In this case, when the linen owner says "20 yards of linen are worth 1 coat," and the owner of the coat says "1 coat is worth 20 yards of linen," exchange between those two parties is possible for the first time. If only one of the two commodities exists in reality, and therefore value-expression is only unilateral, exchange would never take place. However, this certainly does not mean that the subject and object of value-expression are unclear. Two commodities exist actually in this case, so there are two value-expressions, and the question of which is subject or object must of course be decided for each. This means that it is perfectly clear which commodity is in the relative value-form and which is the equivalent form.[8]

---

[7] Uno seems to be confusing two things. As I noted above, it is a clear error to declare that the commodity in the equivalent form does not appear as an actual good; however, it is also a clear fact that the commodity in the equivalent form, *within the value-relation in which it is posited as equivalent*, i.e., as far as being the material for the value-expression of the commodity in the relative form of value, exists as something imagined in the mind. It can be thought that Uno links this fact to the observations he makes, but in so doing he is clearly mistaken. In fact, the opposite supposition should be made, as I note in the main text above.

[8] "Let us consider transactions of exchange between linen-producer A and coat-producer B. Before the deal is struck, A says: 20 yards of linen are worth 2 coats (20 yards of linen = 2 coats), but B says: 1 coat is worth 22 yards of linen (1 coat = 22 yards of linen). Finally, after they have haggled for a long time, they come to agreement. A says: 20 yards of linen are worth 1 coat, and B says: 1 coat is worth 20 yards of linen. In this case, both linen and coat are situated at the same time in relative value-form and equivalent form. But (*nota bene*), the circumstance

In other words, a failure to identify the subject/object of value-expression is not the result of overlooking the want of the commodity owner or of inadequately pondering whether or not a commodity appears in reality. Rather, it is solely the result of not taking a value-equation as a given or of focusing exclusively on its content without considering the *form* of value-expression (thus remaining on the level of the theory of the substance of value). If there is confusion between subject and object, as Uno notes with concern, I think the best way to deal with the problem would be to adopt the standpoint of strict scientific analysis. That is, we should take a certain equation as a given and engage in the elucidation of the value-form, grasping it through an observation of the form of value-expression and extracting and analyzing the relation of value-expression within it. Uno, however, recommends that we consider the want of the commodity owner and the existence (or non-existence) of the commodity, which, from my perspective, is a case of going to an opposite extreme in the hope of preventing an error. There are cases where one must fight one evil with another, but in this case at least I cannot agree with such an approach.

---

obtains for two different persons and in two different value-expressions, which appeared only at the same time. As far as A is concerned, his linen (because for him the initiative has its origin in his commodity) is situated in the relative value-form, and it is the commodity of the other person (the coat) on the other hand which is situated in equivalent form. It is the other way around from the standpoint of B. The same commodity thus never – not even in this case – possesses both forms at the same time in the same value-expression." (Marx, 1976b, pp. 50–51)

Uno's Third Argument:

T he essential difference between the general equivalent form
and the money-form first becomes clear when we consider the
want of the commodity owner. That is, when the general
equivalent becomes money it is no longer limited to the relation
where it is desired for its original use-value, and thus it expresses the
value of a commodity. If we set aside this characteristic, there would
be no essential distinction established between the general equivalent form and the money-form.

Within the developmental stages of the value-form in *Capital*, after
the general equivalent form (form C), Marx takes the further step of
introducing the money-form as the fourth form (form D). However,
Marx says that there is no essential difference between the two
forms. Therefore, at first glance, one may wonder why he bothered to
distinguish between them, and it might seem that Kōzō Uno – in his
argument summarized above – has managed to compensate for
Marx's failure to clarify the essential difference between the two
forms (despite having gone to the trouble of distinguishing between
them). Uno's explanation, which supposes this error on the part of
Marx, adheres to the following line of reasoning:

> For Marx, the "money-form" is merely a matter of the linen, which is
> the equivalent form *qua* "general value-form," changing into gold. He
> says that "form D differs not at all from form C, except that now, in-
> stead of linen, gold has assumed the general equivalent form," but as I
> mentioned earlier, if we clearly suppose the existence of the owner of
> the commodity in the relative value-form, we can understand that in
> the case of the money-form a change occurs so that the liberation from
> its use-value is completed, whereas this had still only been latent in
> the case of the general value-form. (Uno, 1947, p. 164)

It is not clear what use-value is being freed from, exactly, when Uno speaks of the "liberation from its use-value," but the overall gist of his argument seems to concern the liberation of the value-form from the restriction by some individual want, such as the case where a commodity's value is expressed using the object that the commodity owner happens to want. Uno writes:

> The general equivalent is distinguished from other commodities, and "it is not until this exclusion has once and for all confined itself to one specific kind of commodity that the uniform relative value of the whole commodity world gains objective fixity and general social validity" (Marx, 1976a, p. 162). At the same time, it can then no longer be said that this is still a relation where each commodity owner desires the general equivalent because of its use-value and expresses his own commodity's value by means of it. In the case of what Marx calls the general value-form, it can be said that already each commodity is developing such a relation, but for value-expression to be "completely" transformed in that manner it is necessary for the equivalent to be "restricted to one particular commodity." This is precisely the development of the relation where the general equivalent is posited as the "form of general direct exchangeability," on the one hand, while all of the other commodities are posited with the "form of indirect exchangeability," on the other hand. Stated differently, commodities in general make the general equivalent into something able to purchase a commodity at any time, while at the same time those commodities cannot directly purchase each other. ...
>
> Along with the general equivalent becoming this sort of money-commodity, however, as already mentioned, it is not directly the use-value *qua* commodity, as such, that is the desired object, but rather it is set against other commodities as "use-value for everyone, i.e., general use-value" that serves as the "general means of exchange." (Uno, 1947, pp.161–162).

The development of the value-form is also the process of the genesis of a value-form independent of the individual want of the commodity owner. This genesis of the value-form constitutes a necessary moment within the development of commodity production; the value-form is completed with the money-form and at the same time the equivalent commodity comes to be "'use-value for everyone, i.e., general use-value' that serves as the 'general means of exchange.'" All of these points are undeniable truths; but Marx did not overlook them, nor did he fail to identify their importance. Indeed, Marx writes:

> In the direct exchange of products, each commodity is directly a means of exchange to its owner, and an equivalent to those who do not possess it, although only in so far as it has use-value for them. At this stage, therefore, the articles exchanged do not acquire *a value-form independent of their own use-value, or of the individual wants of the exchangers*. The need for this form first develops with the increase in the number and variety of the commodities entering into the process of exchange. The problem and the means for its solution arise simultaneously. Commercial intercourse, in which the owners of commodities exchange and compare their own articles with various other articles, never takes place without different kinds of commodities, that belong to different owners, being exchanged for, and equated as values with one single further kind of commodity. This further commodity, by becoming the equivalent of various other commodities, directly acquires the form of a general or social equivalent, if only within narrow limits. This general equivalent form comes and goes with the momentary social contacts which call it into existence. It is transiently attached to this or that commodity in alternation. But with the development of commodity exchange it fixes itself firmly and exclusively onto particular kinds of commodity, i.e., it crystallizes out into the money-form. ...
>
> *The money commodity acquires a dual use-value. Alongside its special use-value as a commodity* (gold, for instance, serves to fill hollow teeth, it forms the raw material for luxury articles, etc.) *it acquires a formal use-value, arising out of its special social function.* (Marx, 1976a, pp. 182–184)

Marx, in this manner, clearly recognizes that commodities having "a value-form independent of their own use-value, or of the individual wants of the exchangers," is a need that "first develops with the increase in the number and variety of the commodities entering into the process of exchange," and that it is the formation of the general value-form – and further, the money-form – that precisely satisfies this need, with the money-commodity acquiring "a formal use-value, arising out of its special social function." It is worth noting, however, that unlike Uno, who thinks this is a problem pertaining to the theory of the value-form (and that the development of the value-form cannot be understood without focusing on it), Marx makes no mention of it in the theory of the value-form. Marx first raises this problem in the theory of the exchange process because it falls outside of the framework of the particular problem elucidated in the theory of the value-form. It is certainly not the task of the theory of the value-form to discuss every sort of problem related to the value-form, which at any rate would be impossible; just as the discussion of value in Chapter 1 does not (and could not) deal with every conceivable problem related to value.

The task particular to the theory of the value-form is to unravel the riddle of the commodity's price (i.e., the riddle of the money-form), and therefore the riddle of money. The money-form itself is the developed value-form, so the riddle of the money-form is nothing more than the developed form of the fundamental riddle of the value-form. In carrying out his analysis, Marx traces his way back from the money-form so as to reduce it to its elementary form: the simple form of value. He discovers, through this analysis, the core of the riddle of the money-form, which is the peculiar fact that a commodity's value is expressed in another commodity's use-value (the oppositional factor to value). Here we have the riddle of the value-form; and it is the basis of the riddle of the money-form. Without solving the former riddle there is no way to solve the latter – whereas the riddle of the money-form is easily unraveled once the riddle of the value-form has been solved. Marx writes:

> It is clear that the actual money-form does not in itself provide any difficulty. Just as soon as the general equivalent form is penetrated it no longer costs one the least sort of headache to comprehend that this equivalent form holds fast to a specific sort of commodity, like gold; and all the less headache in that the general equivalent form from its nature preconditions the social excluding of one determined sort of commodity by all other commodities. The only problem that remains is that excluding gains objectively social consistency and universal validity, and hence neither happens to different commodities in turn nor possesses a merely local significance in particular circles of the commodity world alone. The difficulty in the concept of the money-form is limited to the comprehension of the general equivalent form, and thus of the general value-form as such, form III. Form III, however, is analyzed reversely into form II, and the constituent element of form II is form I: 20 yards of linen = 1 coat or $x$ commodity A = $y$ commodity B. Now if one knows what use-value and exchange-value are, then

one finds that this form I is the simplest, most undeveloped manner of manifesting a random labor-product (e.g., linen) as commodity, that is, as unity of the opposites use-value and exchange-value. One then easily finds at the same time the sequence of metamorphoses which the simple commodity-form: 20 yards of linen = 1 coat must pass through in order to attain its finished structure: 20 yards of linen = 2 pounds Sterling, i.e., the money-form. (Marx, 1976b, pp. 69–70)

Marx pointed out, in a June 22, 1867 letter to Engels, that earlier economists had not perceived the significance of the simple form of value:

These gentry, the economists, have hitherto overlooked the extremely simple point that the form 20 yards of linen = 1 coat is but the undeveloped basis form of 20 yards of linen = gold of £2, and thus that the simplest form of a commodity, in which its value is not yet expressed as its relation to all other commodities but only as something differentiated from its own natural form, contains the whole secret of the money-form. (Marx, 1987b, p. 384)

Marx's comments do not pertain solely to the orthodox economists who displayed almost no interest in the question of the value-form. He notes that even the "few economists, such as S. Bailey, who have concerned themselves with the analysis of the form of value" (Marx, 1976a, p. 141), not only failed to solve the riddle in the analysis of the simple value-form but were not even aware of its existence and that the "real problem, how it is possible to express the value in exchange of A in the value in use of B – does not even occur to him [Bailey]" (Marx, 1989, p. 335).

In the first of my articles published in *Keizai shirin* (cf. my comments on "Uno's First Argument"), I discussed how the analysis of the simple value-form in *Capital* primarily addresses the task of clarifying the riddle of that form, which Marx brilliantly accomplished in uncovering the "detour" of value-expression. In seeking to unravel the riddle, we must set aside the want of the commodity owner, as Marx did, because introducing that issue there only hinders the solution of the problem at hand and generates confusion. In response to my article, Uno quickly presented a counter-criticism in an article of his own entitled "The Tasks of the Theory of the

Value-Form: A Response to Professor Kuruma's Criticism," published in the June 1950 issue of *Keizai hyōron*. One of the main grounds of his argument presented in that article is the idea that the position of the simple value-form within the developmental process of the value-form could not be understood if we abstract from the want of the commodity owner. Below, in italics, are passages quoted from Uno's article (*Keizai hyōron*, No. 6, 1950, pp. 79–80) where he presents his argument, followed by my response in brackets (to avoid having to quote the same passages twice).

*In the simple value-form, even though the coat, "as a specific use-value, takes on significance as the direct embodiment of human labor, becoming the value-body"* (Kuruma, 1957, p. 70), *it becomes such as a result of the owner of the linen positing the coat as the equivalent, so that it is not the equivalent generally for other commodities.*

[It certainly is true that in the case of 20 yards of linen = 1 coat, the coat only has significance as the equivalent vis-à-vis the linen – rather than generally as the equivalent for every other commodity too – but this fact should not be explained in terms of the equation being the outset of the value-form. Rather, the fact that it is merely the initial form should be explained on the basis of it only having significance as the equivalent vis-à-vis the linen, which itself can be explained by the fact that the coat is only equated to the linen and not to any other commodities. In other words, it is a fundamental fact that, no sooner than a commodity is equated to another commodity, it becomes the form of that other commodity's value. The theoretical problem at hand ultimately comes down to grasping the "how" pertaining to this fact.]

*Professor Kuruma, however, draws the distinction in the following terms: "The coat is posited as the equivalent form because it is an object that the linen owner wants, but the reason the coat is able to express the value of the linen is not because it is a desired object"* (Kuruma, 1957, p. 69). *This sounds reasonable enough, to be sure ... but this idea does not elucidate the fact that in this simple form of value the coat expresses the value of the linen or the fact that the value of the linen is not adequately expressed, nor does it clarify the fact that the form of value must therefore necessarily be developed.*

[This is a matter of course. My discussion there was entirely related to problems common to the value-form, or what might be called the problem of the value-form itself (i.e., the fundamental mechanism of value-expression), so it is natural that the defects of the simple value-form and the necessity for it to develop beyond that level were not clarified by that discussion.]

*As I mentioned earlier, my own view is that this point constitutes the theoretical task regarding the value-form.*

[If the question is whether the task of the theory of the value-form concerns the elucidation of the fundamental mechanism of value-expression or the elucidation of the development of form, I do not have an answer because both are crucial to that theory. Still, from my perspective, the ultimate task of the theory of the value-form is to solve the riddle of the commodity's money-form, and thereby also solve the riddle of the money-fetish. And those riddles themselves are merely the riddle of the developed value-form or the development of the fundamental riddle concerning the value-form. In order to unravel this fundamental riddle, Marx analyzes and traces back the money-form, reducing it to the simplest form of value so that he can clarify the fundamental mechanism of value-expression. Then, starting out once again from this point, while limiting himself to that mechanism of value-expression, Marx follows the developmental process of the value-form from the simple value-form to its completion as the money-form. This is my view regarding the nature of the theory of the value-form in *Capital* and the approach one should take in dealing with that theory. Clarifying the fundamental mechanism of value-expression and clarifying the development of the value-form are partial tasks indispensable to the solution of the ultimate theoretical task concerning the value-form; so both must be accomplished before we can arrive at the theory of the value-form. However, if the question is which of the two tasks is the fundamental one to be carried out first, it is of course the former; because without clarifying the fundamental mechanism of value-expression we cannot basically understand how the development of the value-form is possible. Moreover, I do not hesitate to say that it is the former task that also poses the greatest challenge for the understanding of the value-form. Marx describes it as "the point where all the difficulties originate which hinder an understanding of the *value-form*" (Marx, 1976b, p. 21); whereas once that problem has been solved, one "easily finds at the same time the sequence of metamorphoses which the simple commodity-form: 20 yards of linen = 1 coat must pass through in order to attain its finished structure: 20 yards of linen = 2 pounds Sterling, i.e., the money-form" (Marx, 1976b, p. 70).]

*Kuruma says that the "fact that the use-value of the coat, in its given state, becomes the form of value for the linen can, if not very carefully reflected on, foster the illusion that the coat as a useful thing is capable in that given state of expressing the value of the linen by being an object that the linen owner wants"* (Kuruma, 1957, p. 65); *but could it then be said that in the simple value-form "the coat as a useful thing" without "being an object that the linen owner wants" is "capable in that given state of expressing the value of the linen?"*

[This manner of quoting me is rather unbecoming for a person who I respect as much as Professor Uno. I certainly did not say that the coat as a useful thing, without being a desired object for the linen owner (and therefore without being equated to the linen), is capable *in its given state* of expressing the value of the linen. As should be clear from the sentence Uno quotes just prior to this, I am saying that the coat, in its given state, does not express the value of the linen by being a useful object desired by the linen owner. I explained this earlier in my article in more detail as follows: "Certainly the coat is posited as the equivalent form because it is an object that the linen owner wants; but the reason the coat is able to express the value of the linen is not because it is a desired object. The coat is able to express the value of the linen because the tailoring labor objectified in the coat is equated to the weaving labor objectified in the linen by means of the coat being equated to the linen. Thus, the tailoring labor in its existence as specific concrete labor becomes the realization-form of human labor in common with the weaving labor. The coat, as a specific use-value, takes on significance as the direct embodiment of human labor, becoming the value-body; and it is in its existence as such that the coat can express the value of the linen." (Kuruma, 1957, pp. 69–70) I also dealt with this issue in the following passage: "There is no question that the owner of the linen is the one who posits the coat as the equivalent form, and that he does this because he wants the coat. Yet no matter how long we might dwell on that fact, it is of no use in elucidating the fundamental problem at hand. That problem remains even after the role of the commodity owner has been clarified. It is first posed in an independent form when the process through which a certain value-equation is created (according to the want of a commodity owner) is set aside and the equation is taken as a given. We have two separate issues, belonging to what might be called two different dimensions. It is an intentional act on the part of the commodity owner that posits a specific commodity in the equivalent form. This is a point that can be grasped easily by normal human cognition. In contrast, the process whereby the use-value of the commodity in the equivalent form becomes the value-form for the commodity in the relative value-form takes place independently of the consciousness of the commodity owner. The subject is the commodity, not a human being, and in place of human language we have a fetishistic world where the 'language of commodities' is spoken. This is precisely why – when considering this issue that is the core of the riddle of the value-form – the commodity owner must be abstracted from, by taking a certain equation as a given." (Kuruma, 1957, p. 80)]

*The problem is that if, in the simple value-form, a division is made, in the manner of Professor Kuruma, between "the coat being posited in the equivalent form" and "the coat in the equivalent form being able to express the value of the linen," the position of the simple value-form within the developmental process of the value-form becomes unclear.*

[It does not become unclear at all. As Marx plainly notes: "One sees right away the insufficiency of the simple form of value, of this embryonic form which must undergo a series of metamorphoses before ripening into the price-form. The expression of the value of commodity A in terms of some other commodity B merely distinguishes the value of A from its own use-value, and therefore also only places A in an exchange-relation with one particular different kind of commodity, instead of representing A's qualitative equality with all other commodities and its quantitative proportionality to them. To the simple relative form of value of a commodity there corresponds the isolated equivalent form of another commodity. Thus, in the relative expression of value of the linen, the coat possesses the form of equivalent, the form of direct exchangeability, only in relation to this one kind of commodity, the linen. However, the simple form of value passes by itself into a more complete form. Although this simple form expresses the value of commodity A in only one commodity of another kind, it is a matter of complete indifference what this second commodity is, whether it is a coat, iron, corn, etc. Different simple expressions of the value of one and the same commodity arise therefore according to whether this commodity enters into a value-relation with this or that other kind of commodity. The number of such possible expressions of commodity A is limited only by the number of the different kinds of commodities distinct from A. The isolated expression of A's value transforms itself therefore into the indefinitely expandable series of different simple expressions of that value" (Marx, 1976a, p. 154). The reason that the simple value-form is incomplete as a value-form, as well as the circumstances of its transformation to form B, can thus very well be explained through an analysis that concentrates solely on form – without considering the factor of the want of the commodity owner and hence the reason why a certain commodity (say a coat rather than wheat) is posited as the equivalent form.]

The point noted by Marx in the passage I just quoted concerns the simple value-form; but in the case of the developed value-form as well, the form's defect – and its development into the general equivalent form – can be fully explained through an analysis of the form alone, as is immediately apparent from reading *Capital*. There is some room for doubt, however, regarding the transition from the general value-form to the money-form, as mentioned earlier. That transition, likewise, bears no relation to the want of the commodity owner, but unlike the previous cases, the change in form is not an essential one. Marx writes:

> Fundamental changes have taken place in the course of the transition from form A to form B, and from form B to form C. As against this, form D differs not at all from form C, except that now instead of linen gold has assumed the general equivalent form. Gold is in form D what linen was in form C: the general equivalent. The advance consists only in that the form of direct general exchangeability, in other words the general equivalent form, has now by social custom irrevocably be-come entwined with the specific bodily form of the commodity gold. (Marx, 1976a, p. 162)

Given Marx's view that no "fundamental change" has taken place, why did he go to the trouble of recognizing the money-form as the fourth form, in distinction from the general value-form? At first glance it seems a meaningless distinction. Uno's view is that the shift from the general value-form to the money-form has great signifi-cance. He commends Marx for drawing a distinction between the two forms, but then criticizes him for merely distinguishing between the two without clarifying the true significance of the distinction. The reason that Marx falls short, in Uno's mind, is that he failed to con-sider the vital factor of the want of the commodity owner, which ap-parently demonstrates that the owner's want should not be abstracted from in the theory of the value-form. This is the view Uno proposed in the article from which I just quoted at length, but I think it should now be fully apparent that it lacks validity. The crux of Uno's explanation is the discovery that the characteristic of the money-form centers on the fact that when the general equivalent becomes the money-commodity, "it is not directly the use-value *qua* commodity, as such, that is the desired object, but rather it is set against other commodities as 'use-value for everyone, i.e., general use-value' that serves as the 'general means of exchange.'" Uno's view, however, amounts to nothing more than making "serv[ing] as the general means of exchange" the basis or premise of the conceptual determination within the theory of the value-form. Granted, the function as a "general means of exchange" is one that the money-commodity inevitably comes to acquire along with the development of the value-form into the money-form. Yet this is certainly not a function in the expression of value but rather a function in the exchange process. It is thus a methodological error to make it the premise for unfolding the theory of the value-form – just as it would be wrong to carry out an examination of the function of money as the measure of value by presupposing the function of money as the means of circulation. It is true that the function of money in value-expression takes on even greater concrete significance through the development of the function of money in the exchange process, but it is not acceptable to have the latter as a premise of the former. The conceptual determinations within the theory of the value-form are extremely abstract and formalistic, but this is a necessity from a methodological standpoint, and through the subsequent development our understanding gradually becomes more concrete.

Yet there remains the question of why Marx made a distinction in the theory of the value-form between the general value-form and the money-form. Is there a distinction between them apart from the idea of becoming a "general means of exchange"?

I have already noted my view that Marx, in the theory of the value-form, first clarifies the fundamental mechanism of value- expression by analyzing the simple value-form, and then (while restricting himself to that mechanism) clarifies the process whereby the form of value-expression develops sequentially until it reaches completion as the money-form. The mechanism of value-expression necessarily deals with riddle of the equivalent form, and since the developmental process of the value-form is at the same time the developmental process of the riddle of the equivalent form, the elucidation of the developmental process of the value-form also clarifies the developmental process of the riddle of the equivalent form that crystallizes in the money fetish that dazzles people's eyes. We recognize, from the perspective of the development of the riddle of the equivalent form, the extremely important meaning of the fact that the general equivalent form adheres ultimately to the natural form of a particular sort of commodity (i.e., the fact that the general form of value becomes the money-form); for this adherence accompanies the tremendous unfolding of the fetish-character of the equivalent form. This is illustrated by the fact that vulgar economists have tried to elucidate the riddle of money fetish (i.e., the riddle of gold and silver) by listing the names of commodities that have played the role of general equivalent other than gold or silver:

> The relative value-form of a commodity, of the linen for example, expresses the value-existence of the linen as something quite different from its body and bodily properties, namely, for example, as something which looks like a coat. This expression itself therefore indicates that it conceals a social relation. It is the other way around with the equivalent form. The equivalent form consists precisely in this, that the commodity-body, the coat for instance, this thing in its unadorned figure, expresses value, and is therefore endowed with the value-form by nature itself. Admittedly this holds good only within the value-relation, in which the commodity linen relates itself with commodity coat as its equivalent. However, the properties of a thing do not arise from its relation to other things; they are, rather, merely activated by such relations. The coat, therefore, seems to have its equivalent form – its property of direct exchangeability – just as much from nature as its property of being heavy or its ability to keep us warm. Hence the riddling character of the equivalent form, which only impinges on the crude bourgeois vision of the political economist when it confronts him in its fully developed shape, that of money. He then seeks to explain away the mystical character of gold and silver by substituting less dazzling commodities for them and, with ever-renewed satisfaction, reeling off a catalogue of all the inferior commodities which have played the role of the commodity-equivalent at one time or another. He does not suspect that even the simplest expression of value, such as 20 yards of linen = 1 coat, already presents the riddle of the equivalent form for us to solve. (Marx, 1976a, pp. 149–150)

The following passage from *Capital*, which supports the view I have presented thus far, also deals with the gist of the theory of the value-form:

> We have already seen, from the simplest expression of exchangeable value, *x* commodity A = *y* commodity B, that the thing in which the magnitude of the value of another thing is represented seems to have the equivalent form independently of this relation, as a social natural-property which it possesses. We followed the process by which this false semblance solidified itself. *This semblance was completed when the general equivalent form adhered to the natural form of a particular commodity or crystallized into the money-form. Although a particular commodity only becomes money because all other commodities express their values in it, it seems, on the contrary, that all other commodities universally express their values in a particular commodity because it is money. The movement through which the process has been mediated vanishes in its own result, leaving no trace behind.* Without any initiative on their part, the commodities find their own value-figure ready to hand, in the form of the body of a commodity existing outside and alongside them. This physical object, gold or silver in its crude state, becomes, immediately on the emergence from the bowels of the earth, the direct incarnation of all human labor. *Hence the magic of money.* (Marx, 1976a, p. 187)

We can see, then, that the main theoretical issue at hand can be more easily understood if we consider why the general value-form is recognized as the stage prior to the money-form, rather than concentrating on why Marx recognized the money-form independently of the general value-form. What is posited before us in reality is the money-form, and thus it is natural to think of it as the final form. Our task is to solve the riddle of this money-form, but to do so we must first reduce it to the general value-form. *It is in the form where every sort of commodity is on the left of the equation, and a special commodity is on the right, that for the first time the inherent relation becomes clear wherein "all other commodities universally express their values in a particular commodity because it is money." In the money-form, "the movement through which this process has been mediated vanishes in its own result, leaving no trace behind." When the list of commodities on the left in the general value-form is dissolved, the value-form at first glance takes the form of price identical to the simple value-form. This also completes the peculiar riddle of money. Making the reduction to the general form of value is the indispensable first step towards solving the riddle of money.*

This, at any rate, is the manner in which I understand the distinction between the general value-form and the money-form. So I do not think that the significance of this distinction will be misunderstood if we do not consider the want of the commodity owner. It is true, of course, that by taking the want of the commodity owner into consideration we can understand that there is additional significance to the transition from the general form of value to money-form, and our understanding thus becomes more concrete. However, as I have repeatedly emphasized, approaching the issue from that perspective does not help us solve the task inherent to the theory of the value-form, and in fact hinders a solution by blurring the issue at hand. If we become too engrossed in the fact that the coat is posited as the equivalent of the linen because of the want of the linen owner, for instance, we would end up overlooking the fundamental riddle of the value-form which concerns exactly how it is possible for the use-value of the coat (in its given state) to become the value-form of the linen; and we would also be unable to clarify the "detour" of value-expression that is the key to solving this riddle. This demonstrates why Marx had to abstract from the want of the commodity owner in the theory of the value-form. – That is the gist of my view.

# PART TWO

Marx's Theory of the Genesis of Money
(A Discussion with Teinosuke Otani)

# The Questions "How, Why and Through What"
## (The Genesis of Money)

O TANI: I want to begin by discussing the content of the first of the *Marx-Lexikon zur Politischen Ökonomie*[1] volumes on the topic of money, particularly issues related to Part 1 of that volume, entitled "The Genesis of Money." Since the time of your debate with Kōzō Uno in the late 1940s, scholars have offered a variety of arguments regarding the genesis of money in *Capital*; or regarding, more specifically, the content and interrelation of (1) the theory of the value-form, (2) the theory of the fetish-character, and (3) the theory of the exchange process. Some have inherited the fundamental aspects of Uno's viewpoint (although there have been splits among them so that now there are numerous positions within the "Uno school"); while others have viewed your explanation as fundamentally correct, but felt the need for a partial revision of it. Even though the latter camp seems to be close to your standpoint, there are a number of differences (or misunderstandings) concerning key points. There is also no shortage of scholars claiming to have funda-

---

[1] [*Marx-Lexikon zur Politischen Ökonomie* – edited by Kuruma with the help of Teinosuke Otani, his son Ken Kuruma, and others – is a 15-volume collection of passages (in German and Japanese) from Marx's complete works, organized according to the five main topics of "competition" (1 vol.), "method" (2 vols.), "the materialist conception of history" (2 vols), "crisis" (4 vols), and "money" (5 vols.), along with a one-volume index. This project was based on Kuruma's vast collection of note cards containing passages from Marx and other writers. For *Marx-Lexikon*, Kuruma organized this material under the main topics and then further divided the passages under headings and subheadings. Each volume of *Marx-Lexikon* also came with a booklet around 20 pages long featuring a discussion on the given topic of the volume, usually led by Kuruma. The first volume was published in 1968 and Kuruma continued his editorial work right up to his death in 1982. – EMS]

mentally gone beyond both you and Uno, but to list up every view would probably be quite time-consuming. I am curious, at any rate, about the extent to which you were aware of such opinions when editing Part 1 on the genesis of money in that *Marx-Lexikon* volume, and what sort of points you paid attention to.

**KURUMA:** I have not read many books of that sort in recent years, so I did not edit that volume of *Marx-Lexikon* on the basis of any awareness of the types of arguments being advanced. Colleagues have gone to the trouble of sending me a great number of books and articles, but because my energy has been directed so exclusively towards editing *Marx-Lexikon*, in most cases I have not had the time to carefully read them. Much of what I have read more or less carefully was connected to the questions you posed for the booklet inserted in that first volume on the topic of money. I had read some works criticizing my book *Theory of the Value-Form & Theory of the Exchange Process* (and then re-read a few of them to answer your questions); but when editing the first volume on the topic of money I was not that aware of the articles and books to which you are referring and only addressed the criticism expressed in those works in order to answer your questions.

**OTANI:** Looking at the content of Part 1 of the first *Marx-Lexikon* volume on money, there is an introductory chapter entitled: "How Did Marx Pose the Question for the Genesis of Money? – How, Why, and Through What Is a Commodity Money?" which is followed by three chapters that address, respectively, the questions of how, why, and through what a commodity is money. The title of the introductory chapter does not seem to be a heading that appears in *Capital or A Contribution to the Critique of Political Economy* [hereafter: *Contribution*].

**KURUMA:** That's correct. I did not simply incorporate the headings from *Capital* because Marx did not introduce an independent section on the genesis of money. Marx did analyze the commodity and clarify how money necessarily emerges from out of the commodity world in the first chapter of *Contribution* and the first two chapters of

*Capital*.[2] In *Capital*, the genesis of money is dealt with directly in Section 3 and 4 of Chapter 1, as well as in Chapter 2, but none of these parts addresses the "genesis of money" as its primary topic. They all differ, therefore, from Chapter 3 of *Capital* (or Chapter 2 of *Contribution*), where money is directly taken up as the main subject.

Thus, in order to deal in one place with the references to money in the first two chapters of *Capital*, I had to set up an independent heading that does not exist in *Capital* or in *Contribution*. "The Genesis of Money" seemed an appropriate heading to address the issue in its entirety. Still, there was the question of how to further organize the information and what other sorts of headings to create. One approach might have been to incorporate the headings from *Capital* – regarding the theory of the value-form, fetish-character, and the exchange process – or it also might have been possible to establish headings according to the topic of the *necessity* of money. Despite such alternatives, however, I did not hesitate to introduce the questions "how, why, and through what" as the three main organizational pillars.

As you know, I think that the best expression of Marx's investigation of the genesis of money is found in his sentence on how the "difficulty lies not in comprehending that money is a commodity, but in discovering how, why and through what a commodity is money" (Marx, 1976a, p. 186). I felt that raising those three questions would best reflect Marx's real intention in the first two chapters of *Capital from the perspective of the genesis of money*; and this is the second reason why I did not incorporate the headings from *Capital*.

**OTANI:** Already in *Theory of the Value-Form & Theory of the Exchange Process* you offered a clear and detailed account of how to read Marx's analysis of money in the first two chapters of *Capital*. In Part 1 of that book, near the beginning, you indicate the following three questions that naturally enter the mind of someone encountering the first three chapters of *Capital*:

1. What is the relation between the examination of money in the

---

[2] The content of Chapter 1 and 2 of *Capital* corresponds to Chapter 1 in *Contribution*.

first two chapters and the "theory of money" in Chapter 3?

2. If the examination of money in the first two chapters is introductory (as compared to the theory of money *proper* in Chapter 3), what is the peculiar significance of the analysis of money presented, respectively, in the theory of the value-form, theory of the fetish-character, and theory of the exchange process?

3. Why is Chapter 2, which may be thought to be introductory, also positioned as an independent chapter, parallel to the much longer Chapter 1 that includes four sections which are each longer than the entire second chapter?[3]

Near the end of the first part of *Theory of the Value-Form & Theory of the Exchange Process* you responded to each of these questions. That explanation provides us with a good understanding of your fundamental thinking, so that we can also grasp the meaning of the structure of Part 1 of the first of the *Marx-Lexikon* volumes on money. Do you have anything to add regarding that explanation?

**KURUMA:** My thinking has not changed since then, but there is one point that I was aware of at the time but did not emphasize. That is, near the end of Part 1 of *Theory of the Value-Form & Theory of the Exchange Process*, I said that Marx examines the simplest form of exchange-value ($x$ commodity A = $y$ commodity B) from a different perspective in Section 1 than in Section 3. However, that equation is of course an abstraction from the commodity's appearance as it immediately presents itself to people in the course of their activities in a commodity production society. That abstraction is made in order to purely grasp the object of analysis. What is immediately visible to people, needless to say, is the shape of the commodity in the equation $x$ commodity A = $y$ money-commodity, which is the money-form of the commodity or its price-form. In other words, the form: commodity = money. In terms of their respective relations to the money-form,

---

[3] [I have summarized the content of a passage quoted by Teinosuke Otani from Kuruma's *Theory of the Value-Form and Theory of the Exchange Process* that sketches the theoretical tasks in each of the four sections of Chapter 1 and in Chapter 2 of *Capital*, in addition to briefly touching on Chapter 3. That passage appears at the beginning of Part One of this book. – EMS]

the theory of the value-form, the fetish-character, and the exchange process clarify the *how*, *why*, and *through what* of that form. Marx offers us following observation regarding this in the section in *Capital* on the fetish-character:

> Man's reflection about the forms of social life, and therefore also his scientific analysis of these forms, takes a course directly opposite to the actual development of these forms. He begins "after the feast" with the completed results of the development process. ... It was only *the analysis of the prices of commodities* which led to the determination of the magnitude of value, and only *the common expression of commodities* in money which led to the fixation of their character as values. (Marx, 1976a, p. 168)

As early as the seventeenth century economists had emphasized, in their analysis of commodity prices, that money is a commodity, but no one prior to Marx had clarified "how, why, and through what a commodity is money." Marx writes:

> That money is a commodity is therefore a discovery only for those who proceed from its finished shape in order to analyze it afterwards. ... In the last decades of the seventeenth century the first – but for that time well taken – step in the analysis of money, the discovery that money is a commodity, had long been taken; but this was merely the first step, and nothing more. The difficulty lies not in comprehending that money is a commodity, but in discovery how, why and through what a commodity is money. (Marx, 1976a, pp. 184–186)

As for why economists prior to Marx, particularly the Classical economists, had been unable to pose the question in this way (and were thus unable to solve the problem), I would recommend looking at the passages in the first section of Chapter 1 in that *Marx-Lexikon* volume on money.[4] The important point to note, at any rate, is that

---

[4] [The passages Kuruma is referring to include the following:

"In order to decipher how the simple expression of the value of a commodity is embedded in the value-relation between two commodities, we must, for now, look at the value-relation independently of its quantitative aspect. The usual procedure is the precise opposite of this: one sees in the value-relation only the proportion in which definite quantities of two sorts of commodity count as equal to each other. One overlooks that the magnitudes of different things only become

Marx ultimately is analyzing the *price-form of the commodity*.

**OTANI:** As for the three interrogatives, *how*, *why*, and *through what*, three independent sentences are posited in the headings of Part 1 of the *Marx-Lexikon* volume, in place of the phrase "commodity is money." Those sentences are:

1. How is money generated?
2. Why does the labor that is socially necessary for the production of commodities take the form of the value of commodities (or why does the value of commodities take the form of money)?
3. Through what circumstances does the genesis of money become necessary (or through what praxis is money generated)?

Could you explain the content of those three in more detail?

**KURUMA:** My aim with the headings was to more clearly state the distinctive content of each of the three questions, although fundamentally speaking it could be said that the content is already indicated by each of the three interrogatives themselves. Of course, each of those headings is based precisely on what is discussed, respec-

---

comparable in quantitative terms when they have been reduced to the same unit. It is only as expressions of such a common unit that they are of the same denomination, and are therefore commensurable magnitudes." (Marx, 1976a, pp. 140–141)

"It is one of the chief failings of Classical political economy that it has never succeeded in finding, from the analysis of commodities and more specifically of commodity value, the form of value, i.e., that which turns value into exchange-value. Even its best representatives, Adam Smith and David Ricardo, treat the form of value as something quite indifferent or extraneous to the nature of the commodity itself. The reason for this is not solely that their attention is entirely absorbed by the analysis of the magnitude of value. It lies deeper. The value-form of the product of labor is the most abstract, but also the most general form of the bourgeois mode of production; by that fact it stamps the bourgeois mode of production as a particular species of social production, and therewith as one of a historical and transitory character. If one considers it to be the eternal form of social production, one necessarily overlooks the specificity of the value-form as well – and consequently that of the commodity-form, together with its further developments, the money-form, the capital-form, etc." (Marx, 1976a, p. 174). – EMS]

tively, in the three parts of *Capital* where the three questions are elucidated. I chose the headings so that the reader could grasp, to some degree, the content of the three questions "how, why, and through what" – for in the case of *Marx-Lexikon*, the headings are the reader's most reliable guide.

# Riddle of the Money-Form and
# the Riddle of Money

O TANI: Next, I want to consider a view of the *riddle of money* expressed by Naomichi Hayashi in an article entitled, "On the So-called 'Riddle of Money': The Problem of How, Why, and Through What," published in the December 1975 issue of the journal *Keizaigaku zasshi*.

KURUMA: I don't recall the title of that article, but I believe Hayashi's view is that the "riddle of money" refers to the entire issue of "how, why, and through what a commodity is money." Is that right?

OTANI: Yes. In the introduction to his article, Hayashi says that the problem "will be referred to hereafter as the problem of the 'riddle of money,'" after which there is a heading entitled "The Significance of Elucidating the 'Riddle of Money.'" Even though the title of the article includes the word "so-called" and the riddle of money is placed in quotation marks, Hayashi does not seem to be saying that he finds this manner of expression to be mistaken. And in the main body of the article as well he repeats the view that the "riddle of money" refers to the entire issue of "how, why, and through what."

KURUMA: I see. But in that case, why does Hayashi use the term "riddle of money"? I cannot really understand his point, because, first of all, the word "riddle" conveys the idea that a problem is difficult to respond to because it is presented in a crooked or twisted (rather than straightforward) manner. But the question of "how, why, and through what a commodity is money," is precise and to the point – not convoluted. Yet "riddle" also has the meaning of something not easily solved, so in that sense I suppose the question of "how, why, and through what a commodity is money" is a difficult question that might be called a "riddle."

In Hayashi's case, though, he starts from the view that the French edition of Volume one of *Capital*, which Marx himself thoroughly revised, is superior to the original German edition, and he notices that the passage in the French edition is quite different from the original German. Hayashi points out that the German expression, "*wie, warum, wodurch Ware Geld ist*" (how, why, and through what the commodity is money"), becomes "*comment et pourquoi une merchandise devient monnaie*" (how and why a commodity becomes money) in the French edition. He thinks that "*une merchandise*" (a commodity) in the passage signifies gold, so that the question is: "Why does *gold* become money?" That question, far from being difficult or confusing, can be easily answered by saying that gold becomes money because it is the commodity whose physical properties are best suited to the functions of money. There is no "riddle" here, in any sense.

But what would be the case if "*une merchandise*" is not referring to the specific commodity gold? What if "*une*" is referring to a numeral, rather than an indefinite article, so that Marx is speaking of *one* commodity? Well, that would merely suggest that a single commodity, rather than two or more commodities, should function as money. So the question would center on the reason why bimetallism does not function well. Here, again, we are hardly grappling with a riddle.

As for how Marx himself understood the riddle of money in *Capital*, we can look to the following passage from Section 3 of Chapter 1, which he added to the second edition:

> Every one knows, if nothing else, that commodities have a common value-form which presents a marked contrast to the varied natural forms of their use-values: the money-form. Here, however, we have to perform a task never even attempted by bourgeois economics; namely, to show the genesis of this money-form, i.e., to pursue the development of the expression of value contained in the value-relation of commodities, from its simplest, almost imperceptible shape, to the dazzling money-form. When this has been done, the riddle of money disappears also at the same time. (Marx, 1976a, p. 139)

When Marx says here that the task is to "show the genesis of this money-form, i.e., to pursue the development of the expression of value contained in the value-relation of commodities, from its simplest, almost imperceptible shape, to the dazzling money-form," he seems to be illuminating the issue of *how* a commodity is money. And it is through the elucidation of this problem that "the riddle of money disappears also at the same time." We can get a better idea of what Marx means by the expression the "riddle of money" by looking at other things he has written, such as the following passages:

> Now this fetish-character, to be sure, reveals itself much more strikingly *in the equivalent form* than in the relative value-form. The relative value-form of a commodity is mediated; namely, by its relation to another commodity. Through this value-form, the value of the commodity is expressed as something completely distinct from its own sensible existence. Within this fact it is comprised at the same time that existence as value can only be a relation which is alien to the thing itself and hence its value-relation to another thing can only be the form of appearance of a social relation concealed behind it. *It is the other way around with the equivalent form. It consists precisely in the fact that the bodily or natural form of a commodity counts immediately as the social form, as the value-form for another commodity.* Therefore, within our practical interrelations, to possess the equivalent form appears as the social natural property of a thing, as a property that thing inherently has, so that hence it appears to be immediately exchangeable with other things just as it exists for the senses. Because, however, within the value-expression of commodity A, the equivalent form inheres in commodity B by nature, it seems also to belong to the latter by nature, even outside of this relation. Hence, for example, *the riddling character of gold*, which appears to *possess, along with its other natural properties* (its dazzling color, its weight, its non-oxydizability in air, etc.), also *the equivalent form by nature*, that is, the social quality of being directly exchangeable with all other commodities. (Marx, 1976b, p. 60)

> The relative value-form of a commodity, of the linen for example, expresses the value-existence of the linen as something quite different from its body and properties, namely, for example, as something which looks like a coat. This expression itself therefore indicates that it conceals a social relation. *It is the other way around with the equivalent form. The equivalent form consists precisely in this, that the commodity-body, the coat for instance, this thing in its unadorned fig-*

*ure, expresses value, and is therefore endowed with the form of value by nature itself.* Admittedly, this holds good only within the value-relation, in which the commodity linen relates itself with the commodity coat as its equivalent. However, the properties of a thing do not arise from its relation to other things; they are, rather, merely activated by such relations. The coat, therefore, seems to have its equivalent form, its property of direct exchangeability, just as much from nature as its property of being heavy or its ability to keep us warm. *Hence the riddling character of the equivalent form, which only impinges on the crude bourgeois vision of the political economist when it confronts him in its fully developed shape, that of money.* He then seeks to explain away the mystical character of gold and silver by substituting less dazzling commodities for them, and, with ever-renewed satisfaction, reeling off a catalogue of all the inferior commodities which have played the role of the commodity-equivalent at one time or another. *He does not suspect that even the simplest expression of value, such as 20 yards of linen = 1 coat, already presents the riddle of the equivalent form for us to solve.* (Marx, 1976a, pp. 149-150)

We have already seen, from the simplest expression of exchangeable value, x commodity A = y commodity B, that the thing in which the magnitude of the value of another thing is represented seems to have the equivalent form independently of this relation, as a social natural-property. We followed the process by which this false semblance solidified itself. This semblance was completed when the general equivalent form adhered to the natural form of a particular commodity, or crystallized into the money-form. Although a particular commodity only becomes money because all other commodities express their values in it, it seems, on the contrary, that all other commodities universally express their values in a particular commodity because it is money. The movement through which the process has been mediated vanishes in its own result, leaving no trace behind. Without any initiative on their part, the commodities find their own value-figure ready to hand, in the form of the body of a commodity existing outside and alongside them. This physical object, gold or silver in its crude state, becomes, immediately on the emergence from the bowels of the earth, the direct incarnation of all human labor. *Hence the magic of money. The merely atomistic behavior of men in their social process of production, and hence the fact that their own relations of production take on an objectified figure which is beyond their control and independent of their conscious individual striving, manifest themselves at first in the fact that the products of labor generally take the form of commodi-*

*ties. The riddle of the money fetish is therefore merely the riddle of the commodity fetish itself that has become visible and blinding to the eyes.* (Marx, 1976a, p. 187)

We can see, from the passages just quoted, that Marx uses the term "riddle" to refer to how the natural form of the commodity in the equivalent form – or developed further, the natural form of gold or silver – appears to inherently have the thoroughly social attribute of *direct exchangeability*. Bourgeois economists were unaware of the fact that "the riddling character of gold" is the developed form of "the riddling character of the equivalent form," so that the fundamental key to unraveling the riddle must be found through analyzing the simple value-form. Instead of doing that, economists tried to solve the riddle of money by "explain[ing] away the mystical character of gold and silver by substituting less dazzling commodities for them, and, with ever-renewed satisfaction, reeling off a catalogue of all the inferior commodities which have played the role of the equivalent at one time or another." The nature of the riddle, however, is not such that it can be unraveled by such means.

**OTANI:** In *Theory of the Value-Form & Theory of the Exchange Process*, you mention the "riddle of the *money-form*" in distinction from the "riddle of money." Some have criticized your use of that term, saying that Marx did not use that expression; and I am curious to hear your view of such criticism.

**KURUMA:** As for whether or not Marx himself used the expression "riddle of the money-form," I was never concerned enough to look into the matter. I imagine that those who say that he did not might be correct if they have investigated it carefully. Marx did, however, use the expression, "*secret* of the money-form." There may be other examples, but the one I have in mind is his June 22, 1867 letter to Engels, in which he writes:

> These gentry, the economists, have hitherto overlooked the extremely simple point that the form 20 yards of linen = 1 coat is but the undeveloped basis form of 20 yards of linen = gold of £2, and thus that the simplest form of a commodity, in which its value is not yet expressed as its relation to all other commodities but only as something differen-

tiated from its own natural form, contains the whole secret of the money-form and thereby, *in nuce*, of all bourgeois forms of the product of labor. In my first presentation [*Contribution*], I avoided the difficulty of the development by providing an actual analysis of the expression of value only when it appears already developed and expressed in money. (Marx, 1987b, pp. 384-385)

Another point of reference is the following passage from *Capital* that I quoted a bit earlier, which appears near the beginning of the theory of the value-form:

Every one knows, if nothing else, that commodities have a common value-form which presents a marked contrast to the varied natural forms of their use-values: the *money-form*. Here, however, we have to perform a task never even attempted by bourgeois economics; namely, to show the *genesis of this money-form*, i.e., to pursue the development of the expression of value contained in the value-relation of commodities, from its simplest, almost imperceptible shape, to the dazzling money-form. When this has been done, the *riddle of money* disappears also at the same time. (Marx, 1976a, p. 139)

Here, in relation to the elucidation of the "riddle of money," Marx speaks of showing the "genesis of this money-form" and pursuing the "development of the expression of value contained in the value-relation of commodities, from its simplest, almost imperceptible shape, to the dazzling *money-form*." If we can grasp the connection this has to the elucidation of the "riddle of money," I think that not only the "riddle of money" but also the meaning of the "riddle of the money-form" will be understood.

My own view is that the connection involves the following three aspects. First, money is the outcome of the development of the equivalent form, *so the riddle of money is nothing more than the development of the riddle of the equivalent form*. Second, the equivalent form is the moment that constitutes the pivot of value-expression (or the pivot of the form of value-expression: the value-form), so the riddle of the equivalent form necessarily constitutes the riddle of the value-form. Third, the money-form is the developed value-form, so the riddle of the value-form develops to become the riddle of the money-form. With regard to this, Marx writes:

If one considers in the simple relative expression of value, $x$ commodity A = $y$ commodity B, only the quantitative relation, one will also only find the laws developed above about the movement of relative value, which are all based on the fact that the magnitude of value of the commodities is determined by the labor-time necessary for their production. However, if one considers the value-relation of the two commodities according to their qualitative side, one uncovers in every simple value-expression the *secret of the value-form, and therefore, in nuce, that of money.* (Marx, 1976b, p. 22)

Marx clearly indicates in this passage the indivisible relation between the *secret of money* and the *secret of the value-form* – as well as the secret of the *money-form* as the developed form of the latter. In my own case, taking into consideration the sort of points mentioned thus far, I have used the expression the "riddle of the money-form" in addition to the "riddle of money," but I did not see the need to explain this in my book.

**OTANI:** In one of the passages you quoted, there is also a reference to the "riddle of the money fetish," with Marx saying that the "riddle of the money fetish is therefore merely the riddle of the commodity fetish that has become visible and blinding to the eyes." Judging from the use of the term "money fetish" or "commodity fetish," could it be said that the "riddle of the money fetish" is something elucidated to a greater extent in the theory of the fetish-character in Section 4 than in the theory of the value-form?

**KURUMA:** My view is basically that Marx analyzes the commodity in Chapter 1 of *Capital*, particularly up to and including Section 3, with his analysis naturally carried out by means of examining the fundamental form in which a product appears as a commodity: $x$ commodity A = $y$ commodity B. After clearly indicating that a commodity is both a use-value and a value, Marx elucidates that the substance of value is labor. Then he makes clear the twofold character of the labor that appears within a commodity, where labor has a concrete character in terms of creating a use-value and an abstract character in terms of creating value. Here Marx already clarifies that in the value of a commodity the *social character of labor takes the form of the value-character of a labor-product, i.e., the form of a thing.*

143

This is followed, in Section 3 on the value-form, with Marx underscoring the fact that the value of a commodity is not manifested in the body of that commodity itself, but rather in the *bodily shape of another commodity that is equated to it*, so the other commodity's given bodily shape becomes the form of value. Marx, in other words, further clarifies that the *social character of human labor appears in the form of a thing*. In the second edition of Capital, however, in examining the substance of value and the value-form as well, Marx *merely indicates this point as a fact, without offering any unified explanation of how the fact is a manifestation of the fetish-character particular to commodity production*. It is in Section 4 of Chapter 1 that he first offers that other explanation. The earlier analysis of the commodity clarifies various facts that are manifestations of the fetish-character of the commodity, but in Section 4 Marx looks back on these facts and uncovers the fetish-character of the commodity that runs through them. It is from this new perspective that Marx then explores the causes of the fetish-character, while reconfirming the results of his previous analysis.

The preceding is the case for the second German edition of *Capital*, but in the first edition that examination is presented within the analysis of the value-form. For instance, at the end of the passage discussing the general equivalent form in the first edition, Marx writes:

> Indeed all use-values are commodities only because they are products of mutually independent private labors, private labors, which however materially depend on one another as special, even though autonomized, branches of the naturally-grown system of division of labor. They are thus socially connected exactly by their diversity, their particular usefulness. It is exactly because of this that they produce qualitatively different use-values. Did they not do this, these use-values would not become commodities for each other. On the other hand, their different useful quality does not yet turn these products into commodities. If a peasant family produces coat, linen, and wheat for their own consumption, then these objects confront the family as different products of their family labor, but they do not confront each other as commodities. If the labor were immediately social, i.e., joint labor, then the products would obtain the immediately social character of a joint product for their producers, but not the character of commodities for each other. Yet we do not have to go far in order to find

what is the social form of the private labors that are contained in the commodities and independent of one another. This was already clarified in the analysis of the commodity. *The social form of private labors is the relationship with each other as equal labor*, i.e., since the equality of altogether different labors can only consist in an abstraction from their inequality, *their relationship with each other is as human labor in general*: expenditures of human labor-power, something which all human labors, whatever their content and their mode of operation, indeed are. In every social form of labor, the labors of the different individuals stand also in a relation to each other as human labor, but here, this relationship itself counts as the specifically social form of the labors. *It is true that none of these private labors in its natural form possesses this specific social form of abstract human labor, just as little as the commodity in its natural form possesses the social form of mere congelation of labor, or of value. By the fact that the natural form of one commodity, here the linen, becomes the general equivalent form (because all other commodities refer themselves to the latter as the form of appearance of their own value), the linen weaving labor also becomes the general form of realization of abstract human labor,* or it becomes labor in immediately social form. The measuring stick for "being social" must be borrowed from the nature of the relations peculiar to each mode of production, not from the imaginations alien to it. Just as it was shown a minute ago that the commodity, by nature, excludes the direct form of general exchangeability, that therefore the general equivalent form can only develop antagonistically, the same is true for the private labors contained in the commodities. *Since they are not immediately social labors, it follows first that the social form is a form different from the natural forms of the actual useful labors, a form that is alien to them and abstract, and secondly, all kinds of private labor obtain their social character only antagonistically, by all of them being equated to an exclusive kind of private labor, here the linen weaving.* By this, the latter becomes the immediate and general form of appearance of abstract human labor, and thus labor in immediately social form. It represents itself therefore also immediately in a socially valid and generally exchangeable product. (Marx, 1976b, pp. 31–32)

This description from the part dealing with the theory of the value-form in the first edition of *Capital* was moved (although not in its exact original form) to the independent Section 4 in the second edition, where Marx examines the theory of the fetish-character. This merely suggests, however, that Marx's descriptive approach changed, in terms of where it seemed most appropriate to discuss the issue. I should note, incidentally, that in the discussion of the value-form in the first edition of *Capital*, as is clear from the passage just quoted, the word "fetish" does not yet appear, but in the appendix on the value-form that Marx included in the first edition, we do find the heading: "The fourth peculiarity of the equivalent form: The fetishism of the commodity form is more striking in the equivalent form than in the relative form." Under that heading, Marx includes the following:

> But within our practical interrelations, these social characters of their own labors appear to the producers as social properties pertaining to them by nature, as objective determinations of the labor-products themselves; the equality of the human labors appears as the value-property of the labor-products; the measure of the labor by the socially necessary labor-time appears as the value-magnitude of the labor products; and finally, the social relation of the producers through their labors appears as a value-relation or social relation of these things, the labor products. ... [T]he commodity-form and the value-relation of the labor-products have absolutely nothing to do with their physical nature and the material relationship which is derived from it. It is only the determined social relation of people itself which in this case assumes for them the phantasmagoric form of a relation of things. Thus in order to find an analogy we must flee into the nebulous region of the religious world. Here it is that the products of the human head appear as independent figures endowed with their own life and standing in relationship to one another and to men. That is the way it is in the commodity world with the products of the human hand. That is what I call the fetishism which clings to labor-products as soon as they are produced as commodities, and which is thus inseparable from commodity production.
>
> Now this fetish-character, to be sure, reveals itself much more strikingly *in the equivalent form* than in the relative value-form. ... Hence, for example, the riddling character of gold, which appears to possess, along with its other natural properties (its dazzling color, its weight, its non-oxydizability in air, etc.), also the equivalent form by nature, that is, the social quality of being directly exchangeable with all other commodities. (Marx, 1976b, pp. 59–60)

But the question you raised, I believe, centers on how Marx says that "the riddle of the money fetish is therefore merely the riddle of the commodity fetish that has become visible and blinding to the eyes," which would seem to suggest (judging from the expression "riddle of the money fetish" and "riddle of the commodity fetish") that this is something that should be analyzed in the theory of fetish-character, rather than in the theory of the value-form. Is that correct?

**OTANI:** Yes, that's right.

**KURUMA:** I have just mentioned a number of things related to that question, but my argument could be summed up as follows.

First of all, in the section in which Marx analyzes the substance of value, as well as in his examination of the value-form, he already elucidates the fetish-character as a fact. In this examination of the substance of value, Marx shows that in the case of the value of a commodity, the socially necessary labor for its production presents itself in the form of the value-character of a product, a thing. He then indicates, in the analysis of the value-form, that the value of the commodity is not manifested in the body of that commodity itself, but rather is expressed in the natural, bodily form of another commodity that is equated to it – and ultimately in the natural form of the money-commodity, gold. Marx, in other words, has elucidated all of these points *as facts*.

However, to note the second point, we need to be aware of the difference between recognizing a fact as such, through the analysis of the commodity, and examining this fact as something particular to commodity production (where production is immediately carried out as private production); or as a necessary moment for the commodity producers' immediately private labor to become social labor and thereby gain determinate being as one part of the total social labor.

Third, it seems difficult to make a sweeping declaration regarding where that examination should be presented. Indeed, there is a major difference on this point between the first and the second edition of *Capital*, as is already clear from the passage I quoted from the first edition.

Fourth, from that perspective, I think that there may be room to reconsider the way you posed the question – based on Marx's statement that the "riddle of the money fetish is therefore merely the riddle of the commodity fetish that has become visible and blinding to the eyes" – in terms of whether the issue should be examined in the theory of the fetish-character instead of in the theory of the value-form

The fifth and final point is that the passage you mentioned regarding the riddle of the money fetish, which comes at the end of Chapter 2 in which the process of exchange is dealt with, can also be found in exactly the same form in the first German edition, under heading: 2). Regarding this, we should note first of all that when Marx wrote that part he must have had in mind what he had written concerning the commodity in Chapter 1 – or under heading 1) in the first German edition; and then second there is the question of why Marx raised this in the theory of the exchange process rather than in the theory of the value-form or the theory of the fetish-character.[1]

If we give due consideration to the first point, regarding how Marx had the entire first chapter in mind, I think it is clear that it is impossible to provide a definitive answer if we pose the question in terms of whether it is a problem that is examined in the theory of the value-form or in the theory of the fetish-character.

As for the second question, I think the following answer is possible. In the first German edition of *Capital*, the development of the value-form does not proceed up to the money-form. Money first appears as an outcome of the exchange process. Thus, it was not possible to raise the issue of the "riddle of the money fetish" prior to the theory of the exchange process. In the appendix on the value-form in the first German edition, the development of the value-form *does* proceed up to the money-form. However, that appendix was added upon the recommendation of Kugelmann, and Marx did not rewrite the main text of the first edition (including the part where he presents the theory of the exchange process) to accommodate it. This means that when raising the issue of the "riddle of the money fetish" at the end of the analysis of the exchange process, Marx was unlikely to have had the appendix in mind.

But there remains the question of why the passage concerning "the riddle of the money fetish" is included, in the same form, in the theory of the exchange process in the second edition as well. My

---

[1] In the first German edition of *Capital*, Marx did not clearly distinguish between those two theories by placing each in a separate section, but we can ascertain the point up to which he is analyzing the value-form.

view regarding this question is as follows. As Marx notes in his afterword to the second edition of *Capital*, for that new edition "Chapter 1, Section 3 (on the value-form), has been completely revised" and the last section of the first chapter, 'The Fetish-Character of the Commodity and its Secret,' has been altered considerably" (Marx, 1976a, p. 94). In contrast, Chapter 2 on the exchange process is the same as the first edition, apart from the revision of a few expressions. So it could be said that the passage in question remains as the outcome of that situation.

# 3.

Difference between the First and
the Second Edition of *Capital*

OTANI: There is a significant difference in the way the theory of the value-form is developed in the first German edition of *Capital* as compared to the second edition. In particular, the development of the value-form in the first edition ends with the independent form IV, rather than the money-form. At the same time, in the first edition, Marx already includes the sentence: "The difficulty lies, not in comprehending that money is a commodity, but in discovering how, why, and through what a commodity is money." This sentence appears in the part on the exchange process that corresponds to Chapter 2 in the second edition. Thus, the expression "*how* ... a commodity is *money*" (at least in the case of the first edition) would not seem to be referring to the theory of the value-form, as that theory does not develop up to the money-form. Moreover, the theory of the fetish-character in the first edition, influenced by the way the theory of the value-form unfolds, does not refer *directly* to money, which would seem to suggest that the expression "*why* ... a commodity is *money*" is likewise not indicating the theory of the fetish-character. – I would be interested to hear your view on these points.

KURUMA: Perhaps I can begin by considering the theory of the value-form. Certainly, it is true that the development of the value-form in the main body of the first German edition only goes up to the general value-form. However, as Marx notes, the advance [from form C to form D] consists only in that the form of direct general exchangeability, in other words the general equivalent form, has now by social custom irrevocably become entwined with the specific natural form of the commodity gold" (Marx, 1976a, p. 162), and the "only difficulty in the comprehension of the money-form is that of grasping the general equivalent form" (Marx, 1976a, p. 163; 1976b, p. 70). In other words, the examination of the general value-form already clarifies, *theoretically*, the question of how the money-form is established. Thus, in the theory of the exchange process, when Marx considers the necessity of money to mediate the contradiction confronting the commodity owner in the case of direct barter, he can say (in the first German edition as well as in the second edition) that "they [commodity owners] can only relate their commodities to each other as values, and therefore as commodities, if they place them in a polar relationship with a third commodity that serves as the general equivalent" and that "we concluded this from *our analysis of the commodity*" (Marx, 1976a, p. 180). Here there is no room for doubt that the "analysis of the commodity" basically refers to the theory of the value-form.

The fact that the theory of the value-form does not proceed up to the money-form in the first German edition should indeed trouble Naomichi Hayashi, because he said that theory deals with the "how question," in terms of how one commodity (*gold*) becomes money. Thus, according to his view, it would have to be said that in the first edition *that* "how question" was not yet elucidated within the theory of the value-form.

Next we can consider the theory of the fetish-character. As I just noted, there is no essential difference between the general value-form and the money-form, from the perspective of the development whereby the value of a commodity progressively comes to acquire a more complete form of expression. But the "fetish-character" peculiar to commodity production manifests itself in the value-form, particularly the equivalent form, so from this perspective the fetish-character undergoes a marked development when the general value-form turns into the money-form and the general equivalent form adheres to gold. In the main body of the first German edition, however, the development of form in the theory of the value-form does not reach the money-form, so it is not possible to present the fetish-character of money there. This issue can only first be presented when money appears in the theory of the exchange process. Thus, at the end of the theory of the exchange process, Marx writes the following about the fetish-character of money:

We have already seen, from the simplest expression of exchangeable value, *x* commodity A = *y* commodity B, that the thing *in which* the magnitude of the value of another thing is represented seems to have the equivalent form independently of this relation, as a social *natural property*. We followed the process by which this false semblance solidified itself. This semblance was completed when the general equivalent form adhered to the natural form of a particular commodity, or crystallized into the money-form. Although a particular commodity only becomes money because all other commodities express their values in it, it seems, on the contrary, that all other commodities universally express their values in a particular commodity because it is *money*. The movement through which the process has been mediated vanishes in its own result, leaving no trace behind. Without any initiative on their part, the commodities find their own value-figure ready to hand, in the form of body of commodity existing outside and alongside them. This physical object, gold or silver in its crude state, becomes, immediately on the emergence from the bowels of the earth, the direct incarnation of all human labor. Hence the magic of money. The merely atomistic behavior of men in their *social* process of production, and hence the fact that their own relations of production take on an *objectified* figure which is beyond their control and independent of their conscious individual striving, manifest themselves at first in the fact that the products of labor *generally* take the *form of commodities*. The *riddle of the money fetish* is therefore merely the *riddle of the commodity fetish itself* that has become visible and blinding to the eyes. (Marx, 1976a, p. 187 – Marx's emphasis)

Incidentally, this passage also appears in the second edition of *Capital*, in the same form except for the deletion of the word "exchangeable in the first sentence" and the word "itself" after "commodity fetish" in the final sentence. Because the development of the value-form in the second edition leads up to the money-form, it would seem that this part should be moved to an earlier place, but this trace of the first edition remains.[1]

At the beginning of the passage I just quoted, Marx says: "We have already seen ... "; which suggests that this part is connected to what was presented earlier. If we examine what he is referring to, we

---

[1] It could be related to this circumstance that in the French edition of *Capital* the final two sentences have been deleted (starting from "The merely atomistic behavior ...").

find the following passage at the end of the analysis of the general value-form in the first German edition:

> As the *immediate social materialization of labor*, the linen, the general equivalent, is the *materialization of immediately social labor*, while the other commodity bodies, which represent their values in linen are the materializations of *not immediately social* labors.
>
> Indeed all use-values are commodities only because they are *products of mutually independent private labors*, private labors, which however materially depend on one another as special, even though autonomized, branches of the naturally-grown system of *division of labor*. They are thus socially connected exactly by their *diversity*, their *particular usefulness*. It is exactly because of this that they produce qualitatively different use-values. Did they not do this, these use-values would not become commodities for each other. On the other hand, this different useful quality does not yet turn these products into commodities. If a peasant family produces coat, linen, and wheat for their own consumption, then these objects confront the family as different products of their family labor, but they do not confront each other as commodities. If the labor were *immediately social*, i.e., joint labor, then the products would obtain the immediately social character of a joint product for their producers, but not the character of commodities for each other. Yet we do not have to go far in order to find what is the *social form* of the *private labors* that are contained in the commodities and independent of one another. This resulted already from the analysis of the commodity. Their social form is their relationship with each other as *equal labor*, i.e., since the *equality* of altogether *different* labors can only consist in an *abstraction from their inequality*, their relationship with each other is as *human labor in general*: *expenditures of human labor-power*, something which all human labors, whatever their content and their mode of operation, indeed *are*. In every social form of labor, the labors of the different individuals stand also in a relation to each other as human labor, but here, this *relationship itself* counts as the *specifically social form* of the labors. It is true that none of these private labors in its natural form possesses this specific social form of abstract human labor, just as little as the commodity in its natural form possesses the social form of mere congelation of labor, or of value. By the fact that the natural form of one commodity, here of the linen, becomes the general equivalent form (because all other commodities refer to the latter as the form of appearance of their own value), the linen weaving labor also becomes the general form of realization of abstract human labor, or it becomes labor in immediately social form. The measuring stick for "being so-

cial" must be borrowed from the nature of the relations peculiar to each mode of production, not from imaginations alien to it. Just as it was shown a minute ago that the commodity, by nature, excludes the direct form of general exchangeability, that therefore the general equivalent form can only develop *antagonistically*, the same is true for the private labors contained in the commodities. Since they are *not immediately social* labors, it follows first that the *social form* is a form different from the natural forms of the actual useful labors, a form that is alien to them and abstract, and secondly, all kinds of private labor obtain their *social* character only *antagonistically*, by all of them being *equated* to an exclusive kind of private labor, here the linen weaving. By this, the latter becomes the immediate and general form of appearance of abstract human labor, and thus labor in immediately social form. It represents itself therefore also immediately in a socially valid and generally exchangeable product.

The semblance, as if the equivalent form of a commodity springs from its own material nature, instead of being the mere reflection of the relations of the other commodities, solidifies itself with the development of the *single* to the *general* equivalent, because the oppositional moments of the value-form no longer develop *evenly* for the commodities placed in relation with each other, because the general equivalent form distinguishes one commodity as something quite apart from all other commodities, and finally because this form of that commodity is indeed no longer the product of the relationship of any one *individual* other commodity. (Marx, 1976b, pp. 31–32 – Marx's emphasis)

As a further point of reference, we can also look at the appendix on the value-form that Marx inserted in the first German edition of *Capital*, which deals with the question of the fetish-character. The following passage from the appendix comes under the heading, "Fourth peculiarity of the equivalent form: the fetishism of the commodity form is more striking in the equivalent form than in the relative form":

The fact that products of labor (such useful things as coat, linen, wheat, iron, etc.) are *values, definite magnitudes of value* and, in general *commodities*, are properties which naturally pertain to them only *in our practical interrelations*, not by nature like, for example, the property of being heavy, retentive of heat, or nourishing. But *within our practical interrelations*, these things relate to one another *as commodities*. They *are values*; they *are measurable as magnitudes of value*, and their common *property of being values* places them into a *value-relation* with one another. Now, the equation that *20 yards of linen = 1 coat*, for example, or *20 yards of linen are worth 1 coat*, expresses the fact that, (1) the *different sorts* of labor necessary for the production of these things *count equally as human labor*; (2) the *quantity* of labor expended in their production is *measured* in accordance with definite social laws; and (3) tailors and weavers enter into a definite *social relation of production*. It is a *definite social relation of the producers*, in which they *set* their different sorts of useful labor *equal, as human labor*. It is not to a lesser extent *a definite social relation of the producers*, in which they *measure* the magnitude of their labors *by the duration of expenditure of human labor-power*. But *within our practical interrelations, these social characters* of their own labors *appear* to the producers as social *properties pertaining to them by nature*, as *objective* determinations *of the labor-products themselves*; the equality of the human labors appears as the *value-property* of the labor-products; the *measure* of the labor by the socially necessary labor-time appears as the *value-magnitude* of the labor products; and finally, the social relation of the producers through their labors appears as a *value-relation* or *social relation of these things*, the labor products. Precisely because of this, the labor-products *appear* to them as *commodities*, sensibly supersensible or *social things*. Likewise, the light-impression of a thing upon the optic nerve does not manifest itself as the subjective excitation of the optic nerve itself, but in the *objective form* of a thing outside of the eye. But in the act of seeing, what happens in realty is that light is thrown from a thing (the external object) onto another thing (the eye). It is a physical relationship between physical things. In distinction from this, the *commodity-form* and the *value-relation* of the labor-products have absolutely nothing to do with their physical nature and the material relationship which is derived from it. It is only the determined *social relation of people* itself which in this case assumes for them the phantasmagoric form of a *relation of things*. Thus in order to find an analogy we must flee into the nebulous region of the *religious world*. Here it is that *the products of the human head appear* as *independent figures* endowed with their own life and standing in relationship to one another and to men. That is the way it is in the *commodity world* with the *products of the human hand*. That is what I call the *fetishism* which clings to labor-products as soon as they are produced as *commodities*, and which is thus inseparable from *commodity production*.

Now this fetish-character, to be sure, reveals itself much more strikingly *in the equivalent form* than in the *relative value-form*. The relative value-form of a commodity is *mediated*; namely, *by its rela-*

*tion to another commodity*. Through this value-form, the value of the commodity is *expressed* as something *completely distinct* from its own sensible existence. Within this fact it is comprised at the same time that *existence as value* can only be a relation *which is alien* to the thing itself and hence its *value-relation* to another thing can only be the *form of appearance* of a *social relation* concealed behind it. It is the other way around with the *equivalent form*. It consists precisely in the fact that the *bodily or natural form* of a commodity *counts immediately as the social form*, as the *value-form* for another commodity. Therefore, *within our practical interrelations, to possess the equivalent form appears as the social natural property* of a thing, as a property that thing *inherently* has, so that hence it appears to be *immediately exchangeable* with other things just as it exists for the senses. Because, however, *within the value-expression of commodity A*, the equivalent form inheres in *commodity B* by nature, it seems also to belong to the latter by nature, even *outside of this relation*. Hence, for example, the riddling character of *gold*, which appears to possess, along with its other natural properties (its dazzling color, its weight, its non-oxydizability in air, etc.), also *the equivalent form by nature*, that is, the social quality of being *directly exchangeable* with all other commodities. (Marx, 1976b, p. 60 – Marx's emphasis)

As is clear from the passage just quoted, the fetish-character manifests itself in the value-form of the commodity (particularly in the equivalent form), and reaches completion in the money-form, where the general equivalent form is attached to one particular commodity. This fact is not merely recognized as such in the theory of the value-form in the first German edition, but traced back further to also clarify the "why question" of the fetish-character (i.e., why products of labor take the commodity-form under commodity production, and why the social character of human labor manifests itself in the form of a commodity and ultimately in the form of gold).

In the first German edition, Chapter 1 is not divided into four sections as in the second edition, but if we carefully consider the content we can discern which part is dealing with the theory of the fetish-character. The passage from the main body of the first edition, quoted a moment ago, comes near the end of the examination of the value-form. And I think it can be seen as a sort of bridge linking that theory to the theory of the fetish-character.

In the second edition, however, this examination of the "why question" pertaining to the fetish-character, which is confirmed in the case of the value-form (above all in the case of the equivalent form), can no longer be found in the theory of the value-form. In Section 4 of Chapter 1, the description we just looked at from the theory of the value-form in the first edition can no longer be found, perhaps as the result of Marx dividing the first chapter into four sections. In its place, however, the following passage is inserted:

> Man's reflection about the forms of social life, and therefore also his scientific analysis of these forms, takes a course directly opposite to the actual development of these forms. He begins "after the feast" with the completed results of the development process. The forms that stamp labor-products as commodities, which is therefore presupposed for commodity-circulation, have already acquired the fixity of natural forms of social life, before man seeks to give an account, not of the historical character of these forms – for in his eyes they have already become immutable – but of their content. It was only the analysis of the prices of commodities which led to the determination of the magnitude of value, and only the common expression of commodities in money which led to the fixation of their character as values. It is however precisely this finished form of the commodity world – the money-form – which conceals objectively the social character of private labor and therefore the social relations between the private laborers, instead of revealing these relations plainly. If I say that coats, boots, etc. relate themselves to linen as the general incarnation of abstract human labor, it is plain how bizarre an expression this is. However, when the producers of coats, boots, etc. relate their commodities to linen (or to gold and silver, which does not change the matter in the least) as the general equivalent, the relation of their own private labor to the social aggregate labor appears in exactly this crazy form. (Marx, 1976a, pp. 168–169)

This is followed a bit later with a footnote in which Marx writes:

> It is one of the chief failings of Classical political economy that it has never succeeded in finding, from the analysis of commodities and more specifically of commodity value, the form of value, i.e., that which turns value into exchange-value. Even its best representatives, Adam Smith and David Ricardo, treat the form of value as something quite indifferent or extraneous to the nature of the commodity itself. The reason for this is not solely that their attention is entirely absorbed by the analysis of the *magnitude of value*. It lies deeper. The

*value-form of the product of labor* is the most abstract, but also the most general *form* of the *bourgeois* mode of production; by that fact it stamps the bourgeois mode of production as a *particular* species of *social* production, and therewith as one of a *historical* and *transitory* character. If one considers it to be the eternal form of social production, one necessarily overlooks the specificity of the value-*form* as well – and consequently that of the *commodity*-form, together with its further developments, the *money*-form, the *capital*-form, etc. That is why certain economists who are entirely agreed that labor-time is the measure of the magnitude of value, have the strangest and most contradictory notions concerning *money*, i.e., the finished figure of the general equivalent. This emerges sharply when they deal with banking, where the commonplace definitions of money will no longer do. Hence there has arisen in opposition to the Classical economists a *restored Mercantilist System* (Ganilh etc.), which sees in value only the *social form*, or rather the insubstantial semblance of that form. (Marx, 1976a, p. 174 – Marx's emphasis as in first edition)

In the first German edition Marx places that footnote at the end of the following paragraph, which appears near the end of the part where he deals with the theory of the value-form:

As one sees, the analysis of the commodity yields all *essential* determinations of the *form of value*. It yields the form of value itself in its antagonistic moments, the *general relative form of value*, the *general equivalent form*, finally the never-ending *series of simple relative value expressions*, which first constitute a transitional phase in the development of the form of value, and eventually turns into the *specific relative form of value of the general equivalent*. However, the analysis of the commodity yielded these forms as *forms of the commodity* in general, which can therefore be taken on by every commodity – although in a polar manner, so that when commodity A finds itself in *one* form determination, then commodities B, C, etc. assume the *other* in relation to it. It was however of decisive importance to discover the inner necessary connection between *form* of value, *substance* of value, and *magnitude* of value, i.e., expressed ideally, to prove that the *form* of value springs from the *concept* of value. (Marx, 1976b, pp. 33–34 – Marx's emphasis)

In the second German edition of *Capital*, Marx moves that same footnote to the section on the theory of the fetish-character, attaching it to the second sentence in the following paragraph:

Political Economy has indeed, however incompletely, analyzed value and its magnitude, and has uncovered the content concealed within these forms. But it has never once asked why this content takes that form, that is to say, why labor is expressed in value, and why the measurement of labor by its duration is expressed in the magnitude of the value of the product. These formulas, which have it written on their foreheads that they belong to a social formation in which the production process has the mastery over man, and man does not yet master the production process, are considered by the political economists' bourgeois consciousness to be self-evident and nature-imposed necessities, just as necessary as productive labor itself. Hence the pre-bourgeois forms of the social organization of production are treated by political economy in much the same way as pre-Christian religions were treated by the Fathers of the Church. (Marx, 1976a, pp. 173–175)

It is clear from the passages I have quoted that there is a significant difference between the first and the second German edition of *Capital* in terms of the relation between the theory of the value-form and the theory of the fetish-character. Unlike the first edition, where Marx moves from a recognition of the fetish-character that is concretely manifested in the value-form to a more general consideration of the fetish-character of the commodity, the second edition deals with the question of the fetish-character of the value-form (and therefore the money-form as well) as part of a general consideration of the fetish-character of the commodity. I have my own view regarding why the second edition was revised in this way, but I will not delve into it here. At any rate, we can see that in the second edition – and of course in the first edition – the question of "why" pertaining to the value-form (and therefore to money as well) is dealt with in the theory of the fetish-character. I think that this should be clear, without any room for doubt, if we read *Capital* in a straightforward way, particularly those passages that I have quoted. This is my reason for stating, in *Theory of the Value-Form & Theory of the Exchange Process*, that the "why" of money is elucidated in the theory of the fetish-character.

# 4.

## The Significance of the "Why Question"
### (The Particularity of Commodity
### Production and the Essence of Value)

**O**TANI: Many readers may not have a copy of your book *Keizaigaku shi* (History of Political Economy),[1] but in the third chapter of that book – dealing with the Classical school of political economy – you include a long footnote with a comprehensive, easy-to-understand explanation regarding the "why question" as well the essence of value and the relation of value to its phenomenal forms. Because that explanation appears in a footnote it tends to be overlooked. So here I would like to quote from it to conclude our consideration of problems pertaining to the overall genesis of money. I think this will contribute to a better understanding of the fetish-character that we have been examining in relation to the difference between the first edition and the second edition of *Capital*. Before looking at that footnote, though, I want to introduce the following passage that it is attached to:

> Commodity production is social production carried out under a system of private ownership by private producers who are independent of each other. The labor of the producers, which is private labor, directly speaking, only first takes on an independent social form in the relation of product exchange. In exchange, the products of the producers' labor are mutually equated as value, regardless of their manifold shapes as use-values. The various real differences between types of labor as use-value-producing labor are abstracted from when considered as

---

[1] [My translation of Chapter 3 of Kuruma's *History of Political Economy*, which includes the passage quoted here quoted by Dr. Otani, was published in the 2007 issue of *Research in Political Economy* as an independent article entitled, "A Critique of Classical Political Economy." – EMS]

value-forming labor. In the case of value-forming labor, we are only dealing with indiscriminate human labor, or general human labor in abstraction from concrete differences, i.e., a certain quantity of the simple expenditure of human labor-power And it is in the form of "value" as the crystallization of this general human labor – i.e., in the material form of the value of a product – that a commodity producer's labor first acquires significance as a certain quantity of the total labor-time expended by society to satisfy its needs. (Kuruma, 1954, p. 81)

You attach the following footnote to the end of that passage:

My explanation of the particularity of commodity production and the essence of value in the main body of this book is quite simple, which may conversely make it difficult for many readers to understand. So I would like to offer an additional explanation here. I have placed the explanation in a footnote because it pertains to the principles of political economy, not its history; but I want to underscore the fundamental importance of this issue.

Commodity production, needless to say, is also a type of social production, wherein commodity producers do not produce the objects they themselves need through their own labor. If that *were* the case, it would be possible for them to remain unrelated to each other. But in fact a social division of labor is carried out. Commodity producers, instead of producing the objects they need through their own labor, engage in the production of a particular item that then is provided for the use of other commodity producers, and in return have their own needs met by the labor of those other commodity producers.

In order for this to take place, the various labors of the commodity producers that are respectively engaged in the specialized production of various things must, first of all, in their totality compose an organic system of the social division of labor, thereby integrally responding to the needs of society as a whole. In other words, the total labor-time of society must be distributed to the various spheres of production in such a way as to respond to the various needs of the entire society. Unless this is achieved, in some manner or form, it is not possible for the various things that society requires to be produced in line with necessity. This would not simply mean that it is carried out in an imperfect (rather than ideal) manner, but that it could not be carried out at all.

Secondly, in order for a system of the social division of labor to be feasible, wherein a person produces a particular use-value for other members of society (rather than producing by himself all of the things he requires), and then has his own needs met by the products of the labor of the other members of society, it is necessary that the mode of distribution be decided upon in some manner or form so that the producers are able to receive a certain portion of the total product of society. Unless this is determined, social production is not feasible.

These two points are the general conditions for social production, and without them being realized in some form or another social production cannot be carried out. Commodity production is no exception; but the manner in which these conditions are met under commodity production is fundamentally different from other cases.

In other forms of social production, even if there are differences in the manner of determining how to allocate the total labor-time of society to the various production spheres and distribute the total product of society to the various members of society – that is, whether based on the will of a dictatorial individual (or group of individuals) or rather according to democratic consensus; and whether done in a basically arbitrary manner or instead based on tradition or carried out on the basis of carefully considered plans – this is always carried out according to some decision based on human will, in a way that can be immediately grasped.

Things are different in the case of commodity production, where there is no person who makes such decisions. A commodity producer does not engage in the production of a particular thing according to someone else's direction, but rather completely in line with his own free will and decisions, according to his own responsibility and calculations. The labor-power of the producers is their own private capability as autonomous personalities who constitute the subject of private property, and therefore the labor that is the expenditure of their labor-power is carried out as a private matter. Since the labor-power itself is not social, labor also does not directly have a social character: it remains private labor. Therefore, the products produced do not belong to society, but rather come into the producer's individual possession, so that they cannot be freely disposed of by society. In order for society to decide on the distribution of products, it would have to possess them, just as one cannot freely dispose of something without possessing it.

If there is no one to determine the method of organizing the division of labor and of carrying out distribution, how exactly is commodity production feasible as a system of social production?

Production relations between commodity producers are not formed as direct relations between human beings, but rather are established via the detour of the exchange-relation of their products *qua* commodities.

We need to consider how the production relations between commodity producers are established through the exchange-relation of their products *qua* commodities, and how the exchange-relation between the commodity producers' products *qua* commodities mediates the relations of production between them.

We know from the discussion thus far that the most fundamental condition for social production to be carried out is the social integration, in one way or another, of the labor of individuals so that they are connected with one another as parts of society's total labor. The labor of commodity producers, however, is carried out as private labor, not socially integrated labor. Yet labor must come to have the substance of being one part of the total labor of society, as something that constitutes the overall system of the social division of labor. This represents a fundamental contradiction unique to commodity production. The problem comes down to identifying how this contradiction is mediated via the exchange-relation of labor-products or locating the moment within the exchange of commodity producers' labor-products through which their private labor acquires existence as social labor.

Commodities come in many varieties and are diverse as use-values, which is precisely why they can be exchanged for each other. This exchange presupposes that the use-values of commodities are different; but on the basis of this alone exchange will not be carried out. It is also premised that the thing possessed by person A must be superfluous for him, while being useful to person B; and vice-versa for person B. In this way, the two people are first able to exchange their products. Even though this is unquestionably a precondition for any sort of exchange to occur, on its basis alone the exchange of products as commodities will not necessarily immediately take place. For instance, even if a child with an extra spinning top and another child with extra playing cards exchange these items, we are not dealing with commodity exchange. The children's exchange does not mediate the establishment of a system of social production between them.

What characterizes the exchange of commodities, to repeat, is not merely the mutual difference between things possessed by people as use-values, or the relation between those things and the wants of human beings, but rather a relation whereby commodities are equal as value despite being different as use-values; which is to say: their value-relation. Commodities as use-values come in an infinite variety, but as value they are indistinguishable and equal. This is why commodities all have uniformly the form of being worth such-and-such yen in gold, i.e., a price. And the value indicated in a price is precisely the moment whereby the labor of the commodity producers first comes to obtain unity.

The labor of commodity producers does not directly have social unity, nor does it have a social character. This is the inevitable outcome of labor-power itself not being social. As long as labor-power is private, rather than social, labor as its exertion also remains private and cannot be social. In the case of commodity production, labor-power is not socialized to begin with, nor does it exist as society's total labor-power that is expended for various production purposes (e.g., as tailoring labor or weaving labor). If that were the case, labor in an active state – from the moment it is carried out – would have a social character in its natural form, i.e., directly as labor itself or as specific concrete labor. In the case of commodity producers, however, things are different. The producers' labor is instead objectified in products to form their value. As value, all labor is indiscriminate and equal, differing only quantitatively (not qualitatively). It is in this form – i.e., in the form of the character of the product of labor (rather than the character of the labor itself) and in the form of indiscriminate and qualitatively equal value (rather than use-values for some particular purpose) – that the different types of labor of commodity producers first gain unity, becoming social labor. Labor thus comes to have existence as one part of the total labor-time society expends to satisfy its aggregate wants; as one part of the total labor-power expended by society.

The social relations between producers in the case of commodity production are thus established in a manner completely contrary to that of a planned economy, with everything appearing upside-down. Instead of there first being relations between human beings, followed by the carrying out of social production, there first is the independently carried out exchange of products of private labor, which are equated as value in this exchange, so that the labor of commodity producers becomes identical in terms of producing value and is reduced to indiscriminate abstract human labor. This is how the labor of commodity producers obtains unity in a specific form, becoming one part of the total labor-power expended by society.

Value, in other words, is the distinctive form assumed by the private labor of commodity producers in order to become social labor, forming a moment that mediates the fundamental contradiction of commodity production noted above. Commodity production develops along with this moment (= value), developing at precisely the same pace as it does; while on the other hand the development of value means that products have become commodities so as to exist not merely as use-values but at the same time as value. This means that the contradiction particular to commodity production is sublimated in the form of the commodity *qua* direct unity of use-value and value, so that the contradiction is manifested in the more concrete form of being a contradiction that pertains to the commodity.

The question then becomes how the commodity unfolds and resolves this contradiction. To clarify this we need, above all, to elucidate the necessity for the commodity of a particular form in order for it to express its own value. If we say that a commodity is both a use-value and value, this is something that can first be perceived through theoretical consideration. And the intrinsic value of a commodity – the fact that there are ten hours of social labor included within it, for example – cannot be expressed as is. This is natural from the perspective of the formation of value just explained. It is precisely because the labor of commodity producers does not have existence as a certain quantity of social labor that this labor only first obtains unity *qua* the abstract general labor that produces the value held in common. This is the manner whereby the labor of the producers becomes social labor. It occurs through the exchange of the products of the producers' labor and the relation through which their products are mutually equated within exchange. This means that social labor-time does not exist from the outset; not only does it not exist within labor in an active state, it does not directly exist in an objectified state. If it did exist as such, it could be indicated, as is, as labor-time. However, if that were the case, labor would not be objectified to become value and products would not become commodities. The value of a commodity is not indicated as labor-time because the labor of the commodity producer is not directly social labor, and therefore the labor included in the product is not directly social labor, which means that the product of that labor cannot be grasped as the product of directly social labor.

Precisely how, then, is the value of a commodity indicated? Given that a commodity cannot indicate its value on its own, it is indicated instead by another commodity with which it is in a relation of exchange. Yet in the case of that other commodity as well, its natural form is its use-value (not value); and it does not, on its own, have a form of value in addition to its natural form. The natural form of that other commodity must therefore become the form of value. This is indeed what happens, as is clear from the fact that the value of every sort of commodity today is indicated in the form of a certain quantity of gold. There is still the question, however, of how it is possible (whether in the case of gold or something else) for the natural body of a commodity, its material form, to express the value of another commodity and thus become the form of value. This is the crux of the problem regarding the value-form, which Marx elucidates in Section 3 of Chapter 1 (under the heading: "A. Simple, Isolated, or Accidental

Form of Value"), where he traces the development of the form itself, and by so doing thoroughly solves the riddle of money. But here we will have to omit a further explanation of what Marx elucidates in that part of *Capital*, as well as his explanation of the development of the contradiction of the commodity within the real process of exchange, the necessity of the genesis of money, and the manner in which money mediates the contradiction of the exchange process. (Kuruma, 1954, pp. 82–88)

Following that long footnote, you refer to the defect of the Classical school of political economy in the following way:

Bourgeois economists, however, starting with Smith, failed to grasp the character of value as the specific social form of labor particular to commodity production. Economists were aware that the value of a commodity is in fact labor, but they did not understand why labor, instead of appearing as such, manifests itself in the form of the value of the product; in the peculiar form of being an attribute of a thing, which is an upside-down form that requires scholars to uncover and demonstrate the substance of value. Not only did they fail to understand this pivotal point, it was not even posed as a problem to begin with. This was the inevitable outcome of viewing commodity production as the natural form of social production, equating it with social production itself. As Marx notes: "Political economy has indeed, however incompletely, analyzed value and its magnitude, and has uncovered the content concealed within these forms. But it has never once asked why this content takes that form, that is to say, why labor is expressed in value, and why the measurement of labor by its duration is expressed in the magnitude of the value of the product. These formulas, which have it written on their foreheads that they belong to a social formation in which the production process has mastery over man, and man does not yet master the production process, are considered by the political economists' bourgeois consciousness to be self-evident and nature-imposed necessities, just as productive labor itself." (Marx, 1976a, pp. 173–175) (Kuruma, 1954, pp. 88–89)

# 5

## In What Sense is the Simple Value-Form "Accidental"?

O TANI: Now I want to turn to the "how question" – in other words, the theory of the value-form. My first question concerns the initial value-form, which Marx calls the "the simple, isolated or accidental form of value." The meaning of the adjectives "simple" and "isolated" can be easily grasped from his description, whereas in the case of "accidental" there does not seem to be a single, uniform answer. I should note that the word "accidental" (*zufällig*) does not appear in the first German edition of *Capital* (or its appendix on the value-form); nor does it appear in the second German edition.[1] My question concerns the sense in which that form is "accidental." Should that term be understood in relation to the process of the historical development of the value-form?

**KURUMA:** In the very first paragraph of *Capital*, Marx writes:

> The wealth of those societies, in which the capitalist mode of production reigns, presents itself as "an immense accumulation of commodities." The single commodity appears as the elementary form of this wealth. The analysis of the commodity will therefore be the starting

---

[1] The heading to indicate this initial value-form was gradually modified as follows:

1) "I. First or simple form of relative value" (first edition, 1867)

2) "I. Simple value-form" (appendix of the first edition, 1867)

3) "A. Simple or isolated value-form" (second edition, 1872)

4) "A. Simple or accidental value-form" (French edition, 1872–1875)

5) "A. Simple, isolated or accidental value-form" (third edition, 1883; fourth edition, 1890)

6) "A. Elementary or accidental form of value" (English edition, 1887)

From this, we can see that the adjective "accidental" was first used by Marx in the French edition and then employed by Engels for subsequent editions.

point of our investigation. (Marx, 1976a, p. 125)

If we look at this passage, the commodity that is the object of analysis is the commodity that appears as the elementary form of the wealth of a society in which the capitalist mode of production prevails. I think it is thus clear that we are not dealing with the commodity as in the case of commodity production that has yet to be generalized, where products only *accidentally* become commodities. So the question remains: Why is the simple value-form said to be the "accidental" form of value? In order to answer that question, we can begin by considering the following passage from *Capital*:

> The only difficulty in the comprehension of the money-form is that of grasping the general equivalent form or, more broadly, the general form of value, form C. Form C can be reduced by working backwards to form B, the expanded form of value, and *its constitutive element is form A: 20 yards of linen = 1 coat or x commodity A = y commodity B.* The simple commodity form is therefore the germ of the money-form. (Marx, 1976a, p. 163)

Marx is saying that form A, the simple value-form, is the constitutive element of the expanded form of value known as form B. In the case of form B, if we borrow his example, the linen is in the relative value-form, with a countless number of other commodities in the equivalent form. In this case, the coat exists as one of the countless number of commodities that make up the equivalent form. In the simple value-form, only the coat is in the equivalent form, which just means that from out of the countless number of commodity types in the equivalent form for the expanded value-form, the coat *happens to be* taken out. Tea could have been taken out instead, or coffee, wheat, or anything else, but Marx happens to choose a coat and makes it the equivalent form. It is in this sense that Marx refers to the simple form of value as the "accidental form of value."

We might also consider the fact that the value-form develops to become the money-form (*x* commodity A = *y* money commodity), thus returning to the same shape as the simple value-form, which is the form where there is only one commodity on either side of the equation. Marx writes:

The expression of the value of a commodity in gold – *x* commodity A = *y* money commodity – is its money-form or its price. A single equation, such as 1 ton of iron = 2 ounces of gold, now suffices to express the value of the iron in a socially valid manner. There is no longer any need for this equation to line up together with all other equations that express the value of the other commodities, because the equivalent commodity, gold, already possesses the character of money. *The commodities' general relative value-form has thus the same shape as their original relative value-form: the simple or individual relative value.* (Marx, 1976a, p. 189)

In other words, arriving at the money-form means that the "original shape" of "simple or individual relative value" is again taken. But in the case of the money-form, it is the money-commodity (gold) that is fixed as the equivalent form – rather than a single commodity being *randomly* (or accidentally) selected out from a variety of commodities as in the case of the simple form of value. It seems to me that Marx inserted the adjectives "simple" and "isolated" as well as "accidental" in order to draw attention to this difference.

Regarding your question about whether or not the "accidental" form of value bears a relation to the process of the historical development of the value-form, we can look to the following passage from *Capital*:

The first form, A, brought about equations like this: 1 coat = 20 yards of linen, 10 lb. of tea = 1/2 of iron, etc. The value of the coat is expressed as something which is like linen, that of the tea as something which is like iron, etc. These expressions of the value of coat and tea are therefore as different as linen is from iron. *This form, it is plain, appears in practice only in the early stages, when the products of labor are converted into commodities by accidental occasional exchanges.* (Marx, 1976a, p. 158)

Marx writes that the "form … appears in practice only in the early stages, when the products of labor are converted into commodities by accidental occasional changes." However, the form that Marx is referring to is the form of the equation in which there is just one particular type of commodity on each side of the equation; so it would be a terrible misunderstanding to think that he is referring instead to the simple form of value *qua* fundamental form of value-expression.

The value-form of the commodity is premised on the fact that the product has already become a commodity and that the labor expended on the commodity's production constitutes its value as one part of the total labor expended by society, with the commodity's value-form being the form in which that value is expressed in distinction from the commodity's use-value. What is at issue in the passage just quoted, however, is the "early stages, when the products of labor are converted into commodities by accidental occasional changes," so that the product prior to exchange has yet to become a commodity. Therefore, the value-form of the commodity is not yet under consideration. Of course I do think that it is worthwhile – upon the basis of grasping that distinction – to consider the development of form within the theory of the value-form and how that development corresponds to history.

# 6

# The "Detour" of Value-Expression

**O** **TANI:** One central question is whether the two moments of the mechanism of value-expression – in other words, (1) the linen equating the coat to itself and (2) the linen in this relation expressing its own value in the form of the coat – are in a logical sequential relationship or not. One view is that it is not a unilateral relationship where only one moment premises the other, but rather a relationship in which each of the two moments is the premise of the other. It is not the case that the moment of the linen making the coat the value-body is the unilateral premise of the moment where the linen expresses its own value through this value-body, because the latter is also the premise of the former. The coat becomes the value-body by being equated to the linen, and through this equating the linen expresses its own value using the coat, which is the material for value-expression. Still, there is the question of whether the coat is the value-body only insofar as the linen is expressing its own value, or if the coat alone is the value-body prior to the expression of the linen's value.

**KURUMA:** That sounds like a reasonable question. If I had anticipated that sort of question I probably would have explained myself more clearly in *Theory of the Value-Form & Theory of the Exchange Process*. Still, I do not think that my manner of explanation was necessarily incorrect. And here I can offer a few words of further explanation.

In *Capital* the analysis begins with the simple form of value. Marx notes the respective role played by the commodity on either side of the value-expression equation, which he refers to as the "relative form of value" and the "equivalent form." He confirms the points that are clear at a glance, which in the appendix on the value-form in the first German edition are divided into the following headings: (a) "The inseparability of both forms" (b) "The polarity of both forms" and (c) "Relative value and equivalent are both only forms of commodity value" (Marx, 1976b, pp. 50–51). At this stage, Marx has yet to fully analyze the simple value-form so he speaks of the relation (*Verhältnis*) between the relative form of value and the equivalent form in the following way:

> The relative form of value and the equivalent form are two moments which belong together, mutually condition each other, and cannot be separated; but, at the same time, they are mutually exclusive or oppo-site extremes. They are the two poles of the same expression of value. (Marx, 1976a, pp. 139–140)

One commodity expresses its value using another commodity, while the other commodity serves as the material for value-expression and thus functions as the equivalent. These two moments are "mutually exclusive"; or to use your term, they are "mutually presupposed." At this stage, certainly, we are dealing with a relation of reciprocal pre-supposition. For the linen to express its own value the coat must be made the equivalent, and at the same time for the coat to become the equivalent the linen must express its value in the coat. We are not dealing, therefore, with a relation that has a unilateral premise. However, we must already be careful to note that both moments per-tain to the value-expression of a *single* commodity: the linen. Thus, linen can be said to play an active role, whereas the coat is unable to transform itself into the equivalent. This point is important when we move on to analyze the relative form of value.

In his analysis of the relative value-form (at the beginning of the sub-section in *Capital* entitled: "The content of the relative form of value") – after having clearly indicated that the task is to discover "how the *simple expression of the value of a commodity* is embedded in the value-relation between two commodities" (Marx, 1976a, p. 140) – Marx raises and proceeds to analyze the qualitative aspect of the equation 20 yards of linen = 1 coat. Here we have already gone beyond the relation of mutual exclusion and opposition. The issue now concerns the fact that the *commodity expressing its own value* (= linen) *"relates itself with"* (Beziehung) *another commodity*. Marx notes that those two qualitatively equated commodities do not play the same role: only the *value of the linen* is expressed, not that of the coat. As for how this is this done, Marx's answer is that "in this relation, the coat counts as the form of existence of value, as a thing representing value – for only as such is it the same as the linen" (Marx, 1976a, p. 141). What I refer to as the "mechanism of *value-expression*" concerns precisely this answer provided to the question posed. In using the term "detour" I have attempted to express the key, qualitative content of the answer provided by Marx in a concise and easy to understand manner.

The linen, by itself, is quite unable to express its own value. It must make another commodity the value-body in order to express its own value. The linen equates the other commodity to itself, as value, thus making it the equivalent and positing it with validity as the value-thing. The *linen expressing its own value* – the "how" of which is now under consideration – is *first accomplished by means of* positing another commodity with the formal determination as value-body. I think this is an undeniable fact. In dealing with this issue, it is of no use at all to say that the linen must express its own value using the coat *in order for the coat to be the value-body*. Such a viewpoint, even if not mistaken in itself, poses the question in terms of how the *coat actively* becomes the equivalent. In fact, though, the coat passively comes to acquire this form; and we are not dealing in this case with the question of "how" regarding that. The question, rather, is the "how" of *value-expression.*

The way the linen relates itself with the coat is not by immediately equating *itself* to the *coat.* Such an equating could not occur unless the linen already figured as value for the other commodity. What happens, rather, is that a commodity that does not yet have a form as value equates *the other commodity* to *itself,* so as to relate itself with this other commodity that has thus become *a thing equal to itself.* In this way, for the first time, the linen is able to express its own value.

**OTANI:** Regarding the issue of whether the linen equates the *coat to itself* – or instead equates *itself to the coat* – in *Theory of the Value-Form & Theory of the Exchange Process* you say that Marx's expression "*sich den Rock gleichsetzen*" has been mistranslated in Japanese editions of *Capital.* In that phrase, "*den Rock*" is clearly in the accusative just as "*sich*" is clearly in the dative, so the translation should be: "equates the coat to itself." Yet in all of the Japanese translations of the first German edition of *Capital* we instead find: "equates itself to the coat." Apparently it was not a simple oversight on the part of the translators, given that in other passages there are similarly mistaken translations of "*sich einen Rock gleichsetzen*" and "*sich ihn als Wert gleichsetzen*." The translators seem to have thought that, at least in terms of *content*, the phrase should be translated so that the linen equates itself to the coat.

**KURUMA:** As for that particular passage, I believe that Kōzō Uno, in *Shihon-ron 50 nen* (50 Years with *Capital*), said that either translation is fine, in terms of both grammar and content.

**OTANI:** That is a very strange argument for anyone familiar with the German language to make, so I suppose Uno must have meant that either is fine in terms of *content*. There was, incidentally, a comment regarding this issue made by [Uno's follower] Setsuo Furihata in the discussion published as the 1967 book *Shihon-ron kenkū* (An Inquiry into *Capital*). Furihata said that this translation issue constitutes the basis for your position regarding the detour of value-expression. Then, after referring to what you have to say about the phrase "*sich den Rock gleichsetzen*," Furihata suggests that your position on the detour "incorporates a unique interpretation of that translation." In response to your view that the "linen cannot become the value-body by immediately equating itself to the coat, thereby declaring itself to be equal to the coat, which would be nothing but a 'self-complacent' or 'presumptuous' [*hitoriyogari*] act, so to speak," Furihata offers the following:

> Whether the linen seeks to "immediately equate itself to the coat" or seeks to "equate the coat to itself," in either case there is no difference in terms of the linen being "self-complacent." For the value-form, it seems its fundamental character should be understood as being established through the "self-complacent" act of the commodity in the relative value-form. Regardless of whether the linen "equates itself to the linen" or "equates the coat to itself," the establishment of this equivalent relation is a matter that does not involve the coat. Precisely because of this, the premise of this equivalent relation is that only the

coat is able to have the "attribute of direct exchangeability." In other words, the fact that within this relation it is the owner of the coat, not the owner of the linen, who is able to decide to exchange his commodity with another commodity, is merely the reverse side of the "self-complacent" act of the linen. (Uno et al., 1967, p. 133)

Furihata does not say that either translation is fine grammatically speaking but that both are fine in terms of content.

**KURUMA:** In that case, how does he think the passage should be translated? Is he saying that either translation would be fine?

**OTANI:** I wonder? The strange thing is that the same mistake is made by Jirō Okazaki in his relatively recent translation of the first German edition of *Capital* (Marx, 1976c, p. 45). So there is the question, again, of whether we are indeed dealing with a mere careless mistake.

**KURUMA:** People seem to have a fixed idea regarding that passage. I recall having written some comments in the margins of my copy of *Shihon-ron 50 nen*. Shall we look at them?

**OTANI:** Yes. Uno, in that book, makes the following comment:

> Kuruma says that the linen equates the coat to itself, rather than the linen saying that it is equal to the coat. For Kuruma, the detour is the linen saying that the coat is equal to itself. That may very well be the case. But I don't think there is great significance in saying that the expression of equating the coat to itself, rather than equating itself to the coat, is the detour. (Uno, 1970, p. 714)

Following this, another participant in the discussion says:

> In terms of the linguistic issue, can it really be said that the "*sich*" in "*sich den Rock gleichsetzen*" is definitely not in the accusative?

To which you respond in a margin note:

> How silly! The question is not whether "*sich*" can be in the accusative (which of course it can), but that "*den Rock*" is in the accusative, so

177

that "*sich*" can only be in the dative. If the coat were put in the dative, so that the phrase were "*sich dem Rock gleichsetzen*," then the current translation would be fine. In that case, because the coat is in the dative, the "*sich*" can be exclusively in the accusative. This is because it is not possible for both to be in the dative, or both to be in the accusative.

A different participant in the discussion then adds:

> In terms of that point, even those who specialize in German do not seem to know. I asked Professor Nakano Tadashi about this, and he seems to have investigated the question to a considerable extent when writing his book *Kachikeitai-ron* (Theory of the Value-Form). In the end, even he arrived at the conclusion that either translation is the same. (Uno, 1970, p. 715)

You write in response: "Astounding! What did you ask and how did you ask it? Egregious fool!" Meanwhile, in that discussion, Uno goes on to say:

> The notion of a distinction between a "self-complacent" act and "making a declaration" is a highlight of Kuruma's position. He says that it is not a self-complacent act to "equate to oneself" – but rather is a *declaration*. Kuruma says that to "equate oneself to the other" is to act in a self-complacent way. But I say, instead, that the price-expression of the commodity is originally a self-complacent declaration. It is not simply a self-complacent act. There are other sellers of the same commodity, and depending on circumstances the price is modified. There is, indeed, significance in this fact. (Uno, 1970, p. 715)

In response to Uno's idea that the price-expression of the commodity is a "self-complacent declaration," you write in the margin: "Is he thinking in terms of the level of the price (asking price)? The essential problem of the value-form is elsewhere. He is not even aware of the distinction!" Then, regarding Uno's statement as a whole, you write:

> This is not a question particular to the German language. For instance, there is a difference between person A saying "I equate myself to B" as compared to saying "I equate B to myself." If person A says to per-

son B: "You are my soul," then B can behave as the "soul" vis-à-vis A; whereas if A says to B: "I am your soul," B may very well say, "Get lost, you conceited jerk!" This is what is meant by a "self-complacent" act.

Later in the discussion, Uno says:

> The fundamental point is the want of the commodity owner, which is to say the meaning of value being expressed in the use-value of another commodity, but I think that Marx did not make this clear. I feel there is a merit in my own view concerning this matter. (Uno, 1970, p. 715)

Your comments in the margins deal with that view as well, but I would be interested to hear what you have to say about Furihata's claim that either "equate to itself" or "equate itself to" are acceptable because the linen is acting in a self-complacent manner in both cases.

**KURUMA:** This, in other words, is Furihata's idea that only the linen plays an active role, whereas the coat merely passively becomes the equivalent. That is said to be the "self-complacent" act of the linen and thus the fundamental character of the value-form, so that it is sufficient to understand this point (whereas it matters little whether the linen "equates itself to the coat" or "equates the coat to itself").

This view held by Furihata seems to stem from the idea that the *owner* of the linen desires the coat and for that reason *equates the linen and the coat*, saying that he is *willing to exchange* the linen for the coat. This is seen as the core of the equation: linen = coat. Thus, according to Uno's view as well, if one grasps that it is the *linen owner* who is doing the *equating*, it is inherently a "self-complacent" act because it is done at the owner's discretion – regardless of the owner of the coat. Here we have the fundamental content of Uno's argument, which is merely repeated by Furihata. I criticized that view in *Theory of the Value-Form & Theory of the Exchange Process*, particular in Part 2, where I wrote:

> If a child has some spare playing cards that he wants to trade for a spinning top and then asks if anyone would be willing to give him a

top in exchange for ten cards, because this is not a value-relation between commodities the top does not become the phenomenal form of
the cards' value. What characterizes a value-relation between commodities is the relation of equivalence between commodities as objectified human labor. (Kuruma, 1954, pp. 66)

*If we recognize that the relation between the linen and the coat is a
value-relation,* we abstract from the linen owner desiring the coat, to
focus on the relation of equivalence between commodities as objectified human labor. We need to make clear how the value of the linen
is expressed within this equivalence. By posing the question in this
manner, we can understand the decisive difference between "linen
equating itself to the coat" and "linen equating the coat to itself." We
need to be aware that in the equation, linen = coat, we are dealing
with a relation of equivalence; and that at the same time only the
linen's value is expressed, with only the coat becoming the equivalent. There is a difference in significance between the commodity on
the left of the equation and the commodity on the right. The difference does not concern the fact that the commodity on the right is an
object desired by the owner of the commodity on the left. It is a difference that remains even after we have set that point aside.

In the equation, it is of course the linen that is expressing its own
value. We are dealing with the commodity linen as the *subject*, and
an equating *to it* is carried out. In our example, a coat is equated *to*
the linen. The opposite equation, where the linen is equated to the
coat, would be: coat = linen. Next, there is the question of which
commodity is carrying out the equating: Is it the linen or the coat?
Although we know that the linen owner is the one equating the coat
to the linen, the subject in the *value-expression of the linen* is the
linen and so it is the *linen* (not the coat) that is doing the equating.
The act of equating refers precisely to the linen equating the coat to
itself. If we reverse the linen equating the coat to itself, so that we
have linen *equating itself to the coat,* it would ultimately be the same
as saying that the equation "coat = linen" is created by the linen (i.e.,
the commodity on the right), which would mean that a commodity on
its own accord is able to turn itself into the equivalent. That is certainly *not* possible, however. Even if a commodity were to designate
itself as the equivalent of another commodity, it would merely be a

"self-complacent" act with no validity as far as the other commodity is concerned. A commodity that is directly a use-value cannot count as the value-body for another commodity *at will*. However, if a commodity (e.g., linen) equates another commodity (e.g., a coat) to itself, it is able to posit that other commodity with the formal determination as the value-body. Linen is thus able to indicate its own value through the coat that has been posited with that determination. The linen turns the bodily form of the commodity posited with that formal determination into the form of its own value. As Marx says: "That which it cannot do immediately vis-à-vis itself, it can do immediately vis-à-vis another commodity, thus doing it vis-à-vis itself via a detour" (Marx, 1976b, p. 22). Therefore, we are certainly not dealing, in this case, with a "self-complacent" act on the part of the linen. The outcome is that the coat is posited with the attribute of direct exchangeability vis-à-vis the linen. It is in this sense that there is a decisive difference between saying that the "linen equates itself to the coat" and saying that "linen equates the coat to itself."

I think the reason that Furihata fails to grasp the distinction, as I mentioned a moment ago, is that he does not recognize that it is only by abstracting from the want of the commodity owner – and abstracting from the very existence of the commodity owner – that we can uncover how the simple value-expression of a commodity is encompassed within the value-relation of two commodities.

**OTANI:** We seem to have gone off on a bit of a tangent by discussing the translation issue regarding the linen equating the coat to itself. Shall we return to the topic of the detour of value-expression?

**KURUMA:** Perhaps it isn't such a tangent. I think this issue is important for an understanding of the "detour" we are discussing. At any rate, as I mentioned, there is no question that it is the want of the linen owner for the coat that establishes the equation: linen = coat. But when analyzing the value-form we must set aside the reason why the equation is established. The very existence of the equation means that there is a relation of equivalence, and this is of course equality *as value*. At issue is how the value of the linen is expressed within this equation. And to say that this occurs by the linen relating itself with the coat as the other commodity is merely the first step in answering this question.

It is often said that the relation of the linen to the coat is a *self-reflecting* relation; and there is no question that this is indeed the case, because the linen comes into a relation with itself by relating itself with some other thing. Marx says that "by equating the other commodity to itself as value, the linen relates to itself as value" and "by relating to itself as value, it differentiates itself at the same time from itself as a use-value" (Marx, 1976b, p. 19). So I have no objection to viewing this as a self-reflecting relation, nor would I disagree with those who say that the "detour" is such a self-reflecting relation where value is expressed through the mediation of the commodity relating itself with something else. What I wanted to emphasize in using the term *detour*, however, is the core content of this self-reflecting relation; in other words, the mediating way of value-expression or the pivot of the "content of the relative form of value" that Marx focused upon. This concerns the linen equating the coat *qua* value-thing to itself, thus positing the coat with the formal determination as value-body, which is a formal determination as the embodiment of abstract human labor. It is through this mediation that the linen expresses itself as a value-thing. As long as we are examining the mechanism of value-expression, the term "detour" can only be referring to a detour of this trajectory.

That certainly does not negate, however, that *the coat is posited with the formal determination as value-body* because the linen expresses its own value through it. When Marx moves on to look at the equivalent form, his analysis is premised on what was already elucidated with regard to the relative form of value; but he shifts the angle of analysis to view the matter from the perspective of the equivalent form. A commodity comes to be the equivalent, with the trait of direct exchangeability, because another commodity has equated that commodity to itself and uses it to express its own value. Marx clarifies that the riddling character of the equivalent form arises from the bodily form of a commodity counting, in its given state, as the form of value (thus becoming the "value-body"). Marx speaks of a relationship in which the *genesis of the equivalent is premised on the value-expression of the other commodity*. This is the "how question" pertaining to the equivalent form. But this question is merely one part of a larger "how question" regarding value-expression. If we elucidate that larger question, we at the same time fundamentally clarify the "how question" regarding the equivalent form. This is why Marx, after discussing the equivalent form itself, moves on immediately to deal with the "peculiarities" of that form. Thus, even in his examination of the equivalent form, there are passages that contribute to an understanding of the detour of value-expression. In particular, there are noteworthy descriptions of the second peculiarity of the equivalent form, such as the following passage from the first German edition of *Capital*:

> The coat counts as *value-body* in the linen's value-expression, and the coat's *bodily* or *natural form* therefore counts as the *value-form*; i.e., therefore as the *embodiment of indistinguishable human labor*, of human labor pure and simple. The labor, however, by which the useful thing, coat, is made and obtains its particular form is not *abstract human labor*, human labor pure and simple, but a *particular, useful concrete sort of labor* – *tailoring*. The simple relative value-form demands that the value of a commodity (e.g., linen) be only expressed in *one single other commodity-type*. Just *which* the *other* commodity-type is, is utterly irrelevant for the simple value-form. The linen-*value* could have been expressed in the commodity-type, *wheat*, instead of in the commodity-type, *coat*; or instead of wheat, in *iron*, etc. But regardless of whether in coat, wheat, or iron, the *equivalent* of linen would always count as *value-body* for the linen, and therefore as *embodiment of human labor pure and simple*. And the *particular bodily form of the equivalent* – whether coat, wheat or iron – would always remain *not* an embodiment of *abstract human labor* but of a *particular, concrete, useful sort of labor*, whether that of tailor, farmer, or mine-worker. The *particular, concrete, useful labor* which produces the commodity-*body* of the *equivalent* must therefore always count necessarily in the *value-expression as a particular realization-form or appearance-form of human labor pure and simple*, that is, of *abstract human labor*. The coat, for example, can only *count as value-body*, and therefore *as the embodiment of human labor pure and simple*, insofar as tailoring *counts as the determinate form* in which human labor power is expended or in which abstract human labor realizes itself.
>
> Within the value-relation, and in the expression of value included therein, the abstract and general does not count as the property of the concrete and the sensibly-real, but rather it is the opposite: the sensibly-concrete counts as the mere appearance-form or determinate realization-form of the abstract and general. For example, in the value-expression of linen, the *tailoring-labor* of the *equivalent* coat

does not possess the *general property* of also being human labor. It is the opposite case, where being human labor counts as the *essence of the tailoring labor*, and being tailoring labor only counts as the *appearance-form or determinate realization-form of this essence* of tailoring labor. This *quid pro quo* is unavoidable because the labor manifested in the labor-product only *forms value* insofar as it is indiscriminate human labor, and therefore insofar as the labor objectified in a product is *indistinguishable* from the labor objectified in a different sort of commodity.

The *inversion* whereby the sensibly-concrete counts only as the appearance-form of the abstractly-general, *rather* than the abstractly-general counting as a property of the concrete, characterizes value-expression. At the same time, this makes it difficult to understand value-expression. If I say: Roman Law and German Law are both laws, that is obvious. But if I say, on the other hand, *the* Law, this abstract entity, *realizes itself* in Roman Law and German Law, in these concrete laws, then the connection becomes mystical. (Marx, 1976b, pp. 56–57 – Marx's emphasis)

Marx's use of italics in this passage indicates the points he considers to be particularly important; and I want to draw attention to the following two sentences: "The *particular, concrete, useful labor* which produces the commodity-*body* of the *equivalent* must therefore always count necessarily in the *value-expression as a particular realization-form or appearance-form of human labor pure and simple, that is, of abstract human labor*"; and "In the value-expression of linen, the *tailoring-labor* of the *equivalent* coat does not possess the *general property* of also being human labor. It is the opposite case, where being human labor counts as the *essence of the tailoring labor*, and being tailoring labor only counts as the *appearance-form or determinate realization-form of this essence* of tailoring labor." In terms of the expression of value, the tailoring labor only has significance as a real form of human labor – not as something to create a useful thing that satisfies some need. This is only possible by means of, and insofar as, the linen equates the coat to itself as the equivalent. The linen is not able to endow its own weaving labor with that property. It is instead the tailoring labor that takes on this quality; and it is upon this basis that the linen is able to express its own value, its congealed human labor.

Some people may not see what can be elucidated through this

examination, or even view it as a pointless endeavor. But my view, stated in its most general terms, is that without clearly grasping what is clarified through the analysis of the value-form, we will end up understanding very little at all. Commodity production is a particular system of social production where labor that is directly expended in a private manner must become social labor. Whether commodity production, or communal production, the labor of various individuals comes into a reciprocal relationship as human labor. But under commodity production this has to be carried out in a unique form. And this is manifested in the case of the equivalent form.

Perhaps my presentation in *Theory of the Value-Form & Theory of the Exchange Process* was inadequate in some respects, but in analyzing anything, the manner of analysis will always depend on – or be restricted by – what one sets out to clarify. So it would be a bit pointless to concentrate on someone's use of terminology without being aware of the issue that person is seeking to clarify.

# 7

# The Meaning of the "Formal Content of the Relative Expression of Value"
### (Hegel's Theory of Judgment and Marx's Theory of the Value-Form)

**O**TANI: There are probably other important theoretical points related to the detour of value-expression we could discuss, but I would like to take leave of that topic and move on to other issues. My next question centers on how we should understand the meaning of a footnote in the first German edition of *Capital* in which Marx writes:

> It is hardly surprising that the economists, quite under the influence of material interests, have overlooked the *formal content of the relative expression of value*, because before Hegel the logicians by nature even overlooked the formal content of the paradigms of judgment and inference. (Marx, 1976b, p. 22)

I am curious to hear your view regarding Marx's use of the term, "the formal content [*Formgehalt*] of the relative expression of value"; and what you think he is trying to say in the footnote as a whole.

**KURUMA:** I have given some thought to that footnote where Marx compares economists overlooking the "formal content [*Formgehalt*] of the relative expression of value" to "logicians by nature" overlooking the "formal content of the paradigms of judgment and inference [*Forminhalt des Urteils und Schlussparadigmen*]." I think it becomes clear what Marx means by the expression, "the formal content of the relative expression of value," if we look at the following passage from the second German edition of *Capital*:

> By means of the value relation, therefore, the natural form of com-
> modity B becomes the value-form of commodity A, i.e., the physical
> body of commodity B becomes the mirror which reflects the value of
> commodity A. By relating itself with commodity B as value-body, i.e.,
> as the materialization of human labor, commodity A turns the
> use-value of B into the material for its own value-expression. The
> value of commodity A, thus expressed in the use-value of commodity
> B, has the form of relative value. (Marx, 1976a, p. 144)

Economists, in looking at the equation of value-expression, $x$ commodity A = $y$ commodity B, have been preoccupied with the material
issue concerning the *quantity* of value. In other words, they have focused on the fact that the value magnitudes of both commodities are
equal. As a result, they overlooked the equation's content – which is
to say, the form of value-expression – where the value of the commodity on the left is expressed in the use-value of the commodity on
the right. Because of their approach, the economists did not solve the
further problem of how the bodily form of commodity B is able to
become the shape of value for commodity A. In fact, they were not
even able to *pose* that particular problem. This seems to be Marx's
point when he speaks of how economists "have overlooked the formal content of the relative expression of value."

If this were the extent of the matter it could be grasped by carefully reading *Capital*, but things are a bit trickier because of Marx's
reference to Hegel. In his afterword to the second German edition of
*Capital*, Marx notes that when he was working on that first volume
he was irritated by the popular tendency at the time to irreverently
treat Hegel as a "dead dog." Marx dared to declare himself a pupil of
Hegel and "in the chapter on the theory of value coquetted with the
modes of expression peculiar to him [Hegel]" (Marx, 1976a, p. 103).
The footnote you quoted may be one example of this. But Marx is
doing more than simply mentioning Hegel in passing. We need to
consider the somewhat difficult issue regarding the points of similar-
ity between Marx's theory of the value-form and Hegel's theory of
judgment. To begin, we should note that the footnote in question is
attached to the following passage:

> If one considers in the simple relative expression of value: $x$ commod-
> ity A = $y$ commodity B only the *quantitative* relation, one will also

only find the laws developed above about the movement of relative value, which are all based on the fact that the magnitude of value of the commodities is determined by the labor-time necessary for their production. However, if one considers the value-relation of the two commodities according to their *qualitative* side, one uncovers in every simple value-expression the secret of the value-form, and therefore, *in nuce*, that of money. (Marx, 1976b, p. 22)

This passage is included in the first German edition of *Capital*, under the heading: "First or Simple Form of Relative Value"; however, from the content, it is clear that Marx is discussing the fundamental question of the value-form (up to and including the value-form in general) – not the defect of the simple value-form or the consequent necessity of a development of form. Thus, when Marx, in relation to this, mentions Hegel's theory of judgment (setting aside here Hegel's theory of inference), it is natural to think that he is referring to issues common to judgment in general, rather than to Hegel's examination of the progression of judgment. In Hegel's *The Encyclopedia Logic*, near the beginning of his analysis of judgment, we can find passages that seem to correspond to Marx's statement that "before Hegel the logicians by nature even overlooked the formal content of the paradigms of judgment and inference," Consider, for example, Section 166:

When considering judgment, one usually thinks first of the independence of the extremes (the subject and the predicate): that the first is a thing or determination on its own [*für sich*], and that the predicate likewise is a universal determination outside that subject (for instance in my head), which is then brought together with the subject by me, and is thus "judged." But since the copula "*is*" attributes the predicate to the subject, that external, subjective *subsumption* is again sublated, and the judgment is taken as a determination of the *ob-ject* itself.[1] – The *etymological* meaning of *Urteil* in our language is more profound and expresses the unity of the Concept as what comes first, and its distinction as the *original* division, which is what the judgment truly is.

The abstract judgment is the proposition: "The *singular* is the *universal*." These are the determinations which *subject* and *predicate*

---

[1] [The translators of *The Encyclopedia Logic* use the hyphenated term "ob-ject" to translate *Gegenstand*, which they define as "the ordinary object of experience, in all its modes," as opposed to *Objekt*, which is the "logical concept of the object." (Hegel, 1991, p. xxii) – EMS]

primitively have vis-à-vis each other, where the moments of the Concept are taken in their immediate determinacy or first abstraction. (The propositions: "The *particular* is the *universal*," and: "The *singular* is the *particular*," belong to the further determination of the judgment.) It must be considered a quite amazing lack of observation that <u>we do not find any mention in the logic books [*in den Logiken*] of the fact</u> that a proposition of this kind is expressed in *every* judgment: "*The singular is the universal*," or, more determinately: "*The subject is the predicate*" (e.g., "God is absolute spirit"). It is true that the determinations of singularity and universality, or subject and predicate are also distinct, but the absolutely universal *fact* remains, nonetheless, that every judgment expresses them as identical.

The copula "is" flows from the nature of the Concept: to be *identical* with itself is its uttering; as moments of the *Concept*, the singular and the universal are the sort of determinacies that that cannot be isolated. The preceding determinancies of reflection have among their relationships *also* the relation to each other, but their connection is only one of "*having*," not of "*being*"; it is not *identity posited as such* or *universality*. Hence, only judgment is the genuine *particularity* of the Concept, for it is the determinacy or distinguishing of the Concept which continues to be *universality* all the same. (Hegel, 1991, p. 244 – Hegel's italics; Kuruma's underlining)

We can also take a look the following addendum to the passage I just quoted:

The judgment is <u>usually considered</u> to be a combination of concepts, and indeed of concepts of diverse sorts. What is right in this interpretation is that the Concept certainly forms the presupposition of the judgment, and that in the judgment it presents itself in the form of distinction. On the contrary, it is false to speak of concepts of diverse sorts, for the Concept as such, although concrete, is still essentially *one*, and the moments contained within it must not be considered to be diverse sorts of concepts; similarly, it is false to speak of a *combination* of the sides of judgment, because, when we speak of a combination, we think of the terms combined as occurring also in their own right [*für sich*] outside the combination.

This external interpretation shows up in an even more definite way when the judgment is said to come about through the "*ascription*" of a predicate to a subject. In this view, the subject counts as what subsists "out there" on its own account [*für sich*], while the predicate is what is found in our heads. But the copula "*is*" already contradicts this view. When we say, "This rose *is* red," or "This picture *is* beautiful," what the assertion expresses is that it is not just *we* who, from outside, dress the rose in red, or the picture in beauty, but, rather, that these are the objects' own characteristics. A further defect of the usual interpretation of the judgment in formal logic is the fact that in this perspective the judgment always appears to be something merely contingent, and the advance from the Concept to the judgment is not demonstrated.

But the Concept as such does not abide within itself, without development (as the understanding would have it); on the contrary, being the infinite form, the Concept is totally active. It is the *punctum saliens* of all vitality, so to speak, and for that reason it distinguishes itself from itself. This sundering of the Concept into the distinction of its moments that is posited by its own activity is the *judgment*, the significance of which must accordingly be conceived of as the *particularization* of the Concept. Indeed the Concept is *in-itself* [*an sich*] already the particular, but the particular is not yet *posited* in the Concept as such; it is still in transparent unity with the universal there. So, as we have already [§160 addendum] noted, the germ of a plant, for instance, already contains the particular: root, branches, leaves, etc., but the particular is here present only *in-itself* [*an sich*], and is posited only when the germ opens up; this opening up should be regarded as the judgment of the plant. Consequently, the same example can also serve to make it obvious that neither the Concept nor the judgment is found only in our heads and that they are not merely formed by us. The Concept dwells within the things themselves, it is that through which they are what they are, and to comprehend an ob-ject means therefore to become conscious of its concept. If we advance from this to the judging of the ob-ject, the judgment is not our subjective doing, by which this or that predicate is ascribed to the ob-ject; on the contrary, we are considering the object in the determinacy that is posited by its concept. (Hegel, 1991, pp. 244–245 – Hegel's italics; Kuruma's underlining)

Both of those passages are taken from the first section, entitled "The Judgment." Hegel speaks of the usual ways of thinking, and of the defects of "logic books" or "formal logic." The defect indicated in all of those cases concerns the original meaning of the general form of judgment, where the subject is linked to the predicate via the copula "is"; which is to say, the predicate expressing a certain determination that is originally contained within the subject itself. I think that this is what Marx is referring to when he says that "before Hegel the professional logicians even overlooked the formal content of the paradigms of judgment and inference."

Compared to this, when Marx notes that it is "hardly surprising that the economists, quite under the influence of material interests, have overlooked the formal content of the relative expression of value" (Marx, 1976b, p. 22), he seems to be saying that when economists looked at the equation indicating the value-relation, $x$ commodity A = $y$ commodity B, they only saw the material content, in terms of the commodities on either side of the equation being of equal value. They thus overlooked the complex content of the equation, which concerns the *form* of the commodity's "relative expression of value" wherein the value of the commodity on the left of the equation (corresponding to "subject") is expressed in the bodily form of the commodity on the right of the equation (corresponding to "predicate"). When Marx says that, "it is hardly surprising that the economists … have overlooked the formal content of the relative expression of value, because before *Hegel* the logicians by nature even overlooked the formal content of the paradigms of judgment and inference," he is implying that the situation overlooked by the "professional" logicians prior to Hegel was a relatively simple matter compared to that overlooked by the economists. And indeed this is the case. For example, as we saw a moment ago, Hegel emphasized: "When we say, 'This rose is red,' or 'This picture is beautiful,' what the assertion expresses is that it is not just we who, from outside, dress the rose in red, or the picture in beauty, but, rather, that these are the objects' own characteristics." Of course that is true. At the same time, though, if that were all it means it would be easily understandable, without having to wait for Hegel's explanation. But that natural and self-evident fact is linked in the case of Hegel to his idealistic dialectic, so as to acquire mysterious meaning. For instance, following the passage quoted above, Hegel writes:

> A further defect of the usual interpretation of the judgment in formal logic is the fact that in this perspective the judgment always appears to be something merely contingent, and the advance from the Concept to the judgment is not demonstrated. … This sundering of the Concept into the distinction of its moments that is posited by its own activity is the judgment, the significance of which must accordingly be conceived of as the particularization of the Concept. (Hegel, 1991, p. 245)

Hegel says that the heart of the matter is to clarify the "advance from the Concept to judgment," which seems to correspond to the part of the first German edition of *Capital* where Marx discusses the development of the value-form as follows:

> It was however of decisive importance to discover the inner necessary connection between *form* of value, *substance* of value, and *magnitude* of value i.e., expressed ideally, to prove that the *form* of value springs from the *concept* of value. (Marx, 1976b, p. 34 – Marx's emphasis)

I think that this, like the passage quoted earlier from the afterword to *Capital*, is a typical example of how Marx "coquetted with the mode of expression peculiar to Hegel." But it is necessary to clarify that the "concept of value" is completely different from Hegel's understanding of the Concept. As Marx notes in that afterword:

> For Hegel, the process of thinking, which he even transforms into an independent subject, under the name of "the Idea," is the creator of the real world, and the real world is only the external appearance of the idea. With me the reverse is true: the ideal is nothing but the material world reflected in the mind of man, and translated into forms of thought. (Marx, 1976a, p. 102)

Marx clarifies all of the moments of commodity-value by analyzing the form in which products of labor present themselves as commodities, thereby ultimately reaching an understanding of the nature of commodity-value and at the same time grasping that the value of a commodity must be manifested in the form of value. In this way, he elucidates how the use-value of the commodity in the equivalent form becomes a "mirror of value" for the commodity in the relative form of value. In a Hegelian manner, Marx says that – expressed "ideally" – it is of "decisive importance" to "prove that the *form* of value springs from the *concept* of value."

It may also be helpful, to avoid any misunderstanding and further clarify the matter, if we consider a passage that appears prior to the passage quoted earlier from the first German edition of *Capital*. In it, Marx describes the peculiar social and fetishistic character of the value of a commodity in the following way:

> Indeed all use-values are commodities only because they are *products*

*of mutually independent private labors*, private labors, which however materially depend on one another as special, even though autonomized, branches of the naturally-grown system of *division of labor*. They are thus socially connected exactly by their *diversity*, their *particular usefulness*. It is exactly because of this that they produce qualitatively different use-values. Did they not do this, these use-values would not become commodities for each other. On the other hand, this different useful quality does not yet turn these products into commodities. If a peasant family produces coats, linen, and wheat for their own consumption, then these objects confront the family as different products of their family labor, but they do not confront each other as commodities. If the labor were *immediately social*, i.e., joint labor, then the products would obtain the immediately social character of a joint product for their producers, but not the character of commodities for each other. Yet we do not have to go far in order to find what is the *social form* of the *private labors* that are contained in the commodities and independent of one another. This was already clarified in the analysis of the commodity. The social form of private labors is the relationship with each other as *equal labor*, i.e., since the *equality* of altogether *different* labors can only consist in an *abstraction from their inequality*, their relationship with each other is *as human labor in general*: *expenditures of human labor power*, something which all human labors, whatever their content and their mode of operation, indeed *are*. In every social form of labor, the labors of the different individuals stand also in a relation to each other as human labor, but here, this *relationship itself* counts as the *specifically social form* of the labors. It is true that none of these private labors in its natural form possesses this specific social form of abstract human labor, just as little as the commodity in its natural form possesses the social form of mere congelation of labor, or of value. By the fact that the natural form of one commodity, here of the linen, becomes the general equivalent form (because all other commodities relate themselves to the latter as the form of appearance of their own value), the linen weaving labor also becomes the general realization-form of abstract human labor, or it becomes labor in immediately social form. The measuring stick for "being social" must be borrowed from the nature of the relations peculiar to each mode of production, not from imaginations alien to it. Just as it was shown a minute ago that the commodity, by nature, excludes the direct form of general exchangeability, that therefore the general equivalent form can only develop *antagonistically*, the same is true for the private labors contained in the commodities. Since they are *not immediately social* labors, it follows first that the *social form* is a form different from the natural forms of the actual useful labors, a form that is alien to them and abstract, and secondly all kinds of private labor obtain their *social* character only *antagonistically*, by all of them being *equated* to an exclusive kind of private labor, here the linen weaving. By this, the latter becomes the immediate and general form of appearance of abstract human labor, and thus labor in immediately social form. It represents itself therefore also immediately in a socially valid and generally exchangeable product.

The semblance, as if the equivalent form of a commodity springs from its own material nature, instead of being the mere reflection of the relations of the other commodities, solidifies itself with the development of the *single* to the *general* equivalent, because the oppositional moments of the value-form no longer develop *evenly* for the commodities placed in relation with each other, because the general equivalent form distinguishes one commodity as something quite apart from all other commodities, and finally because this form of that commodity is indeed no longer the product of the relationship of any one *individual* other commodity. ...

As one sees, the analysis of the commodity yields all *essential* determinations of the *form of value*. It yields the form of value itself in its antagonistic moments, the *general relative form of value*, the *general equivalent form*, finally the never-ending *series of simple relative value expressions*, which first constitute a transitional phase in the development of the form of value, and eventually turns into the *specific relative form of value of the general equivalent*. However the analysis of the commodity yielded these forms as *forms of the commodity* in general, which can therefore be taken on by every commodity – although *in a polar manner*, so that when commodity A finds itself in *one* form determination, then commodities B, C, etc. assume the *other* in relation to it. It was however of decisive importance to discover the inner necessary connection between *form* of value, *substance* of value, and *magnitude* of value, i.e., expressed *ideally*, to prove that the *form* of value springs from the *concept* of value. (Marx, 1976b, pp. 31–34 – Marx's emphasis)

This has gotten a bit off track, but my basic point is that, compared to grasping the "formal content of the paradigms of judgment and inference," it is far more difficult to grasp the "formal content of the relative expression of value," which corresponds to the heading in the second edition of *Capital* entitled "The content of the relative form of value." And this is why Marx says it is "hardly surprising" that economists have "overlooked the formal content of the relative expression of value."

# 8.

## How the Development of the Value-form Unfolds
### (Neither a Historical Development
### Nor the "Self-development of a Concept")

**TANI:** I am interested in your view regarding a number of matters raised by Marx in his examination of the simple form of value, but today I want to ask you about the *development* of the value-form. At the end of his analysis of the second form of value, which is the expanded value-form, Marx makes the following transition to the third, or general, form of value:

> The expanded relative form of value is, however, nothing but the sum of the simple relative expressions or equations of the first form. ... But, each of these equations implies the identical equation *in reverse relation*. ... In fact, when a person *exchanges* his linen for many other commodities, and thus *expresses* its value in a series of other commodities, it necessarily follows that the other owners of commodities *exchange* them for the linen, and therefore *express* the values of their various commodities in one and the same third commodity, the linen. If, then, we *reverse* the series 20 yards of linen = 1 coat, or = 10 lb. of tea, etc, i.e., if we formulate the *reverse relation that is in point of fact already implied in the series*, we get the general form of value. (Marx, 1976a, p. 157)

Quite a few scholars have claimed that this transition (via the "reverse relation") is incorrect, or at least inappropriate. Ryōzō Tomizuka, for example, in his book *Keizai genron* (Principles of Political Economy), expresses the following doubt regarding Marx's description of the transition from form B to form C:

> In the current edition of *Capital*, the transition from form B to form C

is explained by Marx in terms of form B merely being the "sum" of the equations of form A, and that each of the equations of form A that constitute form B includes the "reverse relation." But a doubt arises regarding this claim in light of the basis for Marx's own view: i.e., that the commodity on the right of the equation and the commodity on the left are each playing a fundamentally different role. In the explanation of the transition from form B to form C, Marx says: "In fact, when a person exchanges his linen for many other commodities, and thus expresses its value in a series of other commodities, it necessarily follows that the other owners of commodities exchange them for the linen, and therefore express the values of their various commodities in one and the same third commodity, the linen (Marx, 1976a, p. 157). But even if the owner of the linen commodity has developed a relation of value-expression, where the other commodities are made into the particular equivalent, it cannot be said that the owners of the other commodities "necessarily" develop a relation of value-expression in which they make the linen into the general equivalent vis-à-vis their own commodities. Even if such reasoning were possible, the "developed value-form" would be simultaneously developed for every commodity, meaning that the "reverse relation" of value-expression could simultaneously be developed, with all commodities able to become the "general equivalent" at the same time. (In terms of this point, we can gain a hint from "form IV" in the first edition of *Capital*, where it is said that the second form of value is developed simultaneously for each commodity but that the form arrived at through the reversal is not simultaneously developed.) It seems that in the theory of the value-form the question of the transition from form B to form C should only be noted in the main text and then discussed in the theory of the exchange process as the "contradiction of overall exchange." (Tomizuka, 1976, pp. 35–36)

What is your view of Tomizuka's argument?

**KURUMA:** Tomizuka quotes a passage from *Capital* to claim that Marx is mistaken, but from my perspective the person mistaken is none other than Tomizuka himself. The idea that Marx is incorrect stems from a failure to read, with an adequate degree of care, what he actually wrote in *Capital*. Marx emphasizes that the situation where all the commodities commonly express their value in linen is *not* unconditional, noting that "*in fact, when* a person exchanges his linen for many other commodities, and thus expresses its value in a series of other commodities, *it necessarily follows* that the other owners of commodities exchange them for the linen." This is limited, in other words, to a situation where certain conditions are met. Namely, the linen is exchanged in reality with many other commodities. In that case the numerous other commodities also exchange for linen, so linen comes to express the value of these commodities; and Marx says that it is inevitable for this to occur. I find no reason to raise any objection to this perfectly reasonable and correct observation.

In addition, Marx's statement seems closely related to the reason he placed the commodity "linen" in the relative form of value when setting up the simple value-form. Marx did this, I think, because linen is a material used in making clothes, a necessary item for daily life, and is thus a commodity likely to be exchanged with many other types of commodities. The same cannot be said of every commodity, however. And to bring a commodity that is not commonly exchanged into the relative value-form would restrict the sorts of commodities in the equivalent form to a narrow range. This would mean that in the developed value-form there would only be a few commodities in the equivalent form. In such a case, even if we reverse the equation – to view things from the opposite perspective – the common equivalent would not be the *general* equivalent, because only a few commodities would be involved. In the case of the linen, on the contrary, it is indeed possible for it to become the general equivalent. In the passage quoted from *Capital*, Marx is speaking in the form of a "hypothetical judgment" (*hypothetisches Urteil*). Some may object to my view, however, and argue that a problem that should be raised in the theory of the exchange process has been introduced in the theory of the value-form. But that is not in fact the case (as I intend to discuss with regard to the dialectic and the value-form).

I also want to emphasize that the point just made concerns the transition from form B to form C (the shift from the expanded value-form to the general value-form), and does not apply to the transition from form C to form D, which is the transition from the general value-form to the money-form. In the transition from form B to form C, linen becomes the general equivalent because it is exchanged for many other commodities. But that is not the reason why gold becomes money, which occurs instead because gold's natural form is best suited to the functions of money. All commodities express their value in gold and desire to be exchanged for gold because it has already become money, not because gold is the individually desired object. I only mention this point, which should go without saying, because there are respected theories that are based upon ignorance of it.

**OTANI:** You mention the shift from the second to the third form, but from a more general perspective, there is the question of what "motive force" underlies the development of the value-form, determining the shift from one form to the next. If each form *must* shift to the subsequent form – the first precisely to the second, the second precisely to the third, and the third precisely to the fourth form – then I think it must be shown that each form is encompassed within the preceding form. For example, if it is said that form A must develop into another form, and that it can only be form B, it would seem that form B is inherent to form A *itself*. Yet I do not think the same can generally be said for the entirety of the development of the value-form. Although a Hegelian "self-development of the concept" lies outside of our discussion, I should note that the scholar Yoshihiro Niji thinks that the "contradiction between the concept of value and the mode of existence of value" – said to be a contradiction within cognition – represents that sort of "motive force."

**KURUMA:** If we view the first, "simple, isolated, or accidental form of value" as being formed by selecting a random commodity from the numerous equivalent commodities in form B and positing it as the equivalent form, then the shift from form A to form B is natural and there is no reason to think that some "motive force" is necessary. In the transition from form B to form C as well (as I noted in answering the previous question), if form C is seen as merely the reverse side of the equation given in form B, there is no need for any sort of "motive force" underlying the transition.

Form A, of course, has a defect as a form of a commodity's value-expression, and it is true that value-expression progressively becomes more complete with the development of the value-form. From this perspective, one might imagine that the motive force of the value-form underlies the shift from imperfect value-expression to a more completed form. Yet I believe that such an idea is problematic.

Granted, the development of form under examination is a real historical development, and at the same time a formal development stemming from the needs of that reality, so it is not unnatural to think of the realistic needs as the "motive force" of development. However, as I noted already in discussing the term *accidental* in the accidental form of value, the two commodities in *Capital* that first appear on either side of the simple value-form are not commodities as they initially appear historically. That is to say, Marx is not referring to two different products that happen to be exchanged so as to become commodities or (with the continuation of that exchange) two products that are exchanged as commodities from the outset but still not exchanged with any other commodities. Rather, Marx proposes that form to fundamentally elucidate the mechanism of value-expression through an analysis of the fundamental form of that expression. The development of the value-form is a development within a theoretical structure, so it is doubtful whether we need to suppose some "motive force" that underlies the development. Personally I see no such need. Not only does it seem unnecessary, I think that various misunderstandings will arise if the supposition is poorly made. For instance, there are some who mistake the development of form in the theory of the value-form for a historical development, while others see it as a Hegelian self-development of a concept. Instead of looking for a motive force, I think we can be satisfied with what Marx wrote at the end of the analysis of each form regarding the form's defects and the significance of the shift to the subsequent form. It seems sufficient to summarize Marx's observations and note that the development of form has this or that significance in a given case.

# 9

# The Meaning of Abstracting from the Individual Want of the Commodity Owner
## (Nobuteru Takeda's Criticism of Kuruma)

**O**TANI: There are other points related to the development of the value-form that I wish to discuss, but we have already had a long day so I would like to bring our discussion to a close by raising two points that seem to be related to the question of the value-form as a whole. The first issue concerns the connection between the value-form and the individual want of the commodity owner. In *Theory of the Value-Form & Theory of the Exchange Process*, for instance, after pointing out that "the simple value-form of a commodity is not yet a form independent of the want of the commodity owner" (Kuruma, 1957, p. 90), you write:

> The restriction on the commodity's value-form by the want of an indi-
> vidual commodity owner is more than just an inconvenient matter that
> has confounded economists. It is a serious defect for the value-form,
> as it runs counter to the essential nature of value itself. Therefore, the
> value-form, instead of remaining at the simple value-form, must pro-
> ceed to the money-form, where it is first freed from the connection to
> the individual want of the commodity owner, thus reaching comple-
> tion as a form of value. (Kuruma, 1957, p. 91)

Some have disagreed with your view. Are you familiar with that criticism?

**KURUMA:** I became aware of such criticism through a cursory reading of *Kachikeitai-ron* (Theory of the Value-Form) by Yoshihiro Niji, after he sent me a copy. In Niji's book, there are two footnotes where he objects to my position. In the first footnote, he writes:

In considering the value-form, Samezō Kuruma sets aside the want of the commodity owner as a heterogeneous element. But there remains an inconsistency because he sees the selection of the equivalent commodity as always resulting from an individual want. Nobuteru Takeda felt this inconsistency needs to be resolved.[1] He said that the choice of the equivalent commodity, whether in the process of thought or the process of reality, is carried out without regard to a want. This view seems valid, both from the perspective of the example Takeda raises [in his article] and from a theoretical perspective. (Niji, 1978, p. 111)

In another footnote, later in his book, Niji writes:

Kuruma says that the "restriction on the commodity's value-form by the want of an individual commodity owner is more than just an inconvenient matter that has confounded economists," calling it a "serious defect for the value-form" that "runs counter to the essential nature of value itself." He seems to view the value-form as developing from this motive force. And Kuruma sees the development of the value-form as a process of "emancipation" from the individual wants. In fact, as I note in the main body of this book, that is not case. And I want to look at Takeda's view regarding this matter. (Niji, 1978, p. 197)

We can gather from the footnotes that Nobuteru Takeda adopted a position contrary to mine; and if we look for the part of his article that Niji is referring to, we find the following:

Kuruma sees the equivalent commodity as always being the object of the commodity owner's individual want, but when discussing the value-form, he says that we must take the value-equation created on the basis of such a want as a given and abstract from that factor. In other words, the factor of the want is only abstracted from within thought. Even though Kuruma's conclusion differs from that of Uno, who emphasizes the role played by that want within the theory of the value-form, both of them share the same premise. But is it in fact the case that the equivalent commodity must always be an object desired by the commodity owner? Is it impossible for the commodity owner to

---

[1] Niji is referring to Takeda's 1974 article entitled "Theory of the Value-Form & Theory of the Exchange Process", part 1, published in No. 75 of Aichi University's *The Journal of the Association of Legal, Political and Economic Science*, pp. 41-43.

use a commodity other than one he wants as the material for carrying out value-expression? Is it truly impossible to abstract from the process through which a value-equation is created?

Marx raises the example of the primitive exchange of products on the coast of West Africa, where in the case of the exchange of two commodities, each commodity is first equated to a "bar" that signifies iron. The commodity on one side might be expressed by one bar, and the commodity on the other side by two bars, and then their exchange would be carried out at that proportion. As we can see, the bar is the material that expresses the value of a commodity prior to its exchange, but the bar itself is certainly not an object desired by a commodity owner. If we look at the writings of Homer, various commodities in ancient Greece were "priced" using cattle. For example, a cast bronze shell is five head of cattle, a large three-legged bronze cauldron is twelve, a female slave skilled in all matter of arts is four, and a kettle with an engraved flower pattern is one head of cattle. We need to note that cattle is neither the object desired by the owner of the shell or the female slave, nor the object of exchange, but merely the material to expresses the value of each commodity. Such facts indicate that the equivalent commodity is not always a desired object. The choice of the equivalent commodity does not have a direct relation to a want. (Takeda, 1974, pp. 41–42)

A bit further on in his article, Takeda refers to the following passage from my book that you quoted a moment ago, then offers the following criticism of my view:

According to Kuruma, the simple value-form simultaneously encompasses two different relations: the relation of value-expression and the relation of indicating an individual want. Thus, the value-form of the commodity has a fatal defect as a value-form in terms of being restricted by the individual want of the commodity owner. This flaw is overcome once the form is freed of the connection to this individual want of the commodity owner, and Kuruma says that the developmental process of the value-form is a process of completion as the money-form. Is it truly valid, though, to depict the development of the value-form as emancipation from the individual want? ...

The defect of the simple value-form is certainly not that it is restricted by an individual want. In the simple value-form, one commodity (linen) expresses its value in another commodity (coat). However, this equation only expresses the value of the linen in distinction from its use-value. It does not effectively express the essence of value, which is that the linen as value is qualitatively equal to every other commodity and has a proportional quantitative relation to them. And, seen from the opposite perspective, the coat is likewise only the equivalent form for the single commodity linen (not for every other commodity). This is precisely the defect of the simple value-form. In other words, that mode of value-expression is insufficient from the perspective of the essential nature of value, for which there is qualitative equality so that the only distinction is a quantitative one. This flaw is first overcome when a single commodity is excluded from the commodity world as the general equivalent. That is, by means of all commodities expressing their values in a single commodity, in a unified manner, the commodities that differ as use-values are each able to express themselves as a common thing *qua* value. Thus, for the first time, value-expression assumes a mode that suits the nature of value. Marx speaks of how the value-form corresponds to the concept of value. From this perspective, the motive force that gives birth to the development of the development of the value-form is the contradiction between the value concept and its determinate being [*Dasein*].

Thus, the value-form does not develop via the motive force of liberation from an individual want. It is not the case, as Kuruma argues, that the "restriction on the commodity's value-form by the want of an individual commodity owner" is something that "runs counter to the essential nature of value itself." Therefore, it is also not true that the form "reach[es] completion as a form of value" by being "freed from the connection to the individual want of the commodity owner."

Kuruma, however, is not completely unaware of the problem of viewing the developmental process of the value-form as a process of emancipation from the individual want. That is, Kuruma at the same time asserts that the problem of an individual want is not something that must be focused on to understand the development of the value-form, so it can be set aside when elucidating the specific problem posited in the theory of the value-form. This is a view that runs counter to his view that I have looked at up to now. At any rate, Kuruma goes on to quote a passage from Marx indicating the defect of the simple form of value, to which he adds: "The reason that the simple value-form is incomplete as a value-form, as well as the circumstances of its transformation to form B, can thus very well be explained through an analysis that concentrates solely on form – without considering the factor of the want of the commodity owner and hence the reason why a certain commodity (say a coat rather than wheat) is posited as the equivalent form" (Kuruma, 1957, p. 113).

Here, Kuruma does not look to the restriction by the individual want as an explanation of the incompleteness of the simple value-form; therefore, the theoretical basis for depicting the development of the value-form as emancipation from the individual want is lost. Instead, he emphasizes that the incompleteness of the simple value-form and the overcoming of it can be explained solely through the analysis of the form itself, without an explanation regarding some want. In other words, the crux of the matter for Kuruma, when considering the development of the value-form, is sought solely in the analysis of whether or not each value-form is a form appropriate to the essential nature of value. This is precisely the correct perspective. If I could go so far as to speculate, it seems to me that Kuruma first clearly expressed this correct way of thinking when he criticized Uno for having emphasized the significance of the role of a want within the development of the value-form; so this view stemmed less from theoretical necessity than the need to refute Uno. That is a matter of little importance, however. The key point is that an error was corrected. But this point is also not a simple one. Even though Kuruma displays a correct viewpoint, he has not necessarily abandoned the other perspective. The two viewpoints encompassed within Kuruma's theory of the development of the value-form are contradictory perspectives that are heterogeneous and mutually exclusive. Unless one of the two is abandoned, there is no avoiding a theoretical self-contradiction.

Granted, Kuruma does eventually attempt to resolve the theoretical self-contradiction. But instead of rejecting the one perspective in order to reinforce the logic of the other, he attempts what might be called an ambiguous integration of the two. He begins by saying that consideration of the role of a want is not necessary for an understanding of the development of the value-form. In saying this, he is obliged to reject his own depiction of the development of the value-form as emancipation from the individual want, but Kuruma does not go that far. Instead, he posits the want with a new role, saying that "by taking the want of the commodity owner into consideration we can understand that there is additional significance" (Kuruma, 1957, p. 118) concerning the development from the value-form to the money-form – separate from the issue of the expression of value. In other words, Kuruma says that with the expansion of the exchange process, money as the "general means of exchange," which is premised on emancipation from an individual want, must be formed, and that the consideration of the role of the want makes possible an understanding of the formation of money within this exchange process. At some point in his argument, the role of the want shifts from a problem pertaining to the value-form (= value-expression) to a problem pertaining to the exchange process. This is not a resolution of the theoretical self- contradiction, but rather a papering over of it.

> To summarize our argument … Kuruma's initial, seemingly triv-
> ial, mistake of *going no further than abstracting within thought from
> the factor of want in value-expression*, while at the same time thinking
> that a relation indicating a want underlies the expression of value, is
> the source of the self-contradiction that he falls into, and this throws
> his theory into confusion when it comes to dealing with the develop-
> ment of the value-form. This is an example of how all "beginnings are
> difficult." It reminds me of the importance of carefully pondering how
> to establish the starting point, before then taking the first step. (Ta-
> keda, 1974, pp. 47–52)

If we look at the final point made by Takeda in this passage, the basis of my error is apparently that I go no further than "abstracting within thought from the factor of want in value-expression." That criticism also constitutes the main point Takeda makes in the first of the two passages quoted, so I want to look again at the argument he makes in that previous passage.

Takeda begins his criticism by saying that in my argument "the factor of want is only abstracted from within thought"; but it is not clear what Takeda means exactly by "only abstracted from within thought."

The act of "abstracting from" [*shashō*], in the proper sense of the term, is an indispensable step of scientific cognition that involves setting aside or placing out of consideration numerous aspects or moments that make up concrete reality in order to conduct a pure analysis of one aspect or moment. Along with this act of "abstracting from" (or setting aside) those other elements, one then "abstracts" (or extracts) [*chūshō*] the particular aspect that will be considered in a pure form, from out of the totality of complex reality. Needless to say, this involves the operation of the human mind. So both the abstract-ing from what is irrelevant, and the abstraction (or extraction) of the relevant element, solely occur "within thought." Yet because "ab-straction" is the selecting of one element from out of the multi-faceted concrete reality, while "abstracting from" is the mental operation of setting aside the other realistic elements, neither of those two mental operations is unrelated to reality. Indeed, both are *prem-ised* upon it. Therefore, we should not forget that, in addition to the element extracted from reality, the other elements that have been set aside continue to exist. As Marx says in his introduction to *Grun-*

*drisse*: "The real subject retains its autonomous existence outside the head just as before; namely as long as the head's conduct is merely speculative, merely theoretical. Hence, in the theoretical method, too, the subject, society, must always be kept in mind as the presupposition" (Marx, 1973, pp. 101–102).

The role of the commodity owner's want, which is abstracted from in the theory of the value-form but constitutes an important moment within reality, is brought into the field of vision in the theory of the exchange process. Yet even in that theory Marx notes the following about the development of the value-form:

> In the direct exchange of products, each commodity is directly a means of exchange to its owner, and an equivalent to those who do not possess it, although only in so far as it has use-value for them. At this stage, therefore, *the articles exchanged do not acquire a value-form independent of their own use-value, or of the individual wants of the exchangers. The need for this form first develops with the increase in the number and variety of the commodities entering into the process of exchange.* The problem and the means for its solution arise simultaneously. Commercial intercourse, in which the owners of commodities exchange and compare their own articles with various other articles, never takes place without different kinds of commodities, that belong to different owners, being exchanged for, and equated as values with one single further kind of commodity. This further commodity, by becoming the equivalent of various other commodities, directly acquires the form of a general or social equivalent form, if only within narrow limits. This general equivalent form comes and goes with the momentary social contacts which call it into existence. It is transiently attached to this or that commodity in alternation. But with the development of commodity exchange it fixes itself firmly and exclusively onto particular kinds of commodity, i.e., it crystallizes out into the money-form. (Marx, 1976a, pp. 182–183)

Marx says that "in the direct exchange of products ... the articles exchanged do not acquire a value-form independent of their own use-value, or of the individual needs of the exchangers" and that "the need for this [independent] form first develops with the increase in the number and variety of the commodities entering into the process of exchange," resulting in the "general equivalent" and ultimately the crystallization of the money-form.

However, none of these points are raised in the theory of the value-form; they are abstracted from, placed outside of the field of vision. It is of no use to consider those points when we set out to purely examine the value-form as the form of the expression of commodity value and thus concentrate on the *how* of value-expression.

When Takeda criticizes me for only abstracting within thought from the factor of the want in examining the theory of the value-form, he does not understand at all the meaning of "abstracting from" – in the proper sense of the term – as an indispensable step for scientific cognition. Thus, he comes up with the following sort of in-credible argument.

> Kuruma sees the equivalent commodity as *always* being the object of the commodity owner's individual want, but when discussing the value-form, he says that we must take value-equation created on the basis of such a want as a given and abstract from that factor. In other words, the factor of want is only abstracted from within thought. Even though Kuruma's conclusion differs from that of Uno, who empha-sizes the role played by that want within the theory of the value-form, both of them share the same premise. But is it in fact the case that the equivalent commodity must be *always* be an object desired by the commodity owner? Is it impossible for the commodity owner to use a commodity other than one he wants as the material for carrying out value-expression? Is it truly impossible to abstract from the process through which a value-equation is created?

Takeda poses the question in this manner; and in order to prove that it is *not* impossible he introduces the example of "bars" in coastal West Africa or cattle in ancient Greece. However, the bars or cattle in those examples are not merely commodities, but function rather as the general measure of value and have thus become money. When a given commodity becomes money, it is natural that it is no longer the object of some individual want. The question should be whether, when analyzing the value-form at the stage prior to the emergence of money, the abstracting from the want of the commodity owner in-deed only takes place "within thought." Takeda says that my ab-stracting from the want is only within thought, and to counter this view offers the examples above where there is no relation to want (not only within thought but within reality as well). His examples, however, merely demonstrate that once the general equivalent becomes money it no longer has a relation to some human want.

The question of whether abstracting from the want of the commodity owner in the theory of the value-form is "only within thought" cannot be answered by introducing such extraordinary examples, but rather by fundamentally clarifying the meaning for scientific cognition of "abstracting from" and the abstraction obtained through that act.

As I said earlier, concrete reality is comprised of many moments and has many aspects. In order to purely consider any one of those aspects it is necessary to set aside the other ones. This is the essential meaning of "abstracting from" [shashō], as an indispensable step in the scientific cognition of a thing. Thus, the act of "abstracting from" the other elements naturally implies that those elements temporarily set aside for the sake of a given theoretical objective still continue to exist within reality. The elements or aspects that are set aside at one point can be considered at a subsequent stage, which is also indispensable to the scientific understanding of a thing.

Takeda, however, does not seem to grasp this elementary methodological issue regarding scientific cognition, and thus offers the following sort of argument:

> Kuruma begins by saying that consideration of the role of a want is not necessary for an understanding of the development of the value-form. ... [But in other passages he says that] "by taking the want of the commodity owner into consideration we can understand that there is additional significance" (Kuruma, 1957, p. 118) concerning the development from the [general] [2] value-form to the money-form – separate from the issue of the expression of value. ...
> At some point in Kuruma's argument, the role of a want shifts from a problem pertaining to the value-form (= value-expression) to a problem pertaining to the exchange process. This is not a resolution of the theoretical self-contradiction, but rather a papering over of it. (Takeda, 1974, pp. 51–52)

---

[2] In *Theory of the Value-Form & Theory of the Exchange Process*, I use the term "*general* value-form" but Takeda has deleted "general," which results in confusion regarding my point.

This is followed by Takeda's "overview" of my theory, which he evaluates as follows:

> Kuruma's initial, seemingly trivial, mistake of going no further than abstracting within thought from the factor of want in value-expression, while at the same time thinking that a relation indicating a want underlies the expression of value, is the source of the self-contradiction that he falls into, which throws his theory into confusion when it comes to dealing with the development of the value-form. This is an example of how all "beginnings are difficult." It reminds me of the importance of carefully pondering how to establish the starting point, before then taking the first step. (Takeda, 1974, p. 52)

"Beginnings *are* difficult." – And Takeda's error stems from failing to understand the significance of "abstracting from" as the first step of scientific cognition. As a result, when Takeda sees that what was abstracted from at one stage of analysis is dealt with at a subsequent stage, he regards this as a "theoretical self-contradiction" and develops a rather audacious but off-target argument on that basis.

# 10.

## What is the "Dialectic" in the Case of the Value-Form?

**O**TANI: I would like to raise a final question concerning the value-form. In making corrections to the beginning of the first German edition of *Capital*, Marx sent the manuscript to Engels in 1867 to solicit his comments, and in response Engels wrote him the following in a June 16 letter:

> Compared with your earlier presentation [*Contribution*], the dialectic of the argument has been greatly sharpened, but with regard to the actual exposition there are a number of things I like better in the first version. (Marx, 1987b, p. 382)

Marx wrote back on June 22:

> With regard to the development of the *form of value,* I have both followed and *not* followed your advice, thus striking a dialectical attitude in this matter, too. … Anyway, the issue is crucial for the whole book. These gentry, the economists, have hitherto overlooked the extremely simple point that the form *20 yards of linen = 1 coat* is but the undeveloped basis form of *20 yards of linen = gold of £2*, and thus that the *simplest form of a commodity*, in which its value is not yet expressed as its relation to all other commodities but only as something *differentiated* from its own natural form, contains the *whole secret of the money-form* and thereby, *in nuce, of all bourgeois forms of the product of labor*. (Marx, 1987b, p. 384 – Marx's emphasis)

Looking at the two letters, we can see that the "dialectic" is said to play a major role in the theory of the value-form. Some have wondered what aspects of the theory are in fact manifestations of the dialectic. What are your thoughts on this?

**KURUMA:** Engels says that "the dialectic of the argument has been greatly sharpened," compared to *Contribution*, to which Marx responds by saying "I have both followed and *not* followed your advice, thus striking a dialectical attitude in this matter" and emphasizing that the core of the theory of the value-form is the simple form of value. I think that in responding to Engels (who seemed to have in mind the development of the value-form itself in speaking of the noticeable advance in the precision of dialectical development compared to *Contribution*), Marx emphasizes that the pivot of the theory of the value-form is the analysis of the simple value-form and that he necessarily adopted a dialectical attitude. The question then becomes what aspect of the analysis of the simple value-form can be considered dialectical. Marx has not written anything about this matter himself, so I can only speculate as follows.

The analysis of the commodity first clarifies that the commodity is a use-value and a value (a direct unity of two opposites), and as such it is in a contradiction. But the opposition between use-value and value is an opposition within the *same* commodity. In contrast, when we come to the value-form, the internal opposition is externalized to become an oppositional relation between two commodities. The natural form of the commodity in the relative form expresses that commodity's use-value, while its value is expressed using the natural form of the commodity in the equivalent form. In this way, the opposition between use-value and value within a single commodity is objectified as the oppositional relation between two commodities. The bodily form, or use-value, of the commodity in the equivalent form (in its given state) becomes the form of the value of the commodity in the relative form of value. In *Contribution* this was not yet posed as a problem, however. It is only in *Capital* that Marx first clarifies this fundamental point, in his analysis of the simple form of value. Upon the basis of that explanation, Marx goes on to analyze the development of the value-form. The development of the value-form, from this perspective, is thus the development of the form in which the commodity's value is distinguished from its use-value.

I think that this is the "dialectical attitude" Marx is referring to when he tells Engels that, "with regard to the development of the *form of value*, I have both followed and *not* followed your advice, thus striking a dialectical attitude in this matter, too." We need to note that the development of the value-form is premised on the analysis of the simple form of value, and is first constituted on its basis. Therefore, the locus of Marx's "dialectical attitude" in the theory of the value-form must be fundamentally uncovered in the analysis of the simple form of value.

\* \* \* \* \*

**OTANI:** There are still things that I would like to ask you about the "genesis of money." And even for the topics that we did discuss, I think that there might have been somewhat different responses on your part if I had posed the questions in a more complete form. I regret also that we did not make it to the theory of the exchange process. Still, we will have to end our discussion here, as I know that you must be quite tired, Professor Kuruma. I look forward to continuing our discussion on another occasion. Thank you very much for taking so much time today to patiently answer my questions.

# References

Böhm-Bawerk, E. 1984, *Karl Marx and the Close of His System*, Orion Editions, Philadelphia.

Hegel, G. 1977, *Phenomenology of Spirit*, Oxford University Press, Oxford.

Hegel, G. 1991, *The Encyclopaedia Logic*, Hackett Publishing Company, Indianapolis.

Inwood, M. 1992, *A Hegel Dictionary*, Blackwell Publishers, Oxford.

Kuruma, S. 1954, *Keizaigaku shi* (History of Political Economy), Iwanami Shoten, Tokyo.

Kuruma, S. 1957, *Kachikeitai-ron to kōkan-katei-ron* (Theory of the Value-Form & Theory of the Exchange Process), Iwanami Shoten, Tokyo.

Kuruma, S. (ed.) 1969, "Shiori" (booklet), in *Marx-Lexikon zur Politischen Ökonomie*, Otsuki Shoten, Tokyo.

Kuruma, S. 1979, *Kahei-ron* (Theory of Money), Otsuki Shoten, Tokyo.

Lenin, V. 1976, *Philosophical Notebooks*, in *Lenin Collected Works*, vol. 38, Progress Publishers, Moscow.

Marx, K. 1973, *Grundrisse*, Penguin, London.

Marx, K. 1976a, *Capital*, vol. 1, Penguin, London.

Marx, K. 1976b, Chapter 1 and Appendix of First Edition of *Capital*, in *Value: Studies by Marx*, New Park, London.

Marx, K. 1976c, *Shihon-ron dai-1-kan shohan* (Partial Translation of First German Edition of Volume 1 of *Capital*), translated by Jirō Okazaki, Otsuki Shoten, Tokyo.

Marx, K. 1983a, *Marx-Engels Collected Works*, vol. 40, International Publishers, New York.

Marx, K. 1983b, *Das Kapital: Kritik der Politischen Ökonomie*, Erster Band, Dietz Verlag, Berlin.

Marx, K. 1987a, *A Contribution to the Critique of Political Economy*, in *Marx-Engels Collected Works*, vol. 29, International Publishers, New York.

Marx, K. 1987b, *Marx-Engels Collected Works*, vol. 42, International Publishers, New York.

Marx, K. 1988, *Marx-Engels Collected Works*, vol. 43, International Publishers, New York.

Marx, K. 1989a, *Theories of Surplus Value*, in *Marx-Engels Collected Works*, vol. 32, International Publishers, New York.

Marx, K. 1989b, *Theories of Surplus Value*, in *Marx-Engels Collected Works*, vol. 33, International Publishers, New York.

Marx, K. 1991, *Marx-Engels Collected Works*, vol. 45, International Publishers, New York.

Marx, K. 1996, *Wages, Prices and Profit*, Foreign Languages Press, Beijing.

Niji, Y. 1978, *Kachikeitai-ron* (Theory of the Value-Form), Aoki Shoten, Tokyo.

Otani, T. 2001, *Zukai shakai-keizaigaku* (An Illustrated Guide to Political Economy), Sakurai Shoten, Tokyo.

Sakisaka, I., and Kōzō Uno (eds.) 1948, *Shihon-ron kenkyū* (An Inquiry into *Capital*), vol. 1, Kawade Shobō, Tokyo.

Takeda N. 1974, "Kachikeitai-ron to kōkan-katei-ron" (Theory of the Value-Form & Theory of the Exchange Process), part 1, published in *The Journal of the Association of Legal, Political and Economic Science*, No.75, Aichi University.

Tomizuka, R. 1976, *Keizai genron* (Fundamental Theory of Political Economy), Yuhikaku, Tokyo.

Uno, K. 1947, *Kachi-ron* (Theory of Value), Kawade Shobō, Tokyo.

Uno, K. et al. 1967, *Shihon-ron kenkyū* (An Inquiry into *Capital*), vol 1, Chikuma Shobō, Tokyo.

Uno, K. 1970, *Shihon-ron 50 nen* (50 Years with *Capital*), vol. 1, Hosei University Press, Tokyo.

Printed in the United States
140893LV00005B/11/P

9 781432 727314